Royalists and Royalis[ ]
English Civil Wars

Much ink has been spent on accounts of the English Civil Wars of the mid-seventeenth century, yet royalism has been largely neglected. This pioneering volume of essays by leading scholars in the field seeks to fill that significant gap in our understanding by focusing on those who took up arms for the king. The royalists described were not reactionary, absolutist extremists but pragmatic, moderate men who were not so different in temperament or background from the vast majority of those who decided to side with, or were forced by circumstances to side with, Parliament and its army. The chapters force us to think beyond the simplistic dichotomy between royalist 'absolutists' and 'constitutionalists', and suggest instead that allegiances were much more fluid and contingent than has hitherto been recognized. This is a major contribution to the political and intellectual history of the Civil Wars and of early modern England more generally.

Jason McElligott is the J.P.R. Lyell Research Fellow in the History of the Early-Modern Printed Book at Merton College, Oxford. He is the author of *Royalism, Print and Censorship in Revolutionary England* (2007) and the editor of *Fear, Exclusion and Revolution: Roger Morrice and Britain in the 1680s* (2006).

David L. Smith is Fellow and Director of Studies in History at Selwyn College, Cambridge. His previous publications include *Cromwell and the Interregnum* (2003) and, with Graham E. Seel, *Crown and Parliaments, 1558–1689* (2001).

Royalists and Royalism during the English Civil Wars

Edited by

Jason McElligott
Merton College, Oxford

and

David L. Smith
Selwyn College, Cambridge

CAMBRIDGE UNIVERSITY PRESS

Cambridge, New York, Melbourne, Madrid, Cape Town, Singapore,
São Paulo, Delhi, Dubai, Tokyo, Mexico City

Cambridge University Press
The Edinburgh Building, Cambridge CB2 8RU, UK

Published in the United States of America by Cambridge University Press, New York

www.cambridge.org
Information on this title: www.cambridge.org/9780521181471

First published 2007
First paperback edition 2010

A catalogue record for this publication is available from the British Library

ISBN 978-0-521-87007-8 Hardback
ISBN 978-0-521-18147-1 Paperback

In Memory of
Lawrence George Smith (1918–2006)

Contents

Notes on contributors

Barbara Donagan was educated at the Universities of Melbourne and Minnesota. Her work has focused on the processes of choice by which religious and moral dogmas were adapted to meet the demands of practical life, and on the ways in which the codes and conditions of the English Civil Wars affected the conduct of its protagonists. The latter issue is explored in her forthcoming book, *War in England 1642–1649*.

Rachel Foxley lectures in early-modern British history at the University of Reading. Her research interests are in the history of political thought, and she is completing a monograph on the Levellers.

Sean Kelsey has written extensively on the trial and execution of Charles I and the founding of the English commonwealth. His biography of Lord President John Bradshaw is currently proceeding at a rate consistent with the pursuit of a legal career in the City of London.

Mark A. Kishlansky is the Frank B. Baird Professor of English and European History at Harvard University and the author of *A Monarchy Transformed* in the Penguin History of Britain. He is currently at work on a study of the reign of Charles I.

Jason McElligott is the JPR Lyell Research Fellow in the History of the Early-Modern Printed Book at Merton College, Oxford. He is the author of *Royalism, Print and Censorship in Revolutionary England* (2007), *A Biographical Companion to Roger Morrice's Entring Book* (2007), and the editor of *Fear Exclusion and Revolution: Roger Morrice and Britain in the 1680s* (2006). He is currently working on the life, career and books of the radical satirist William Hone (1780–1842).

Michael Mendle is a professor of history in the University of Alabama. He has written extensively on political thought and on pamphlet culture. He is currently at work on a cultural history of shorthand in the seventeenth century and studies of the formation of historical sources in the seventeenth century and their later rediscovery.

Sarah Poynting is a research fellow in the Department of History at Keele University, where she is working on a scholarly edition of *The Writings of Charles I*. Her publications include an edition of Walter Montagu's *The Shepherds' Paradise* (1998), and articles on Charles I's letters in the 1630s and to Jane Whorwood in 1648, as well as on the women of Henrietta Maria's court.

Ian Roy, formerly of King's College, University of London, is an historian of early-modern Britain and Europe, writing especially on the Civil Wars and on English towns. He was Literary Director of the Royal Historical Society, 1978–85, a Trustee of the Royal Armouries, and helped found the Battlefields Trust. He first published work on the royalists in 1962.

David Scott is Senior Research Fellow at the History of Parliament. He has written a number of articles on the Civil War period, and is the author of *Politics and War in the Three Stuart Kingdoms, 1637–49* (2004).

David L. Smith is Fellow and Director of Studies in History at Selwyn College, Cambridge. His publications include *Constitutional Royalism and the Search for Settlement, c. 1640–1649* (1994), *A History of the Modern British Isles, 1603–1707: The Double Crown* (1998), and *The Stuart Parliaments, 1603–1689* (1999).

Malcolm Smuts is a professor of history at the University of Massachusetts-Boston and President of the North American Society for Court Studies. His publications include *Culture and Power in England 1585–1685* (1998), *Court Culture and the Origins of a Royalist Tradition in Early Stuart England* (1987), an edited collection, *The Stuart Court and Europe: Essays in Politics and Political Culture* (1996) and numerous articles on early Stuart culture and politics.

Blair Worden is Research Professor of History, Royal Holloway, London.

Preface

This volume evolved from an international conference entitled 'Royalists and Royalism: Politics, Religion, and Culture, 1640–60' that we jointly organized at Clare College, Cambridge, in July 2004. This conference brought together more than seventy scholars and students from four continents and a variety of disciplines, all of whom shared a common interest in mid-seventeenth-century British royalism. The conference proved extraordinarily lively and stimulating, and we hope that something of that atmosphere will be evident in this collection. More than thirty papers were presented at the conference, spanning the period from the late 1630s to the early 1660s, but in the interests of focus and coherence we have decided to concentrate this collection on the period from about 1638 through to the execution of Charles I. We plan in the near future to edit a related collection entitled *Royalists and Royalism during the Interregnum.*

Sally Johnson, the Conference Manager at Clare College, went out of her way to ensure the smooth running of the conference. She and her colleagues were a model of helpfulness, efficiency and professionalism. We raised close to £10,000 to pay for the conference. We are deeply grateful to the Centre for Research in the Arts, Social Sciences and Humanities (CRASSH) in Cambridge for their generous financial support of the conference, and for providing us with invaluable administrative assistance. The British Academy paid for the flights of a number of scholars from the United States. We also gratefully acknowledge the generous financial help that we received from the Trevelyan Fund of the Cambridge History Faculty, the Royal Stuart Society, the Royal Historical Society, and Christ Church, Oxford. John Morrill has, as always, been a great source of support and encouragement, as have Ronald Hutton and Quentin Skinner.

In the footnotes, place of publication is London unless otherwise stated. Original spelling in quotations from primary sources has been retained and the standard abbreviated forms have been expanded. Dates are given in old style, except that the year is taken to begin on 1 January rather than 25 March.

JASON McELLIGOTT
DAVID L. SMITH
September 2006

Abbreviations

Add. MS	Additional Manuscript
BIHR	*Bulletin of the Institute of Historical Research*
BL	British Library
Bodl.	Bodleian Library, Oxford
Carte (ed.), *Letters*	T. Carte (ed.), *A Collection of Original Letters and Papers, concerning the Affairs of England, from the year 1641–1660*, 2 vols. (1739)
Carte, *Life*	T. Carte, *The Life of James Duke of Ormond*, 6 vols. (Oxford, 1851)
CHR	W. D. Macray (ed.), *The History of the Rebellion and Civil Wars in England by Edward, Earl of Clarendon*, 6 vols. (Oxford, 1888)
CJ	*Commons' Journals*
CSP	Richard Scrope and Thomas Monckhouse (eds.), *State Papers Collected by Edward, Earl of Clarendon*, 3 vols. (Oxford, 1767–86)
CSPD	*Calendar of State Papers Domestic*
CSPV	*Calendar of State Papers Venetian*
DWL	Dr Williams's Library, London
EHR	*English Historical Review*
Gardiner, *HGCW*	S. R. Gardiner, *History of the Great Civil War*, 4 vols. (1987 edn)
Gardiner (ed.), *CDPR*	S. R. Gardiner (ed.), *The Constitutional Documents of the Puritan Revolution 1625–1660* (Oxford, 1906)
HGR	Edward, Earl of Clarendon, *History of the Rebellion and Civil Wars in England*, ed. W. D. Macray 6 vols. (Oxford, 1888)
HJ	*Historical Journal*
HLQ	*Huntington Library Quarterly*

HLRO	House of Lords Record Office
HMC	Historical Manuscripts Commission
HR	*Historical Research*
IHS	*Irish Historical Studies*
JBS	*Journal of British Studies*
LJ	*Lords Journals*
LQHM	M. A. E. Green (ed.), *Letters of Queen Henrietta Maria* (1857)
MPR	Eliot Warburton, *Memoirs of Prince Rupert and the Cavaliers*, 3 vols. (1849)
MSS	manuscripts
NAS	National Archives of Scotland
Nicholas	F. Warner (ed.), *The Nicholas Correspondence: the Correspondence of Sir Edward Nicholas*, 4 vols. (Camden Soc., 1886–1920)
NLW	National Library of Wales
Oxford DNB	*Oxford Dictionary of National Biography*
P&P	*Past & Present*
SP	State Papers
SRP	J. F. Larkin and P. L. Hughes (eds.), *Stuart Royal Proclamations*, vol. II (Oxford, 1983)
STC	Short-Title Catalogue
TNA	The National Archives, Kew
TRHS	*Transactions of the Royal Historical Society*

1 Introduction: rethinking royalists and royalism

Jason McElligott and David L. Smith

I

Royalism has never been particularly fashionable among historians of the English Civil Wars. There has long been an unfortunate tendency to dismiss those who were loyal to the Stuarts as, in the immortal words of *1066 and All That*, 'wrong but romantic', or as the products of unthinking political and religious reaction. We do possess a number of first-class studies of those who were loyal to the monarch,[1] but when one compares this work to the multitude of books and articles on the various parliamentarians and sectaries of the period one is struck by the great imbalance between the two. As long ago as 1981 Ronald Hutton drew our attention to the lack of research on royalism, and a decade later Conrad Russell wrote that

it is the English Royalists, not the English Parliamentarians, who are the real peculiarity we should be attempting to explain ... The intellectual and social antecedents of Royalism have not yet been studied with the care which has for many generations been lavished on the Parliamentarians.[2]

Since then, a number of important studies have been produced by historians and literary scholars, including David L. Smith's *Constitutional Royalism and the Search for Settlement* (1994), Michael Mendle's *Dangerous Positions: The Estates of the Realm and the Making of the Answer to the XIX Propositions* (1985), James Loxley's *Royalism and Poetry in the English Civil Wars: The Drawn Sword* (1997), Jerome de Groot's *Royalist Identities* (2004), and Geoffrey Smith's excellent *The Cavaliers in Exile, 1640–1660* (2003). Despite the high quality of this work we still know far too little about those who were loyal to the Stuarts. This strange neglect of royalism is unfortunate because we can never hope

---

[1] Ronald Hutton, *The Royalist War Effort, 1642–1646* (2nd edn, 1999) and David Underdown, *Royalist Conspiracy in England, 1649–1660* (New Haven, CT, 1960).

[2] Ronald Hutton, 'The Structure of the Royalist Party, 1642–1646', *HJ*, 24, 3 (1981), 553–69; Conrad Russell, *The Fall of the British Monarchies, 1637–1642* (Oxford, 1991), pp. 526, 532.

to unlock the essential characteristics and dynamics of the conflict which engulfed Britain in the 1640s and 1650s until we know far, far more about those men and women from all levels of society who supported the king and thumbed their noses at the puritans and Roundheads.

II

The following ten chapters in this book are intended as a contribution to the task of recovering the royalist experience of Civil War and Revolution. This volume has evolved from an international conference entitled 'Royalists and Royalism: Politics, Religion, and Culture, 1640–60' that we jointly organized at Clare College, Cambridge, in July 2004. This conference brought together more than seventy scholars and students from four continents and a variety of disciplines, all of whom shared a common interest in the phenomenon of mid-seventeenth-century British royalism. The chapters presented here are not, however, merely a random assortment of the papers presented over that wonderfully sunny and convivial weekend by the banks of the River Cam. Rather, we have decided to focus this volume on the decade prior to the regicide; at a later date we intend to produce a collection which examines the sorry tale of loyalism during the Interregnum. For this volume we have selected seven of the almost twenty papers at the conference which examined the years before the regicide; the chosen papers are those which we believe best suit our desire to produce a thematically and chronologically coherent treatment of those who sided with Charles I. We have also commissioned three new chapters (those by Kishlansky, Mendle and Roy) to fill perceived gaps in this volume's coverage of the period under examination. In doing so, we believe that we have assembled an exciting range of high-quality chapters by established and emerging historians and literary scholars. In what follows we shall briefly consider the themes of the contributors' chapters and suggest some of their strengths before turning to some of the possible lacunae within them and between them. We shall then suggest how these issues relate to a number of unresolved (and in some cases, unasked) questions about royalism, before concluding with suggestions as to the most fruitful directions for future research.

The Short Parliament marks an appropriate starting-point for this volume because, as Mark Kishlansky argues in his chapter, it was a watershed in the process by which Charles I himself became the leader of a royalist party. Kishlansky offers a fundamental reappraisal of Charles I's handling of the Short Parliament, arguing that the king displayed 'a

sincere willingness to work with Parliament', that he constantly sought
to achieve a compromise with the parliamentary leaders, and that he
'ventured every conceivable concession in every possible way'. By contrast, the parliamentary leaders, especially in the Commons, were both
provocative and intransigent: they launched repeated assaults on the
royal prerogatives and revenues. Nothing the king could have done or
offered would have placated them. This reassessment of the Short Parliament forms part of Kishlansky's wider reappraisal of Charles I's per-
sonality and political style. It suggests a monarch far more flexible and
conciliatory, and much less arrogant and duplicitous, than that portrayed in much of the existing literature. It also suggests a monarch
who was anxious to reach a compromise with his leading subjects and
who only concluded gradually and reluctantly that he was unable to
agree terms with them.

   This leads us naturally into an examination of how and when a royalist
movement emerged. In his chapter, Malcolm Smuts focuses on the role
of the Court and courtiers in the formation of royalism. He demonstrates
that there were a number of rifts at Court at various points in time but
suggests that the really crucial split occurred in 1640–2 *among* those
courtiers who had favoured pro-Protestant, pro-French policies during
the 1630s. It was this split, he suggests, between men who had often been
friends and allies during the Personal Rule, that was critical in the emergence of a royalist party. Smuts argues that those royalist swordsmen
like Suckling, Goring, Percy and Jermyn, who became involved in the
Army plots, were not – as has sometimes been implied – would-be absolutists or crypto-Catholics. Instead, they were political pragmatists and
religious sceptics, with an interest in military affairs. In terms of their
background and earlier careers, they had much in common with other
courtly figures, some of whom later became parliamentarians. Smuts
also suggests that the apparent differences between the army plotters
and constitutional royalists such as Hyde and Falkland may have owed
more to contingency and short-term tactical decisions than to any fundamental principles. Smuts's chapter thus not only sheds much new
light on the politics of the Court at the beginning of the 1640s, but also
helps to clarify the nature of the various strands of royalism and the
relationship between them.

   One of those strands was epitomized in the king's *Answer to the Nineteen Propositions*, drafted by Falkland and Culpeper, and published in
June 1642. Michael Mendle argues in his chapter that the *Answer* envisaged a mixed monarchy in which the three elements of king, House of
Lords and House of Commons were equated with the three categories of
monarchy, aristocracy and democracy. The functions of these three

elements were kept clearly distinct, other than in the passage of legisla-tion: Mendle explores the striking metaphor by which each 'estate' was imagined as a river that needed to be kept within its proper bounds. The distinction of their functions was crucial, and Mendle argues that this rested on a doctrine of the separation of powers that anticipated that associated with Montesquieu in the eighteenth century. In the *Answer*, the king and his advisers defended the crown's position by arguing that the assumption of executive powers by the two Houses of Parliament threatened to overturn the natural balance of the constitution. In the later 1640s, other royalists, such as Charles Dallison, continued to ad-vocate the doctrine of separate powers, and it enabled other loyalists to forge links with Independents or Levellers (a point also developed in Rachel Foxley's chapter). The doctrine of separate powers was conve-niently flexible and Mendle shows it re-emerged in the Instrument of Government (1653) and was frequently debated in the Protectorate par-liaments; its influence was also apparent in the conceptualisation of the Restoration monarchy in 1660.

In examining what she calls the 'rainbow coalition' of royalism, Barbara Donagan explores the diverse opinions and varying degrees of commitment that lay under the broad umbrella of royalist allegiance. She also notes the remarkable similarities in the constitutional views of moderate royalists and moderate parliamentarians. Perhaps the most important distinction between the adversaries was that for many royal-ists the choice of sides 'seems to have been almost instinctive', and often rested on a strong element of personal loyalty to the monarch or, as Donagan suggests, to local grandees who became royalist officers and decided to offer their allegiance to the king. The role of the personal in the formation of royalist allegiance may help to explain why so many royalists displayed a deep sensitivity to affronts and a notorious pro-pensity to violence and feuds (a theme which is also addressed in Ian Roy's chapter). Donagan is at pains to stress the more personal and irrational aspects of royalism; many sided with the king out of an al-most visceral sense that he was a more convincing safeguard of order, hierarchy and settled institutions, including the established Church of England, than the leading parliamentarians. However, for royalists prag-matism and prudence sometimes ran counter to their natural inclina-tions, and these tensions help to explain why in some cases allegiances were so volatile. The problem of what one contemporary called 'tergi-versatious bats' was by no means confined to the royalists, of course, but the highly instinctive and personal nature of so much royalist allegiance often led, Donagan argues, to a collision between such emotional feelings and more rational ideas and calculations of self-interest. It was this kind of collision that accounts for some of the volatility of the king's armies and the decision of many royalists to retire from the fray at different points in time.

Donagan's emphasis on the role of the personal within royalism connects neatly with David Scott's discussion of the dynamics of counsel and factionalism in the king's party between 1642 and 1646. Scott shows how Charles I's marked preference for personal counsel and for informal discussion ensured that his reliance on 'cabinet counsels' – already evident during the Personal Rule – persisted into the 1640s. Scott argues that as a result, the real seat of policy-making at Oxford lay in the king's bedchamber rather than in the Privy Council or the Council of War. Membership of the bedchamber gave direct access and personal proximity to the king, and this was the basis of the considerable political influence wielded by men such as Richmond, Ashburnham and Porter. The careers of these and other members of the bedchamber reflected what Scott calls the 'triumph of access over high office', a triumph that helps to explain the fierce competition for places in the bedchamber that was apparent throughout this period.

Scott's chapter also attempts to shed light on the nature of – and the relations between – different groupings of royalists. He suggests that an underlying antagonism persisted between the swordsmen and many of the leading civilian councillors. In the wake of the battle of Naseby, there was a hardening of the division between those, such as Richmond, Hertford and Hyde, who continued to seek a negotiated settlement, and those, like Ashburnham, Culpeper, Jermyn and Digby, who favoured trying to bring in foreign support on the king's behalf, beginning with his Scottish supporters. Scott is highly critical of the traditional description of the royalist leaders as either 'absolutists' or 'constitutionalists'. Instead, he posits a novel interpretation of the influence of Machiavelli and Tacitus upon the justifications for the use of force put forward by Lord Jermyn and his allies. He contrasts this allegedly Tacitean politics with the arguments of Hyde, Richmond, Hertford and their allies who tended to emphasize the relationship of trust, loyalty and even love that should ideally exist between king and people.

Charles's relations with his family and closest advisers were reflected most clearly in his private correspondence, and these letters – and the rhetorical strategies that Charles deployed in them – form the subject of Sarah Poynting's chapter. Poynting argues that Charles's deep desire to be 'rightly vnderstood' coloured his letters throughout the Civil Wars until the very eve of the regicide. In particular, the king often added short apostiles to his letters that provide helpful insights into his state of mind. It seems that Charles, far from being aloof, stern and authoritarian, strongly disliked being at odds with those to whom he was close. When Jermyn and Culpepper wrote to him in 'astonishingly blunt' terms about the Newcastle Propositions, Charles's response was to try to cajole and persuade them rather than to command them into agreement with him. His letters to Ormond, Lanark and Hamilton adopted an air of much greater spontaneity and immediacy, while his correspondence from Carisbrooke Castle to Henry Firebrace, Silius Titus and Sir William Hopkins was easy, relaxed and cordial. All in all, Charles adopted a variety of rhetorical strategies and voices in his correspondence, depending on the person to whom he was writing. Poynting's nuanced and intriguing examination of the king's writings reminds us that even now, more than a century and a half after Carlyle's edition of Cromwell's letters and almost seventy years after that of W. C. Abbott, we lack a comparable source for the study of the king. Poynting's forthcoming edition of Charles's writings promises to be a major source which will simultaneously allow for a much more rounded picture of the king than has hitherto been possible, and force us to re-examine much of the received wisdom concerning politics during the 1640s.

Ian Roy's chapter explores various ideals of royalism and the extent to which these were lived out in practice. He traces the positive images of Cavaliers that the king and his advisers sought to project as a recruitment strategy in the summer of 1642. The *Military Orders* of August 1642, together with later royal proclamations, set out codes of conduct that emphasized the importance of loyalty and obedience, as opposed to the 'popularity' associated with the London rebels. In practice, however, the royalists faced widespread problems of poor behaviour, disorder and absenteeism. Roy contrasts the nobility of character displayed by some Catholic martyr-soldiers, such as Sir Henry Gage, with the record of other rather less attractive figures. By 1644–5, pillage by royalists was an increasing problem, and the lofty ideals of royalist loyalty and nobility that the king and his advisers had presented in the summer of 1642 were little more than a distant memory.

Rachel Foxley explores whether the attempts by some royalists to form a rapprochement with the army leaders during the summer and autumn of 1647 were the product of shared, rational principles or the result of grubby, temporary political opportunism. Many of the royalists and the Independents in the army and the two Houses of Parliament certainly had some significant areas of shared ideological ground, not least a hatred of presbyterianism and an increasing resentment of parliamentarian tyranny. A commitment to religious freedom of conscience was something that the Independents and most royalists could also accept, as is clear from the remarkable religious clauses of the *Heads of the*

Proposals, which envisaged a moderated episcopacy, shorn of coercive powers, co-existing with a generous measure of liberty of conscience.

Yet, as Foxley argues, a willingness to build bridges with royalists was not the same thing at all as actually becoming a royalist. There was a genuine gulf of ideology and principle between the two sides in the projected settlement of 1647 over the nature of the king's powers. At a particular moment in time, *individual* royalists were indeed able to open up meaningful links with *individual* Independents and Levellers – as the rapport between John Lilburne and the royalist judge David Jenkins shows – but Foxley argues persuasively that royalists did not compromise their core beliefs in these negotiations. Any alliance that they might have been able to forge would have been a temporary and 'self-conscious and uncomfortable' one. Even as they conducted these ultimately unsuccessful negotiations both sides were undoubtedly aware that they would, in all likelihood, be forced to fight each other at some point in the future.

Blair Worden develops Foxley's theme of the remarkable resilience of royalism during the years of the king's captivity. He argues that 'never was Royalism more buoyant on the page than in the two years that preceded the execution of the King'. Worden's reappraisal of Andrew Marvell draws out the royalist aspects of a poet traditionally classified as a parliamentarian. He argues that between 1648 and 1650, Marvell wrote four poems that reveal a royalist allegiance. In particular, possibly Marvell's most famous poem, *An Horatian Ode upon Cromwell's Return from Ireland* (1650), can in Worden's view sustain a royalist perspective. In the *Horatian Ode*, Marvell's Cromwell is driven by ambition: he is 'restless Cromwell', pursuing his 'fiery way'. The contrast with Marvell's depiction of Charles I, who at his execution 'nothing common did or mean / Upon that memorable scene', is very pronounced and reflects the extent to which Marvell continued to cling to royalist sentiments. He was never drawn to republicanism, or to the idea of a sovereign parliament. Instead, the extraordinarily complex and enigmatic nature of the *Horatian Ode* helps us to chart the painful process of adjustment by which royalist attitudes and allegiances began to come to terms with the regicide.

The essential resilience and plasticity of royalism is also evident in Sean Kelsey's chapter, which claims that some royalists were already beginning, by the autumn of 1648, to think seriously about the possibility of life after Charles I, and to pin their hopes on the prospective succession of Charles II. Kelsey traces Charles I's deep distress at the concessions that he made during the treaty of Newport and his feeling that by making those concessions – however insincerely – he had come too close to accepting his guilt for all of the blood shed during the Civil Wars. Figures such as Hyde and Ormond even wondered, Kelsey claims, if the king had made concessions that were not within his power to make. Kelsey shows how the knowledge that the Prince of Wales was at liberty, and the prospect that he might lead a royalist naval strike from the continent, directly shaped the course of events at Westminster. By the autumn of 1648, he suggests, some supporters of the House of Stuart were coming to regard the prospective succession of Charles II as a glimmer of opportunity, and were as a result more able to reconcile themselves to the possibility of Charles I's trial and execution.

III

There are striking convergences in this book between, say, the work of Donagan and Worden on the nature and extent of changes of allegiance during the conflict. There are also some equally striking tensions between, say, Kishlansky, who sees Charles I as a fundamentally honest character, and Kelsey, who describes the king as essentially duplicitous. Both individually and collectively, all of these chapters present royalism as a complex and fascinating phenomenon, full of vitality and vibrancy, and every bit as creative and worthy of scholarly interest as those whom they fought against on the battlefield and in print. In the light of these chapters it should no longer be possible to view royalism as a static, fixed and unchanging entity. It was an allegiance in the process of constant adaptation in response to changing contexts and circumstances, and it looks different depending on whether we are examining the formation of the royalist party in the early 1640s, the period of actual war-fighting, or the complex series of negotiations which took place after the surrender of the king to the Scots in 1646. The royalists described in this collection were not reactionary, absolutist extremists but pragmatic, moderate men who were not so different in temperament or background from the vast majority of those who decided to side with, or were forced by circumstances to side with, parliament and its army. One is also repeatedly struck by the recurring theme of the importance of contingent and personal factors in the creation and maintenance (or, indeed, recantation) of royalist allegiance. Finally, it is important to point out that not the least of the strengths of this collection is the evident willingness of at least some historians and literary scholars to engage with each other's arguments, sources and methodologies. It is to be hoped that the example of the chapters produced by Poynting and Worden will convince other researchers of the great benefits to be gained by sometimes stepping outside their own disciplines.

There are, however, a number of important gaps and omissions in this collection as a whole, and these weaknesses are symptomatic of some of the most important problems with the current conceptualization of royalists and royalism among the broader scholarly community. These weaknesses include a strangely old-fashioned preoccupation with social elites; a two-dimensional model of allegiance which does not take account of the complexity of politics and war; and a reluctance to define or theorize the exact nature or definition of royalism.

In general, these chapters are preoccupied with the careers and choices of high-status males at the Court, and among the upper echelons of the military and clergy. In particular, a number of authors have concerned themselves with the phenomenon of factional infighting at Court. Such an approach is not intrinsically without merit, as is demonstrated by the wonderfully erudite arguments and conclusions of Malcolm Smuts. Factional struggles among the elite are certainly of interest if one is interested in factional struggles among the elite, but do they illuminate, or even come close to explaining, the wider cultural, social, religious or political culture of royalism? Why, we might ask, when there are so many gaps in our knowledge about the nature and extent of the broader royalist party, do so many scholars feel the need continually to revisit the minutiae of these internecine squabbles? Have these lengthy researches resulted in anything other than the invention of new names for factions that were identified long ago by scholars such as S. R. Gardiner or David Underdown? This question is particularly pertinent in the wake of Geoffrey Smith's recent *The Cavaliers in Exile, 1640–1660* which has argued forcibly that faction is not the key to royalist politics that many imagine it to be: most supporters of the king never adhered to a faction; many people moved between different factions at various times; and there were personal and familial relationships which cut across factions, just as there were intense political and personal disagreements between people who were supposedly members of the same faction.

This emphasis on the petty jealousies and hatreds of the leading loyalists is unfortunate because it contributes to a widely held impression that the royalist party consisted of nothing more than a few dozen grandees with very few followers among the wider population. There is a crying need for more work on at least some of the hundreds of thousands of men and women outside the rarefied milieu of the Court who supported the king during the conflict. One naturally thinks of the tens of thousands of men who enlisted in the royalist armies but it is important to realize that only a minority of the king's supporters ever took up arms; the loyalism of the vast majority of the king's supporters necessarily consisted of less

active or dangerous activities, but those actions were vital to the maintenance of the cause and the ability of that cause to raise, deploy and maintain significant numbers of armed men. To borrow a metaphor from
modern warfare, we need to begin to consider the nature, extent and
composition of the water in which those who actively fought for the king
were nourished and protected.

A study of royalism below the level of the elite has never been attempted
because many scholars in the field share the late Gerald Aylmer's
scepticism as to the validity of research into royalism among lower social
groupings.[3] There has also been little or no attempt to apply the meth-
odology of cultural history to the study of royalists, except in the context
of high culture and entertainment.[4] Until very recently one could have
been forgiven for assuming that, apart from Queen Henrietta Maria,
there were no female royalists.[5] It is surprising that so little has been
published on the use of print by those loyal to the Stuarts during the
Civil Wars. Print has always been seen as a radical, destabilizing force:
an agent of social change, innovation, and revolution.[6] It is high time to
demonstrate how lively, vibrant and exciting the use of print as an agent
of social stability and cohesion could be.[7] In the same way that the
neglect of royalists and the disproportionate emphasis on the parliamentarians has impaired our knowledge of the Civil Wars in general, we can
never hope to understand the role played by print in the conflict until we
know much more about how the royalists approached and used this
medium of communication. The study of royalist print-culture will necessarily transform our understanding of the relationship between royalist activists and the wider population.[8] It is true that there has been

---

[3]   G.E. Aylmer, 'Collective Mentalities in Mid-seventeenth Century England: II. Royalist Attitudes', *TRHS*, 5th ser., 37 (1987), 29.

[4]   R. Malcolm Smuts, *Culture and Power in England, 1585–1685* (1999).

[5]   Hero Chalmers, *Royalist Women Writers 1650–1689* (Oxford, 2004); Jerome de Groot,
'Gorgeous Gorgons: Royalist Women', ch. 5 of his *Royalist Identities* (Basingstoke,
2004); de Groot, 'Royalist Women' and Claire Walker, 'Loyal and Dutiful Subjects:
English Nuns and Stuart Politics', in James Daybell (ed.), *Women and Politics in Early
Modern England, 1450–1700* (Aldershot, 2006).

[6]   The classic statement of this position is Elizabeth Eisenstein's *The Printing Press as an
Agent of Change*, 2 vols. (Cambridge, 1979).

[7]   Jason McElligott, 'Stabilizing and Destabilizing Britain in the 1680s', in Jason
McElligott (ed.), *Fear, Exclusion and Revolution: Roger Morrice and Britain in the
1680s* (Aldershot, 2006), pp. 9–10.

[8]   On this see Jason McElligott, 'Edward Crouch: a Poor Printer in Seventeenth Century
London', *Journal of the Printing Historical Society*, ns, 1 (2000), 49–73; McElligott,
'John Crouch: A Royalist Journalist in Cromwellian England', *Media History*, 10, 3
(2004), 139–55; McElligott, 'The Politics of Sexual Libel: Royalist Propaganda in
the 1640s', *HLQ*, 67 (March 2004), 75–99; and *Royalism, Print and Censorship in
Revolutionary England* (Woodbridge, 2007).

a good deal of recent work on royalist literature but even here, with a few honourable exceptions, there has been a tendency to concentrate on a small range of topics; the *Eikon Basilike* itself, or canonical authors and poets with connections to the royal Court or other prominent loyalists.[9] There were, quite simply, many more royalists and many more different types of royalists than the existing literature might lead one to believe.

A fundamental problem with the current conceptualization of royalism is the inability to think beyond the simplistic and all-too convenient dichotomy between 'absolutists' and 'constitutionalists'. A prime example of the limitations of this hoary paradigm is afforded by David Scott's chapter in this volume. He is loudly critical of the division of loyalism into these two separate, mutually antagonistic groupings. Instead, he argues that the real division was between those drawn to the justifications of the use of force put forward by the classical thinker Tacitus, and those who were opposed to this world view. At its most basic level this new model of royalist politics is open to the objection that it is difficult to establish that any of Scott's 'Taciteans' had ever read Tacitus, let alone digested and appropriated his arguments. More importantly, however, it is clear that we are still being encouraged to think of politics in terms of strict polarities. Some readers may wonder whether Scott offers us not so much a thoroughgoing rethink of royalist politics as a rebranding of the familiar categories with 'Tacitean' replacing 'absolutist' and 'anti-Tacitean' being substituted for 'moderate' or 'constitutionalist'.

The construction and maintenance of a strict dichotomy between 'absolutists' and 'moderates' is problematic because it tends to ignore a whole spectrum of rich and variegated opinion between these theoretical extremes. It also presupposes the same penchant for intellectual clarity, consistency and logical thinking among the supporters of the king as is expected of modern scholars. Only a relatively small number of royalists could ever have experienced the Civil Wars without borrowing bits and pieces of ideological baggage from the theoretical extremes of 'absolutism' and 'moderation' at different times, or perhaps even at the same time. The strict demarcation of two theoretical extremes also leads to a remarkably static view of political allegiance which expects one to accept that people took fixed positions at the start of the conflict which they never altered during the terrible events of the following years. Rather than seeing royalist identity as a choice between two mutually exclusive extremes, we perhaps need to see a broad spectrum of opinion

---

[9]   See, for example, the disproportionate emphasis on the poet Henry Vaughan in Robert Wilcher's *The Writing of Royalism, 1628–1660* (Cambridge, 2001).

between these pure, unsullied ideological positions. If one accepts that the royalist political spectrum is divided into a whole series of bands of different colours which represent different political, religious and cultural positions, then one must also accept that each distinct band of colour shades into and is, to some extent at least, overlapped by the positions on either side of it. One might argue that there were certainly two political positions which can be termed 'absolutist' or 'constitutionalist', but they were distinct points joined by a much bigger, and arguably more interesting and important, spectrum or continuum of inter-related and overlapping positions which could, and did, change over time. Alternatively, one might consider that, apart from a few inconsequential extremists, almost every royalist was a constitutional royalist, as that term has been defined by David L. Smith.[10] Who could not be for law, order, the ancient liberties of the subject and the church 'as by Law established', especially if the criteria for admission to that church could be loosely defined and interpreted? If there is a sense in which 'absolutists' were almost as rare as hen's teeth, then perhaps the danger implicit in 'constitutional royalism' is that the criteria for membership of the club are so broad and general – so commonplace – that the term encompasses almost everyone on the royalist side. We might need then to be open to, and aware of, the broad range of political and religious opinions, strategies and tactics which could be encompassed *within* the mainstream of 'constitutional royalism'.

Scholars have usually been content to define a royalist as somebody who took up arms for the king.[11] This definition has the benefit of simplicity, but it does not enable us to do justice to the vast majority of the population who supported one side or other in the conflict without ever actually taking up arms. It also has the disadvantage of not enabling us to consider how individuals viewed themselves: should we really consider a man to have been a royalist who had no interest in politics but was forcibly enlisted in the king's forces? Is it not time to move beyond *prescriptive* definitions of royalism – what people must have thought or believed in order to qualify for membership of the royalist party – in favour of a *descriptive* definition which examines what actual royalists thought, believed or argued? When one considers the diverse men and women who sided with the king the only acceptable definition of a royalist is this: somebody who, by thought or deed, identified

---

[10]   David L. Smith, *Constitutional Royalism and the Search for Settlement, c. 1640–1649* (Cambridge, 1994).

[11]   James Loxley, *Royalism and poetry in the English Civil Wars: The Drawn Sword* (Basingstoke, 1997).

himself or herself as a royalist and was accepted as such by other individuals who defined themselves as royalists. These royalists could (and did) hold a wide variety of political or theological opinions but they were united by a concern to see the Stuarts return to power on their own terms or, failing that, the best possible terms available. This definition of royalism is admittedly broad, but is not so broad as to be meaningless. It also allows us to realize for the first time that not every expression of antipathy to parliament or sympathy for the plight of the king is evidence of royalism. The members of the New Model Army who advocated a temporary alliance with the supporters of the king in 1647 were not royalists.[12] They never defined themselves as such and were anxious to secure the return of the king to power on the best possible terms for themselves. For the same reasons it is clear that the Scottish army which invaded England on Charles I's behest in 1648 was not a royalist army.[13] Neither did the Catholic confederates of Ireland become royalists when they formed alliances with Ormond and his men.[14] It should also be clear that occasional expressions of sympathy for the personal plight of Charles I by a number of pro-parliamentary writers in the months before the regicide are not evidence of royalism.[15]

What then was the relationship between royalism and loyalism? Both terms were in use among contemporaries during the Civil Wars but the foreign root of the word 'royalist' – 'roy' is the old French word for 'king' – seems to have ensured that the supporters of the king referred to themselves more often as 'loyalists' than 'royalists'. Modern scholars have traditionally drawn a distinction between the royalist, whose obedience was to the person of the king, and the loyalist, whose allegiance was to the office and authority of the monarch. This is a convenient division, yet it is one of the themes of this introduction, and many of the chapters in this book, that the intellectual consistency and clear-cut polarities favoured by many scholars do not accurately describe the muddled and often confusing politics of the period. The nature and course of civil war politics is best explained not by reference to the history of political thought or ideas, but in terms of contingency, opportunism, short-term

---

[12] Michael Mendle, 'Putney's Pronouns: Identity and Indemnity in the Great Debate', in Mendle (ed.), *The Putney Debates of 1647: The Army, the Levellers, and the English State* (Cambridge, 2001), pp. 125–47.

[13] David Stevenson, 'A Revolutionary Regime and the Press: The Scottish Covenanters and their Printers, 1638–51', *The Library*, 6th ser., 7 (1985), 315–37, at 332.

[14] David Scott, *Politics and War in the Three Stuart Kingdoms, 1637–49* (Basingstoke, 2004), pp. 182–3.

[15] Joseph Frank, *The Beginnings of the English Newspaper, 1620–1660* (Cambridge, MA, 1961), pp. 121, 124; F. S. Siebert, *Freedom of the Press in England, 1476–1776* (Urbana, IL, 1965), p. 215.

shifts of tactics, and simply muddling through in the face of unforeseen developments. There may have been a small number of intellectuals at the time who could maintain a distinction between 'royalism' and 'loyalism', but such men (and women) are necessarily few and far between in any age and are unlikely to exert any great influence over political discourse or the course of events during periods of trauma such as that which convulsed Britain during the 1640s. Instead, the vast majority of those who adhered to the king seem to have used the terms 'royalist' and 'loyalist' as synonyms. Indeed, the writer in the leading royalist newsbook of the late 1640s, *Mercurius Pragmaticus*, was adamant that his comrades formed the 'Royall, Loyall party', while another writer appealed to all those with 'honest, royall, and loyall hearts' to stand up for the king.[16] It is for this reason that we have used the terms interchangeably throughout this introduction, often alternating them merely to avoid repetition in the same or succeeding sentences.

IV

To conclude, the chapters in this book offer a variety of fresh and exciting perspectives on royalist politics, religion and culture in midseventeenth-century Britain. They provide us with an opportunity to redress the conventional scholarly focus on parliament, its armies, and the various sectaries who came to the fore during the Civil Wars. Such work will inevitably force us to rethink our assumptions about the royalists *and* their opponents, and will also provide us with a more rounded, and convincing, picture of the society in which they lived. The chapters by Mark Kishlansky and Sarah Poynting are important contributions to a necessary reassessment of the traditionally unsympathetic treatment of Charles I. There is also much that we do not yet know about the leading royalist courtiers, soldiers and clergymen. We have suggested, however, that future research on this relatively small number of men might usefully be broadened away from considerations of political faction-fighting. Scholars must realize that there were many individual royalists and types of royalism that have been almost completely ignored. It is vital to understand that there was such a thing as popular royalism, both in the sense of numerical popularity and the ability to appeal to men and women beyond the upper echelons of society. We need to know much more about royalism in Ireland and Scotland and the way in which loyalists from all three Stuart kingdoms interacted with each other,

---

[16] *Mercurius Pragmaticus*, no. 18B, 11–18 Jan. 1648, sig. 4v; *Mercurius Elenticus*, no. 2, 22–29 April 1650, sig. 1r.

particularly when they were thrown together in less than salubrious conditions in exile on the continent.

Above all else, we would suggest that it is imperative to move beyond simple and simplistic dichotomies – 'absolutist' versus 'constitutionalist' – when describing and analyzing royalist politics and allegiance. A number of chapters in this collection have stressed the temporary, contingent nature of allegiance and drawn attention to a number of individuals whose loyalty shifted over time. These pieces provide fascinating insights which might usefully be mapped onto other individuals or groups of individuals, such as the large number of royalist troops who joined the New Model Army after Naseby, or the surprising number of royalist polemicists who only went over to the side of the king in 1647 or 1648.[17] If, as we suspect, shifts in allegiance were much more common than has hitherto been realized and if, as we also suspect, there were discernible patterns to these shifting allegiances, then these chapters are important milestones in the conceptualization and understanding of political allegiance during the Civil Wars as a whole. We might no longer be able to think of allegiance as a fixed, unchanging and unchangeable entity. This insight may explain why all attempts to find pre-determining factors for political allegiance during the Civil Wars have failed. There was, quite simply, no single, fixed, pre-determined allegiance but a conscious choice to adhere to one side or the other which was dependent on a whole series of entirely contingent factors which differed from time to time, from place to place, and from person to person. What is more, scholars have not been sufficiently aware of the fact that for some people – Marchamont Nedham is the obvious example – we have to explain not one but two, or perhaps even three or more, changes of allegiance. The number of permutations and combinations of factors determining allegiance were enormous, but when one factors *changing* allegiances into the equation then there was never any prospect of finding pre-determining reasons for particular political stances. Royalism emerges from this collection as a much more variegated, complex, heterogeneous and interesting creed than has hitherto been described. We hope that in future years more and more graduate students who wish to work on the Civil Wars and Revolution will begin to examine those remarkably neglected men and women who chose loyalty and royalty. Only then will it finally be possible to come close to a balanced assessment of the causes, nature and effects of that calamitous conflict.

---

[17]   For these turncoats see chapters four and five of McElligott, *Royalism, Print, and Censorship*.

2   A lesson in loyalty: Charles I and the Short Parliament

Mark A. Kishlansky

'Treason doth never prosper; what's the reason? For if it prosper, none dare call it treason.'[1]

I

How did Charles I become a royalist? The question is worth considering. What factors made him willing to turn into the head of only a part of the body politic? There could be no royalism without the king and no king would readily accept that his nation was divided against itself. Loyalty or treason were stark alternatives and Charles only reluctantly decided to pose them. Despite numerous provocations since the onset of the Scottish rebellion, he was acutely aware of the consequences of escalating the situation. 'It is ... my own people, which by this means will be for a time ruined, so that the loss must be inevitably mine', he lamented to the marquis of Hamilton in 1638.[2] The Scots were those 'for whom it was glorious neither to conquer or be conquered'.[3] Though his disinclination to engage in war in 1639 is variously attributed to military or financial weakness, Charles's recognition of this simple fact was equally significant. His campaign against the Scots should 'not be thought to be by way of a war, but by way of a Prince, the Father of his country, his chastising his unruly children, which is never in anger, but in love and for their good'.[4] The king's conception of his obligations to his people necessarily made him a reluctant protagonist.

[1] STC 12777. Sir John Harington, *The Most Elegant and Witty Epigrams of Sir John Harrington Knight* (1625), Book 4, Epigram 5.
[2] STC B5832. Gilbert Burnet, *The Memoires of the Lives and Actions of James and William Dukes of Hamilton* (1667), p. 55.
[3] Esther Cope (ed.), *Proceedings of the Short Parliament of 1640*, Camden Society Fourth Series, vol. XIX (1977), p. 118.
[4] STC, 21906. [Charles I] Walter Balcanquhal, *A Large Declaration Concerning the Late Tumults in Scotland* (1639), p. 5.

Surely the events of 1641–2 provide the proximate answer to this question. The forced execution of Strafford, the removal of the bishops from the House of Lords, the unpalatable legislation that the king was compelled to sign, including the Act against the dissolution of parliament without its own consent, all contributed to his profound alienation from parliament. The continued threat of mob violence and rumours of the queen's impeachment persuaded Charles to risk arresting the Five Members, the gamble that transformed constitutional conflict into Civil War. But Charles's experience of humiliation preceded the calling of the Long Parliament; his sense of grievance against the representatives of his subjects had a longer pedigree. Though it only lasted three weeks, his experience with the Short Parliament had a decisive impact upon the king's psyche. In April 1640 he had appeared before parliament not as a supplicant, but as a partner, asking for the aid of his English subjects in punishing Scottish treason. Though Charles I came to the Short Parliament for money, what he asked of its members was loyalty. He received neither.

Because it was immediately overtaken by a series of transforming events, what happened during the Short Parliament has been predictably overshadowed. But the king could not so easily erase its memory. He approached this first meeting of his subjects in eleven years with a sure sense of the justness of his cause. For two and a half years he had faced a rebellion in his northern kingdom and now was the time to suppress it by force. This was the ancient prescription for summoning parliament. An aggressive army of an ancient enemy camped on England's border, seasoned warriors had returned from Europe to lead it, and all efforts at pacification had failed. The danger faced by the king was a danger shared by his subjects: 'the Scots would gladly change soils with us'.[5]

With his cause just, his need obvious, and the stakes high, Charles I approached the Short Parliament hopefully. He was not unaware that it would be difficult to have subsidies voted quickly or at the beginning of a parliament. Nor was he ignorant that after an eleven-year hiatus members of parliament would have myriad grievances to air. But it was possible that passions had cooled and tensions eased during a decade of prosperity, that nationalistic feelings would stir Englishmen to resent being dictated to by Scots, that support for their monarch would usher in a new alliance between subjects and sovereigns. Even a signal that parliament was willing to fund the king's necessities would have been sufficient encouragement for Charles to continue to work with them. But if the king approached the session with hope, leaders of parliament approached it with despair. 'I find it will be a hard matter to please them',

[5] Cope, *Short Parliament*, p. 71.

the earl of Northumberland wrote on the first day of the session. 'Their jealousies and suspicions appear upon every occasion and I fear they will not readily be persuaded to believe the fair and gracious promises that are made them by the King.'[6] The convergence was like a thunderclap. While the king sought success, key members like Pym, Hampden and Oliver St John pursued failure. The Commons was so deaf to royal appeals for immediate supply that on several occasions members went so far as to attempt to prevent them being heard. They turned back Charles's every effort at compromise and every gesture of conciliation. Nor was there anything subtle about their tactics.[7] Five times the king made direct overtures for supply of his urgent needs and five times they were rebuffed. The Commons treated every plea for haste as an opportunity for delay. Skilled parliamentarians, who had previously perfected the art of seeming cooperation, made no effort in the spring of 1640 even to keep up appearances. Most disconcerting of all, Charles's personal entreaties to be trusted were met with blank refusal. The king appealed to the members' allegiance, to their honour, to their duty. They offered him no response. Though it took only three weeks before the king was goaded into dissolving the session, it was a period long enough for Charles I to learn a lesson in loyalty.

II

By the autumn of 1639 it was clear that the Pacification of Berwick would not hold. 'I do not see how a war can possibly be avoided', the earl of Northumberland lamented in November, echoing the sentiments of many.[8] Within days of the agreement each side complained of multiple violations and each soon learned of the other's plans for military operations in the spring. Emissaries of the king and the Covenanters jostled each other at the Courts of Europe searching for munitions and ordering their men in arms to return home.[9] Charles had initially been reluctant to involve his English subjects in his Scottish affairs, but once he had reliable reports of Scottish war preparations he created a committee of the English Privy Council to advise him.[10] This was the textbook case for summoning

---

[6]   HMC, *De L'Isle and Dudley* MSS (1966), vol. VI, p. 245.

[7]   Cf. Conrad Russell, 'The Scottish Party in English Parliaments, 1640–2', *HR*, 66, no. 159 (1993), 48.

[8]   HMC, *De L'Isle and Dudley*, vol. VI, p. 201.

[9]   Steve Murdoch, *Britain, Denmark-Norway and the House of Stuart, 1603–60* (East Linton, 2000), pp. 90–1.

[10]   S. R. Gardiner, *History of England* (1893), vol. IX, p. 74; Mark Charles Fissel, *The Bishops' Wars* (Cambridge, 1994), pp. 62–8.

parliament, a defensive war necessitating extraordinary finance – 'when his kingdoms and person are in apparent danger'.[11] On 4 December 1639 a marathon meeting of this Council of War debated alternatives before it was agreed to 'advise the king making trial of his people in Parliament, before he used any way of power'. Unexpectedly it was Hamilton, Laud and Strafford – 'those Lords that were all this while most adverse to Parliaments' – who pressed the summoning most vigorously.[12]

Charles I was enough of a believer in the fundamental constitution of his monarchy to think that a parliament meeting in such circumstances would perform its duty: 'in his own inclination he desired the old way'.[13] He was prepared to allow his subjects to debate grievances, propose bills, and criticize his servants as the price to be paid for failing to find a genuine pacification with the Scots as long as these activities followed a grant of sufficient funds to begin the war. But Charles was no starry-eyed optimist. Debate in the Council rehearsed the history of past Caroline parliaments and plans were laid in anticipation of either success or failure. Privy councillors pledged 'to assist the King in extraordinary ways if the Parliament prove peevish'.[14]

It is crucial to understand that in December 1639 Charles did not think that he was violating his often-expressed principle that he would not go to parliament out of necessity. He believed he could finance the opening sallies of a war by emptying the Exchequer, borrowing extensively, and assessing military dues like coat and conduct money. More than two thirds of a £200,000 loan from his councillors was immediately subscribed and in the four months prior to the meeting of parliament the king raised the equivalent of seven subsidies, a remarkable feat.[15] No one imagined that parliament would foot the entire bill, but it was believed that a successful session would make other forms of financing easier to collect.[16] Debate in the Council of War revealed genuine support for a military solution to the Scottish crisis, whatever individuals would later claim. The earl of Northumberland, soon to be appointed Lord General, despaired of financing the fighting, but he knew which side was driving it forward. He reported to his brother-in-law, the earl of Leicester, that the Scots 'go on in their rebellious ways with much

---

[11] *CSP*, vol. II, p. 81.
[12] Arthur Collins, *Letters and Memorials of State* (1746), vol. II, p. 623; W. Scott and J. Bliss (eds.), *The Works of Archbishop William Laud* (Oxford, 1847–60), vol. III, p. 233.
[13] *CSP*, vol. II, p. 81.
[14] Laud, *Works*, vol. III, p. 233.
[15] HMC, *De L'Isle and Dudley*, vol. VI, pp. 212–14; Robert Ashton, *The Crown and Money Market 1603–40* (Oxford, 1960), pp. 176–7.
[16] Conrad Russell, *The Fall of the British Monarchies 1637–42* (Oxford, 1991), p. 72.

constancy and resolution, having respect to nothing but the maintaining of their own wills'.[17] Few doubted the justice of the king's cause, even if many worried about his ability to attain it.

These worries stemmed in part from the realization that not everyone supported the king's objectives in Scotland. Throughout the crisis the existence of English subjects who took the side of the Covenanters and who offered them encouragement if not outright aid was widely known. 'The Scots have many spies which flock about the King ... they know our divisions, and the strength of their own combination and they have a party amongst us.'[18] Who constituted this party remains a matter of speculation for their presence was shadowy and their identity secret, but Charles knew of the disloyalty of some of his English subjects and it remained a matter of concern to him as he prepared for war.[19] Some of the private approaches made by the Scottish commissioners to individual English lords were publicly rebuffed. A petition to the earl of Essex was handed over to the king unread, while overtures to individual peers were rejected.[20] In March 1640 the duke of Hamilton warned his son-in-law, the earl of Lindsay, against depending upon the treachery of the king's English subjects. 'Trust not to that, nor give credit to a few factious spirits, with whom perhaps correspondence may be kept.'[21] Indeed, Charles's antenna was sensitive to betrayal ever since his forces retreated from Kelso.[22]

It was in this context of treason that the revelation provided by the earl of Traquair made such an impression upon the king. Traquair had come into possession of dramatic proof that the Covenanter leaders had held correspondence with a foreign ruler and he presented it to Charles at the end of March.[23] It was a letter directed to Louis XIII requesting 'an assistance equal to your accustomed clemency heretofore, and so often showed to this nation'. The appeal was to be delivered by one William Colville along with an oral narration of the Scots' proceedings and a request for aid. Ominously, the letter was addressed 'Au Roi', a superscription 'never written by any French man to any, but to their own King'.

---

[17] HMC, *De L'Isle and Dudley*, vol. VI, p. 182.

[18] *CSPD 1639*, p. 123.

[19] Alan Macinnes, *Charles I and the Making of the Covenanting Movement* (Edinburgh, 1991), p. 193; David Stevenson, *The Scottish Revolution* (Newton Abbot, 1973), p. 188.

[20] *CSPD 1639*, pp. 155–6; Peter Donald, *An Uncounselled King* (Cambridge, 1990), p. 149; John Nalson, *An Impartial Collection of the Great Affairs of State* (1682), vol. I, pp. 283–4.

[21] Burnet, *Memoires of Hamilton*, p. 164.

[22] John Scally, 'Counsel in Crisis: James, Third Marquis of Hamilton and the Bishops' Wars 1638–40', in John R. Young (ed.), *Celtic Dimensions of the British Civil Wars* (Edinburgh, 1997), p. 20.

[23] Sir James Balfour, *The Historical Works of Sir James Balfour* (Edinburgh, 1824), vol. III, p. 76.

Seven Covenanter leaders, including the earl of Loudoun who was currently in London presenting Scottish demands to the king, had signed the letter.[24] Here was a smoking gun if ever there was one, evidence from their own hands that the Scots were willing to endanger Charles's southern kingdom, 'for if a stranger once take footing in those northern parts, it is not hard to judge how easily he may be invited by such guides as they'. The letter was also proof of the king's belief that the Scottish rebellion was not motivated by arcane matters of religious practice but by a desire to cast aside English rule: 'herein appears first their malignity to us their natural sovereign, in that they had rather prostitute themselves to a foreign government and that such as is different in religion than yield conformity to ours'.[25]

When read the way Charles read it – 'no construction can be made of the letter itself but that they have given themselves to that King' – the 'Au Roi' letter was an act of despicable treason, showing 'that the ground of their rebellion is nothing but a mere opposition to civil and monarchical government'.[26] By addressing Louis as their king, the Scots had implicitly renounced Charles's sovereignty over them. Despite the humiliation of revealing its contents – 'for the honour of our nation we should have concealed this business' – Charles determined immediately that he would have to 'communicate it to our Court of Parliament, that so the world may be no longer abused by their artifices, and pretences of conscience'.[27] To foil what remained of the plot, the king ordered William Colville's brother James detained in London, the earl of Loudoun sent to the Tower and interrogated by the Attorney General, and his ambassador in France the earl of Leicester to undertake an immediate investigation.[28]

On 11 April 1640 a secret emissary brought Leicester detailed instructions that revealed the contents of the letter, what was known of the plot, and the delicate tasks that lay before him. As a measure of how seriously the king regarded the matter, the earl was informed that he was only the third person to know.[29] Leicester had little difficulty locating Colville in

---

24 John Rushworth, *Historical Collections* (1721), vol. III, p. 1120. I am grateful to Eleanor Hubbard for her careful translation of these letters.
25 STC, 9260. *His Majesties Declaration Concerning his Proceedings with his Subjects of Scotland since the Pacification of Berwick* (1640), p. 56. This was also Henry Guthry's assessment: 'many believed the design to be against the King, and whispered anent it; but had not the confidence to speak out'. Henry Guthry, *The Memoirs of Henry Guthry* (1747), p. 68.
26 Collins, *Letters and Memorials*, vol. II, pp. 644–5.
27 *Ibid.*, vol. II, p. 645.
28 *CSPD 1640*, p. 30.
29 William Knowler (ed.), *The Earl of Strafforde's Letters and Dispatches* (1739), vol. II, p. 408.

Paris or in placing an informant at his side.[30] Nor did he wait long for an audience with Louis XIII where the French king denied all knowledge of the affair and any willingness to aid rebels against the government of his brother-in-law.[31] Indeed, the Scottish approach had presented the French king and his chief minister, Cardinal Richelieu, with a dilemma. Deeply committed to war with the Habsburgs they were more eager to have England as an ally than an enemy, but could survive equally well if it were neither. A Scottish military rebellion would at least have the effect of neutralizing Charles I and neutering the hispanophiles at his Court. Thus Richelieu quietly encouraged Scottish hopes.[32]

It was soon apparent to Leicester that the Scots had indeed attempted to forge an alliance with Louis XIII, though whether that included an implied offer of sovereignty was more open to question. Colville's mission was to represent the brutal tyrannies the Scots had suffered through attacks upon their fundamental laws and liberties and to seek French military assistance. He brought with him copies of those Scottish official declarations that had proven such effective propaganda pieces when published in England, though one assumes that their French translations downplayed Charles's supposed imposition of popery.[33] In London, Loudoun's interrogation in the Tower confirmed the authenticity of the letter, though he insisted both that it had never been sent to France and that he was ignorant of its contents since he was unable to read French.[34]

Anti-Scottish sentiment, never far below the surface in England, was another of the factors that led Charles to believe that his subjects would take up his cause. It was building perceptibly since the summer. The gathering Covenanter army was a source of tension for the northern counties and fears of an invasion were sufficiently high that the Scots launched a propaganda campaign to deny that it was their intention 'to invade our neighbour kingdom of England and enrich ourselves by the spoils thereof'.[35] But their actions spoke for themselves and if they did not they were aided by Charles's own appeal to his subjects. The king had never shied away from public explanations, using the declaration

---

[30]   *CSPD 1640*, p. 104.
[31]   Collins, *Letters and Memorials*, vol. II, p. 647.
[32]   M. V. Hay (ed.), *The Blairs Papers 1603–60* (1929), pp. 250–3.
[33]   *CSPD 1640*, p. 104.
[34]   Macinnes claims that the 'Au Roi' letter was 'never delivered' but it is to be found in the French archives and was known to Richelieu. Macinnes, *Making of the Covenanting Movement*, p. 195. Cf. Gardiner, *History of England*, vol. IX, p. 97 where Louis XIII's denial of having seen the 'Au Roi' letter is analyzed.
[35]   STC, 21905. *An Information to all Good Christians within the Kingdom of England* (Edinburgh, 1639), p. 4.

more often and more fully than any of his predecessors to explain and justify aspects of royal policy.

In contemplating war with the Scots he prepared the way with a skilful propaganda campaign. It began with the *Large Declaration*, the longest (430 pages) and fullest royal statement of political affairs that had ever been published. Written by Walter Balcanquhal, but narrated as if by the king himself, the *Large Declaration* provided the royal perspective upon events in Scotland beginning with Charles's accession.[36] Its goal was to answer Scottish propaganda, justify royal policy, and explain the reasons why all the king's efforts to reconcile his differences with the Scots had failed. Charles's self-defence was ample and vigorous. The Jacobean history of the development of the prayer book was related in copious detail beginning with its authorization at the General Assembly of 1616 and its development by James's commissioners 'in substance, frame, and composure much about one with this very service book which we of late commended to them'.[37] The *Large Declaration* printed nearly all the official documents created by crown and Covenanters and placed them within the context of ever escalating Scottish demands and royal concessions to them. Its central oft-repeated thesis was that the events in Scotland were an anti-monarchical rebellion under colour of religion: 'the question indeed is neither more nor less than this, whether we and our successors shall be any more kings of that kingdom'.[38]

As the history detailed in the *Large Declaration* ended with the Pacification of Berwick, the king and his councillors saw fit to produce a sequel, *His Majesty's Declaration Concerning his Proceedings with his Subjects of Scotland*. This account was penned by Secretary Windebank but again written as if Charles were the narrator and presented in the form of a royal declaration 'by the King'. Its central themes were the king's willingness to enter into the Pacification and the manifold Scottish violations of its terms. In it Charles repeatedly stressed how disinclined he was to shed the blood of his own subjects and how ready he had been to offer concessions to the Scots. But every instance of 'Princely goodness and mildness' had been met with 'extreme ingratitude and insufferable insolencies'.[39] These public sentiments matched his private ones.

[36] STC, 21906. Balcanquhal, *Large Declaration*. The king read and annotated the *Large Declaration* as well as responded to queries from Balcanquhal and was thus directly involved in its production. David Laing (ed.), *The Letters and Journals of Robert Baillie* (Edinburgh, 1841–42), vol. II, pp. 429–30.

[37] STC, 21906. Balcanquhal, *Large Declaration*, p.17.

[38] *Ibid.*, p. 428.

[39] STC, 9260. [Sir Francis Windebank] *His Majesties Declaration Concerning his Proceedings with his Subjects of Scotland, since the Pacification in the Camp near Berwick* (1640), pp. 1–2.

The previous year he told the earl of Rutland 'there was not above 5 or 6 Lords in the Covenant whom he had not done courtesies to'. He condemned the ingratitude of the earl of Argyle 'for those many and great favours he has conferred upon him'.[40] After pardoning countless instances of treason, forgiving blatantly rebellious conduct, and overlooking personal slights, Charles still found himself betrayed. Covenanter pamphlets 'stuffed full of calumnies against our regal authority' continued to pour from the presses in such profusion that the Privy Council urged the king to issue a proclamation against them, which was done on 30 March.[41]

Indeed it was to counter *An Information from the Estaites of the Kingdome of Scotland* that Charles's *Declaration Since the Pacification* was produced.[42] It was timed to be published just as parliament convened, as Windebank informed the earl of Leicester on 11 April.[43] By waiting until the last minute, it was hoped that the *Declaration* would sway those who came to Westminster without preconceptions about supplying the king. Windebank was thus able to report the generosity of the Irish parliament that had convened in Dublin at the end of March and voted Charles four subsidies 'and if more than these four shall be requisite ... they will grant more'.[44] When Wentworth crossed the Irish Sea in April he brought several hundred copies of the letter detailing this grant, supposing that its distribution in London might loosen English purse strings as well.[45] But most fortuitously, the *Declaration* was able to include the first public notice of the 'Au Roi' letter, laying out the circumstances in which it was obtained, and printing it in French and English, 'to fill up the measure of their treasons'.[46]

Thus the king had every reason to wish for and work for the success of the spring parliament just as he had done whatever was in his power to clear the way for it. As he would proclaim in his opening speech, he had 'sequestered the memory of all former discouragements'.[47] Sir Benjamin Valentine and Sir William Strode, imprisoned since 1629 for their role in the adjournment riot, were released so as not to be provocative symbols

---

40   HMC, 12th Report, *Manuscripts of the Earl of Rutland* (1888), vol. IV, p. 504; *CSPD 1639*, p. 52.
41   *SRP*, vol. II, pp. 663, 703–5.
42   STC, 91216. *Information from the Estaites of the Kingdome of Scotland, to the Kingdome of England* (Edinburgh, 1640). *SRP* confuses this tract with the similarly entitled STC, 21917 that was published after the Short Parliament.
43   Collins, *Letters and Memorials*, vol. II, p. 644.
44   Rushworth, *Historical Collections*, vol. III, p. 1099.
45   Knowler, *Letters and Dispatches*, vol. II, p. 403.
46   STC 9260. *His Majesties Declaration Concerning his Proceedings*, pp. 55–9.
47   *CJ*, vol. II, p. 4; Cope, *Short Parliament*, p. 116.

of past contentions. Sir John Finch was elevated to a peerage both to secure him from potential retaliation and to remove an obvious flash-point. Viscount Saye and Sele and Lord Brooke, both of whom had defied the king by their refusal to take the military oath at York in 1639, nevertheless received writs of summons to avoid a privilege dispute.[48] On the king's side, Roger Maynwaring, now bishop of St David's, was ordered to stay away so as not to revive complaints about his 1627 sermons *Religion and Alegiance*.[49] With the advice of his Council of War in 1639, the king had cancelled a large number of patents for monopolies, including several that had been granted to his chief servants.[50] He now issued a proclamation to reform the collection of debts and prevent receivers from abusing the royal prerogative.[51] These actions signalled a willingness to redress further grievances. Whatever might happen, the king had done everything he could to pre-pare to meet his subjects in the spring of 1640.

III

Charles held out hope that 'there may be such a happy conclusion of this Parliament that it may be a cause of many more meetings with you'.[52] A harmonious session with his subjects would not only replenish his coffers, it would end speculation that England was a paper tiger power-less to engage in continental military activity. Despite the long decade of peace, the king had never given up hope that he would participate in the restitution of the Palatinate. Even as his domestic problems mounted, he was vigorously engaged in negotiations to broker a deal in favour of his nephew, the Elector Palatine. Moreover, a willing vote of supply would go far to amend 'what discouragements he hath formerly had ... in preceding assemblies of Parliament'.[53] Both sessions of the parliament of 1628 had ended badly and the king took no pleasure in the rupture of relations that had resulted. He had cause to hope that the long hiatus would have calmed the passions that had flared in 1629 when otherwise sober parliamentarians rioted in their own chamber rather than have their session adjourned for a week. Finally, because of the

---

48   *CSPD 1639–40*, p. 522; Marc Schwarz, 'Viscount Saye and Sele, Lord Brooke and Aristocratic Protest to the First Bishops' War', *Canadian Journal of History*, 7 (1972), 23.
49   Cope, *Short Parliament*, pp. 82–3; *LJ*, vol. IV, 58. STC, 17751; Roger Maynwaring, *Religion and Alegiance in Tvvo Sermons Preached before the Kings Maiestie* (1627).
50   Fissel, *Bishops' Wars*, pp. 68–70.
51   *SRP*, vol. II, pp. 705–7.
52   Rushworth, *Historical Collections*, vol. III, p. 1119.
53   STC, 9262. *His Majesties Declaration*, p. 3.

extreme pressure of time, Charles had set the Short Parliament a simple agenda, completion of the bill for tonnage and poundage and the vote of supply. Thus he would know immediately whether his hopes of success might be fulfilled.

Charles opened the Short Parliament with two requests and a promise.[54] First, he desired passage of the bill for tonnage and poundage that each of his previous parliaments had failed to complete. The king had never claimed that this subsidy for naval defence was his by right – 'he hath taken it only de facto'.[55] But without parliamentary authorization, collection of tonnage and poundage had led to 'questions and disputes' and Charles went so far as to have the legislation prepared for the Commons.[56] His second entreaty was for subsidies sufficient to carry out war with the Scots. Here Lord Keeper Finch did not mince his words. The Scots had committed 'rebellious treason unparalleled' and 'foul and horrid treason'. Their 'mutinous behaviour' threatened not only the king but also his kingdoms, for the Scots had invited into Britain foreign armies 'that may as in former times find out a postern gate'. To defend the English nation Charles beseeched parliament to provide 'so many subsidies as you in your hearty affections to his Majesty and to the common good shall think fit'.[57] His promise was that he would receive all of parliament's petitions for redress of grievances that time allowed before his armies took the field and if necessary would convene another session in the winter to allow them to complete their work. This promise was unequivocal: 'to stay till your just grievances be heard and redressed. And his Majesty doth assure you he will go along with you for your advantage.'[58]

Time was pressing. Even as the members assembled in London, royal forces were being gathered in the North of England and Covenanter armies in the South of Scotland. Though no one knew for certain, it was credibly believed that hostilities would be underway by June. If the subsidies were to do the king good, they would have to be approved quickly. 'The summer must not be lost nor any minute of time foreslowed to reduce them.'[59] Thus Charles desired that supply precede grievances, asking parliament to trust his pledge that the session would

---

[54] There are two good narrative accounts of events, Kevin Sharpe, *The Personal Rule of Charles I* (New Haven, 1991), pp. 852–84 and Russell, *Fall of the British Monarchies*, pp. 90–123.

[55] Cope, *Short Parliament*, p. 121; Judith Maltby (ed.), *The Short Parliament (1640) Diary of Sir Thomas Aston* (1988), p. 7.

[56] Cope, *Short Parliament*, p. 121.

[57] *CJ*, vol. II, p. 3; Cope, *Short Parliament*, pp. 120, 119.

[58] Cope, *Short Parliament*, p. 121.

[59] Cope, *Short Parliament*, p. 120.

not terminate upon the passage of the subsidy bill.[60] Though it was more common for grievances and supply to progress together through the stages of parliamentary approval, the king's proposal did not involve much risk.[61] Since subsidies were raised at intervals specified in the Act, the king could be gratified and the parliament protected simply by setting future dates for their collection. If the king did not keep his promise, he would threaten this revenue. Certainly the emergency warranted the request, for in the king's view delay was equivalent to denial and the consideration of grievances would inevitably create delay. Even in the best of circumstances, creating petitions of grievances was a time-consuming enterprise involving hearings, committees, drafting and debate before decisions could be taken in just one House of Parliament. To underscore the urgency of his needs, the king himself followed the Lord Keeper's presentation with the disclosure of the 'Au Roi' letter and the danger that it posed to England.[62]

The response to the royal revelation was a blow to Charles I. On 17 April Secretary Windebank was sent to the Commons to present the intercepted letter officially and to inform the members that the earl of Loudoun had admitted to having signed it. Despite the dramatic nature of his presentation, it elicited but a single comment, that 'the French king did never receive much less entertain the notion'.[63] No committee was appointed to examine either the letter or the Scottish lord who had signed it and no one moved for the topic to be considered subsequently. The king of England had informed his Commons that the Scots had invited a French invasion force into their country and his Commons responded with silence. Nor did Charles fare better in the Lords. There it was introduced by Lord Cottington who was challenged not on his account of the letter – like Windebank he was only asked when it was written – but on his appearance in the upper House before being formally admitted.[64] A request to have the letter read in English was even refused and it passed into the same oblivion as it had in the Commons.[65]

---

[60] There was not much trust required as he offered to accept 'a proviso in the Act' to that effect. Cope, *Short Parliament*, p. 120.

[61] Thomas Cogswell, 'A Low Road to Extinction? Supply and Redress of Grievances in the Parliaments of the 1620s', *HJ*, 33 (1990), 285, 291–2. While Cogswell argues persuasively that redress along with, rather than before or after, supply was the most common experience, he also provides examples in which supply did precede redress and could therefore serve as precedent, if precedent was desired. These were well known to Members of Parliament.

[62] Cope, *Short Parliament*, pp. 121–2.

[63] Maltby, *Diary of Sir Thomas Aston*, p. 7. The assurance was given by John Pym and could only have been based on consultation with the Scottish commissioners.

[64] Cope, *Short Parliament*, p. 58.

[65] *Ibid.*, pp. 58, 97.

Charles's smoking gun had turned into a damp squib. The emotional impact he had expected the 'Au Roi' letter to have created never materialized and the way in which it was contemptuously brushed aside demonstrated that there was nothing he could do to influence the parliamentary agenda.

Parliament's refusal to examine the 'Au Roi' letter was a slap in the face to the king. Here was an easy opportunity to condemn Scottish behaviour without committing to funding the war, to express horror at Scottish treason without actually doing anything about it. Sympathy for a traduced king could have come cheaply. The same was true about the Bill for tonnage and poundage. As the king had a text already prepared, appointing a committee would have demonstrated at least an inclination to satisfy his desires. Consideration of tonnage and poundage had gone to committee in each of Charles's previous parliaments so sending it there again did not oblige the Commons to any particular course of action. Yet it too, foundered. A Bill did not receive a single mention in the records of the debates and no committee was ever appointed to consider it. If Charles was searching for a signal 'that the King may delight in his people' it did not come in the opening days of the Short Parliament.[66] On the contrary, the first recorded speech in the House took up a theme that had been heard in 1626, that Englishmen faced greater perils at home than abroad: 'the more dangerous because it is home bred and runs into the veins'.[67] This was followed the next day by John Pym's sensational two-hour oration 'that left not anything untouched'. He listed at least thirty-six separate grievances contained under the headings of liberty of parliament, matters of religion, and affairs of state.[68] He outlined a programme for reform that would have necessitated months of committee work and debate before either a petition of grievances or a remonstrance could have been produced.

It is hard to imagine how the parliamentary leaders could have behaved more provocatively. Though Clarendon, who was a member, believed that the Short Parliament represented the king's best opportunity for comity with his subjects, this was an observation only validated by hindsight. It should not suggest that parliament's leaders would have allowed the king to achieve his goals in the Short Parliament. The few 'who brought ill purposes with them' were probably in direct contact with the Scots and certainly in sympathy with their cause.[69] They must

---

[66] Rushworth, *Historical Collections*, vol. III, pp. 1138–9.
[67] Cope, *Short Parliament*, p. 135.
[68] Dorothy Gardiner (ed.), *The Oxinden Letters, 1607–1642* (1937), p. 163; Cope, *Short Parliament*, pp. 148–157.
[69] *CHR*, vol. I, p. 183; Donald, *An Uncounselled King*, pp. 191–7.

have known from the councillors amongst them that the king's fuse would be a short one and that they would have to go some way toward meeting his needs if the session was to hold. When they were faced with a similar constraint in 1628, they had enforced a moratorium on criticism of the duke of Buckingham until after the king assented to the Petition of Right. Now the price of gaining redress of grievances was simply doing their duty, supplying the king in time of extraordinary need. Sir Benjamin Rudyard pointed the way on the opening day of business: 'Parliament is the bed of reconciliation betwixt King and people', he averred. 'I would desire nothing more than that we proceed with such moderation as the parliament may be the mother of many more happy parliaments.'[70] His moderate views received no more consideration than had the 'Au Roi' letter.

Instead, attacks upon the king's prerogatives began almost immediately. A debate over the break-up of the 1629 session led to assertions that the Commons rather than the king held the power of dissolution, precisely the assertion that had led to war in Scotland. When Edward Herbert, the Queen's Solicitor General, 'told them they were putting the greatest question that ever was put in a Parliament and said it manifestly trenched the prerogative', Oliver St John denied that the king had any such prerogative: 'nay he said ... the court must adjourn itself. He concluded therefore that the adjourning was not legal.'[71] This represented an ominous change of opinion, for as Hampden's counsel St John had argued that only the king 'summons, continues, and dissolves' parliament.[72] If Charles did not have power to adjourn parliaments, neither did it appear that members believed he held the power to summon them. In the debate over institutional grievances it was asserted that the king was required to summon parliament annually according to statutes from the reign of Edward III.[73]

These direct assaults upon royal prerogatives did not escape the king's notice. He would begin his declaration of May 1640 justifying the dissolution with the statement 'that the calling, adjourning, proroguing and dissolving of Parliaments are undoubted prerogatives inseparably annexed to his imperial crown'.[74] Nor was he unaware of the insidious attacks upon his revenues that developed from Pym's list of grievances.

---

[70] Cope, *Short Parliament*, pp. 139–40.
[71] Cope, *Short Parliament*, p. 163; Maltby, *Aston's Diary*, p. 19. Cf. Russell, *Fall of the British Monarchies*, pp. 108–9.
[72] Gardiner (ed.), *CDPR*, p. 112.
[73] 'By the law should be once every year.' Cope, *Short Parliament*, p. 155; Maltby, *Aston's Diary*, pp. 58–9.
[74] STC, 9262. *His Majesties Declaration*, p. 1.

This included forest and knighthood fines, monopolies and patents, even fees for building permits. Members of the Commons seemed intent on reducing Charles's ordinary revenue to his rental income. It was soon apparent that tonnage and poundage would be ransomed for the surrender of the right to collect impositions.[75] Ship Money was attacked as illegal. Coat and conduct money as well as other military fees were declared breaches of the Petition of Right. Ominously, a parliamentary committee continued to examine accounts of the 1624 Treasurers at War.[76] Impositions and Ship Money were seemingly impervious to parliamentary attack since both rights had been confirmed in law cases. Thus one of the first acts of the Short Parliament was to send for the records in Bate's and Hampden's cases with the intention of having the judgments vacated. Despite the presence of so many lawyers in the House, hardly anyone seemed troubled by the Commons' assumption of the power of judicial review or the unseemliness of defendants and their lawyers acting as their own judges. The only concession the royal spokesmen could achieve was to allow the king's Counsel to be heard before Ship Money was declared illegal. This was grudgingly accepted although many speakers regarded it as unnecessary as they had already made up their minds.

Taken together this was a staggering assault on the royal prerogative and the nature of the English monarchy. Parliamentary leaders aimed their attacks at the foundation of the king's rights rather than at putative abuses of them. It was not specific patents and monopolies that were grievous; it was the class of grants itself.[77] The Petition of Right, which king and parliament had agreed only confirmed traditional liberties, was given the most radical interpretation possible. No taxation could be raised without explicit parliamentary approval no matter how strong the precedent or ancient the practice.[78] Legal decisions were deemed not binding either because the judges 'were different in their opinions' or because their opinions were 'contrary to all other judgment of the law'.[79] Nor were these criticisms any longer veiled by placing the blame upon unnamed 'evil councillors'. Pym named the Privy Council, the judges, and the king himself – 'I have now gone as high as I can upon earth' – in apportioning blame.[80]

[75]   Rushworth, *Historical Collections*, vol. III, p. 1134; Maltby, *Aston's Diary*, p. 24; *CJ*, vol. II, pp. 7–8.
[76]   *CJ*, vol. II, pp. 7–8.
[77]   Cope, *Short Parliament*, p. 154.
[78]   Maltby, *Aston's Diary*, p. 17.
[79]   Pym's speech, Cope, *Short Parliament*, pp. 152–3.
[80]   *Ibid.*, p. 155. Cf. *ibid.*, p. 149.

It took Charles barely a week to respond. He was doubtless informed of the wide front on which the Commons had opened its offensive and his observation that 'from their first assembling until the 21 of April the House of Commons did nothing that could give his Majesty content' was a delicate understatement.[81] But he was willing to meet his subjects more than half way. As tempting as it might have been to lecture the Commons on their responsibilities, Charles summoned them to the Banqueting House simply to reassert his urgent needs. 'If the supply be not speedy it will be of no use at all, for the army is now marching.' Bargaining with himself, the king lowered his demands, requesting 'not a great and ample supply . . . [but] such a supply (as without which) the charge will be lost, and the design frustrated'.[82] In addition, he offered to abandon the collection of Ship Money if parliament could provide a substitute that would fund maritime protection. Clearly his councillors must have believed that this was the real sticking point because his explanation of Ship Money was full and frank. It was a levy that was paid directly to the naval treasurers, every penny of the money went for seaborne defence, and as much as he had hoped to suspend its collection, the international situation was more dangerous than ever. The king had no objection if parliament wished to place the most severe restrictions on such revenue 'that it may never come to the least benefit and advantage to himself'.[83]

Once again Charles promised to redress the grievances of his subjects if they would provide him with aid. By now the king knew what some of those grievances would be and to announce in front of the assembled members of both Houses 'that he will hear them with a gracious ear, and give them such an answer, as you and all the Kingdom shall have reason to joy therein' was to make a royal vow.[84] There was still a chance that this could become 'the most blessed and most happy Parliament that ever was' and that chance lay in its members 'putting an obligation of trust and confidence upon him, which shall more secure you than all you can invent . . . It is a course that good manners, duty, and reason should require of you.'[85] The king had now personalized the issues so that continued opposition to an immediate vote of supply would be viewed as opposition to the king, himself. On 21 April he again asked for the loyalty of his subjects in a cause that touched his honour and theirs.

Charles's reappearance so soon after the opening of parliament, his offer to take less than he needed and to give more than he wanted, and his

---

[81] STC, 9262. *His Majesties Declaration*, p. 10.
[82] Rushworth, *Historical Collections*, vol. III, p. 1137.
[83] *Ibid.*, p. 1139.
[84] *Ibid.*, p. 1137.
[85] *Ibid.*, p. 1139.

frank and ingenuous promises all represented a sincere willingness to work with parliament. The royal statement was carefully crafted to appeal to a presumed moderate majority who would be swayed by 'good manners, duty, and reason'. Charles did not go on the offensive, as he had in appearances before previous parliaments. He did not complain about the attacks on his judges and ministers, the misrepresentations of his policies, or even the aspersions cast on his own character. In fact, there was not a whisper of criticism of the proceedings of the past week, not an adjective that could conceivably give offence. The statement ended on such a hopeful note as to make it nearly impossible to deny the king's good intentions.[86]

The king's entreaties fell upon stony ground, not to say salted earth. When, on 22 April, the Speaker, Sir John Glanville, attempted to present Charles's message officially to the House, objections were raised about whether to receive it. Pym and others argued that only written messages should be presented since oral reports were liable to error. The royal councillors in the House strenuously objected to this assertion – 'report ever hath been made by the Speaker'. Vane and Windebank reminded the members that this was an extraordinary message delivered personally by the king and therefore of even greater weight than one sent in writing. Solicitor General Herbert added furiously: 'the king commands attendance to receive and hear, he himself commands'. There could be no question that the report should be delivered. The queen's solicitor, Sir Peter Ball, was apoplectic: 'when four times delivered his Majesty's command no man to spend time and dispute form'.[87] For the Commons to refuse to receive the king's message upon a punctilious technicality was further than even the most obstructionist members could persuade the House to go. After all, most of the members had already heard the speech in the Banqueting House and knew its contents. To demand a copy in writing was a plain insult. Thus it was ultimately conceded that the Speaker could provide the details. But those who agreed to hear did not agree to listen. The Commons voted to delay consideration of the king's requests.[88]

Though debate of the king's second appeal was postponed only a day, it was enough to dash any hope that the Commons intended to cooperate with the crown. It was also a preview of the outcome of the deliberation. In the committee of the whole House debate alternated between royal

---

[86]   Dorothy Gardiner, *Oxinden Letters*, p. 172.

[87]   Maltby, *Aston's Diary*, pp. 26–7. This sentence is somewhat garbled but the meaning is clear: when delivered four times no one should dispute his Majesty's command. None of the diaries printed by Cope provide an account of this debate.

[88]   Maltby, *Aston's Diary*, p. 29.

councillors demanding that the question of supply be put and members clamouring for yet more grievances to be incorporated into a petition. When Sir Benjamin Rudyard suggested 'let us trust him first that we may trust him hereafter' he was met with 'a long pause. No man speaking.'[89] But then came a cascade of voices in favour of pressing on with grievances. Every effort to force the House to a statement of its willingness to provide for the king was beaten back. Even Sir Henry Vane's transparent warning that 'if we do not supply the king we shall hardly relieve our grievances' fell on deaf ears.[90] Worse still, Pym's motion that the heads of grievances be presented to the Lords carried the day. Bringing the Lords into the process before the Commons' committee of grievances had completed its own work simply guaranteed a raft of needless disputes and repetitive decisions.[91] Wily parliamentarians knew that no course of action would take longer than this one.

Observers interpreted the Commons' provocations as parliament's death knell. 'We have this day declined the supply of the king and have resolved the grievances shall take place wherefore the king resolved to dissolve us tomorrow. They are in council now but it is to confirm the King's sense by the vote of the council.'[92] But once again the king proved pliant. He had asked for parliament's trust and it was not forthcoming. Was there anything else he could do now that the Commons had ignored his two direct appeals? Once the lower House began presenting their lists of grievances to the Lords, the session would be lost. It was already clear that they intended to have Ship Money declared illegal, but that could only be done by a process of reversal in which the Lords, sitting in their capacity as a court of appeals, would essentially rehear the case and then examine the justification for each of the judges' decisions. Charles Jones's estimate that such a procedure by itself would take six weeks was uncontested.[93] Charles did not believe he had six weeks to spare. Thus the very next day he appeared in the House of Lords in a desperate attempt to gain a vote of supply. For the third time in less than two weeks he confessed, 'my necessities are so urgent, that there can be no delay'. Had he time, he would not insist that supply precede redress, but in such an emergency all he asked was that 'if the House of Commons will trust

---

89   *Ibid.*, p. 36.
90   Maltby, *Aston's Diary*, p. 41; Cope, *Short Parliament*, p. 173.
91   See Strafford's account of what would be necessary to determine the legality of Ship Money. Cope, *Short Parliament*, pp. 74–5.
92   This was the report of Henry Percy, who sat for Portsmouth. HMC, *De L'Isle and Dudley*, vol. VI, p. 252. The earl of Northumberland also believed parliament would be dissolved on 23 April. *Ibid.*, p. 254.
93   Strafford, Cope, *Short Parliament*, p. 74; Bridgewater, *ibid.*, p. 77.

Me, I will make good what I have promised'. Trust was now the paramount issue. Without it 'all my business this summer will be lost'. Then the king asked the Lords not to join with the Commons in pressing grievances ahead of supply in consideration 'of your own honours and mine'.[94] Over objections from a number of peers, the upper House voted to report to the Commons the substance of the king's speech as well as their own sense that on this occasion supply should take priority over grievances.[95] 'They all resolved to trust him and said they would take the word of a King, and that some also added of a gentleman.'[96]

No matter how delicately the Lords put the proposition, and an entire morning was spent attempting to ensure that they would not breach the privileges of the Commons, their intervention was heaven-sent to those who sought ways to delay a vote of supply. Rather than debate the substance of the Lords' appeal members of the Commons focused on their institutional privileges. Money matters were initiated in the Commons. Their language was of high principle and moral absolutes. 'The liberties of Parliament were our inheritance', intoned Sir Walter Earle; 'this was the greatest liberty we had', added John Pym. 'Break a rule and our liberties are gone', urged one of Hampden's Ship Money attorneys; 'a main violation', assessed the other.[97] Nor was it likely that the Lords would accept the rebuke the Commons had in store for them. After the lower House spent two full days debating their privileges and preparing for a conference to defend them, the Lords spent the next two days in the same activities. Nor would they be outdone in defence of the privileges of their institution. 'This house was never made such ciphers', thundered the Earl Marshal; 'let us consider whether we are not any more than circuit judges only to serve their turns', fumed the Lord Chamberlain.[98] Conferences between the Houses absorbed yet another two days and still the substance of the Lords' report was ignored. When it was not occupied with its privilege dispute, the Commons pressed forward with its grievances. 29 April was taken up with a laundry list of complaints about religion, the thirtieth with the first examination of the records of the Ship Money case.

On 24 April Charles had appealed to the Lords for haste and a week later that appeal languished unheard in the lower House. At this point it might be reasonably concluded that parliament would be dissolved. It

---

[94] *LJ*, vol. IV, p. 65.
[95] These decisions were made only after divisions of the House. *LJ*, vol. IV, p. 67; Cope, *Short Parliament*, p. 79.
[96] Cope, *Short Parliament*, p. 177.
[97] *Ibid.*, pp. 178–9; Maltby, *Aston's Diary*, p. 72.
[98] Cope, *Short Parliament*, p. 84.

appeared there was nothing the king could do to impress upon the Commons the exigencies he faced. He could not even redress their grievances for none had yet been presented. Twice he had made personal appearances, three times he had asked for personal trust. Nothing had moved the Commons to consider his appeals. They were obdurate that they would do their own business before they did the king's and they had not provided even a chink of hope to the contrary. No committees were appointed to prepare Bills for either tonnage and poundage or subsidies, and no commitments were made to grant either. It was hard to see what else the king could do. Nevertheless, Charles was reluctant to give up and simply walk away. If he did there would never be another parliament voluntarily summoned during his reign. The Commons' leaders were playing for very high stakes indeed, and as Windebank had written

if his people should not cheerfully, according to their duties, meet him in that exigent when his kingdom and person are in apparent danger, the world might see he is forced, contrary to his own inclination, to use extraordinary means.[99]

So the king made one more attempt. On 2 May, his Secretary, Sir Henry Vane, delivered a terse message directly to the Commons.

That his Majesty hath divers times, and by sundry ways, acquainted this House with the urgent necessity of supply and ... hitherto hath received no answer at all, his Majesty doth again desire them to give him a present answer concerning his supply.[100]

The king's demand was direct and unequivocal. Only one question seemingly remained, would the Commons make any move to grant him supply? Debate began promisingly enough when Sir Francis Seymour said that if he could have immediate satisfaction regarding Ship Money then he 'should trust the king with the rest'.[101] Numerous speakers echoed this position and while it was not exactly what Charles had suggested when he challenged parliament to find some other source of revenue for naval defence, it was at least a concrete proposal. Had it carried in debate it might have ended the impasse. But a chorus of parliamentary leaders spoke against such harmony. Hampden, whose very person was associated with the naval levy, argued that institutional liberties were more important. William Strode and others insisted upon the Commons' hard-line position that all of their grievances go forward. But it was Pym who raised the stakes. Fearful that a compromise on Ship

---

[99]   *CSP*, vol. II, p. 81.
[100] *CJ*, vol. II, p. 19.
[101] Cope, *Short Parliament*, p. 189. This was a position from which he retreated the following day.

Money might lead a majority to vote supply, he spoke for the first time against the war. Pym argued that while it was the prerogative of kings to declare hostilities, it was the prerogative of parliaments to support them. 'He said this war with Scotland was of dangerous consequence and since we were not obliged to maintain a war he thought as yet we had not proofs enough to engage ourselves.' If Charles required subsidies he should justify his request, a position so startling that Sir Thomas Jermyn, Comptroller of the Household, blurted, 'he expected not what was last spoken of'.[102] Examining the causes of the Scottish war would have allowed those who supported the Covenanters to have aired their case and rehashed every detail of the previous three years of conflict.[103] Beyond anything else, it would also have created even longer delays. Debate raged the entire day and into the evening. The king's councillors attempted to have a series of direct questions put to the House and each effort was beaten back by more debate.[104] Finally it was resolved to defer the question entirely. The next day was Sunday, and Monday had already been set aside for a hearing on Ship Money. Tuesday would be time enough to resume consideration of whether or not to provide the king with an 'immediate' answer to his demand for supply.

Again Charles was stymied, but incredibly he attempted another compromise – his fifth. Saturday's debate had revealed sentiment that if the king would yield Ship Money, the Commons might vote supply. While this was not an attractive fiscal exchange for the crown, it did have counter-balancing political advantages.[105] It would avoid an ugly legal dispute in the Lords, allow a successful conclusion to the parliament, and secure funding for the war. Following Sunday prayers and sermons, Charles decided to make the deal. On Monday morning, 4 May, Secretary Vane rose with yet another royal message. In return for an immediate grant of twelve subsidies, the king would abandon Ship Money forever.[106] To those members who had come to Westminster to do both the king's and the people's business, this was a handsome offer. They could satisfy their monarch and their neighbours all at once as well as look forward to a further session to redress particular complaints. To those who had come with other motives, the offer posed a daunting

---

[102]   Cope, *Short Parliament*, p. 190.

[103]   *CSPD 1640*, pp. 144–5 for what may have been preparation for this debate.

[104]   Cope, *Short Parliament*, pp. 192–3.

[105]   The calculation is that Charles was selling Ship Money at three years' purchase, that is that twelve subsidies amounted to roughly £600,000 as did three years' collection of Ship Money. Most land was bought at ten years' purchase. Cf. Esther Cope, 'Compromise in Early Stuart Parliaments: The Case of the Short Parliament of 1640', *Albion* 9, no. 2 (1977), 137.

[106]   Maltby, *Aston's Diary*, p. 128.

challenge. Sir Walter Earle suggested that the House should take no notice of the message; Pym moved that they proceed as previously scheduled. But the offer was far too attractive for it to die unheard.

Despite attempts by the leading speakers to prevent it, the House went into a committee of the whole and many who had taken little part in previous discussion now spoke in favour of the offer. Against them came every possible objection. Nothing had been done about religion or the liberty of the subject. Coat and conduct money weighed even more heavily. Impositions had not been challenged. As for the proposal itself, the cost was too great and the concession too small. Oliver St John actually asserted that necessity should be judged by parliament rather than the king, a stunning reversal of sovereign power.[107] For most of the day, opponents of the king's bargain groped for a stick with which to beat it back. It was Sir Hugh Cholmley who finally found it when he observed that if Ship Money were illegal 'he knew no reason to buy it out'.[108]

This brought the Commons back to the question they had intended to resolve that day, the legality of the judgment in Hampden's case. The Attorney General had been scheduled to appear before the House to defend the prosecution before the royal proffer had pre-empted him.[109] As Alexander Rigby aptly summarized, 'if illegal our grant a great gift, if legal it is far too little'.[110] This was the winning line for it played upon genuine anger over Ship Money. Lawyers rose to cast doubt on the king's ability to abandon a part of his prerogative: 'his Majesty could not alienate it from the crown'. It was not his to give. He had made them an offer they had to refuse.[111] Soon they were clamouring for the House to declare Ship Money illegal, a resolution that would then be used to vitiate the deal.[112] On the offensive in the morning, the king's councillors were driven to fighting a holding action by nightfall. Now they were the ones attempting to prevent any resolution coming to a vote.[113] But by arguing that Ship Money should not be judged without hearing its defence, they were back to where they had started two weeks ago, at the beginning of a legal process that could take months to resolve. They achieved a pyrrhic procedural victory when the House adjourned without ever returning to formal session. Once again,

---

[107] Cope, *Short Parliament*, p. 209.
[108] *Ibid.*, p. 194.
[109] Maltby, *Aston's Diary*, p. 128.
[110] *Ibid.*, p. 130.
[111] This was the opinion of Robert Holborne, one of Hampden's lawyers in the original case. Cope, *Short Parliament*, p. 194.
[112] At one point Vane even asked if they would accept the king's offer if Ship Money was declared legal. He was ignored. Maltby, *Aston's Diary*, p. 142.
[113] *Ibid.*, p. 138.

Charles's efforts fell stillborn, but this time there would be no attempt to reconceive them; parliament was dissolved the following day.

IV

It is conventional to blame Charles I for the failure of the Short Parliament. The tradition stretches back to Edward Hyde who maintained the polite fiction that it was Charles's advisers, particularly Sir Henry Vane, senior, who were at fault.[114] Like many of the members, Hyde was stunned when parliament was dissolved, for he too refused to believe the warnings of the king and his councillors that delay was equivalent to denial. The mist of memory may also have erased his own role in obstructing the crown's desires.[115] Nevertheless, Clarendon believed the dissolution premature. Had the king asked for fewer subsidies he would have been gratified, a conclusion reached by several contemporaries but one that was at odds with the content and character of the debate over the offer on 4 May.[116] Realization that the Short Parliament was a lost opportunity was not long in coming to future royalists as so many of them had failed to support the king at this critical juncture. Hyde and Falkland had added fuel to the fire of grievances in the early days, Sergeant Glanville and Sir Hugh Cholmley declared Ship Money illegal in the crucial debate on 4 May. It was easier to repent the king's actions than their own.

Historians have followed participants. 'If ultimate responsibility for the failure of compromise in the Short Parliament had to be placed somewhere, it belongs to the King.'[117] They have offered numerous explanations for Charles's 'precipitate' action.[118] Some have blamed his 'obstinacy' and 'lack of flexibility'.[119] Others his excessive self-regard: 'He was reluctant to lose time or honour in talking.'[120] Criticisms of his management of the parliament also suggest Charles's culpability. His opening speech was too brief and it made no mention of Ship Money; his summons of the members to the Banqueting House was peremptory;

---

[114] *CHR*, vol. I, p. 182.
[115] Though Kevin Sharpe produces a full and reliable account of the debates, I cannot agree with his conclusion that Falkland and Hyde were willing to accept the offer of trading subsidies for Ship Money alone. Sharpe, *Personal Rule*, p. 870.
[116] At no point in the surviving record of the debates on 4 May is there any suggestion that a price reduction would have yielded agreement.
[117] Esther Cope, 'Compromise in Early Stuart Parliaments', p. 145.
[118] Charles Carlton, *Charles I: The Personal Monarch* (2nd edition, 1995), p. 212.
[119] Conrad Russell, 'The Scottish Party in English Parliaments', p. 48; Cust, *Charles I: A Political Life*, p. 255.
[120] Donald, *An Uncounselled King*, p. 233.

his appeal to the House of Lords led inevitably to a dispute over privilege.[121] He had not learned that he had to 'bargain' with parliament rather than appeal to loyalty and duty.[122] Ever since Gardiner, historians have repeated the unsubstantiated allegation that Charles dismissed the parliament rather than face a sudden remonstrance against his Scottish policies.[123] 'The Short Parliament was broken by the fears of a conspiracy.'[124] This was another way of highlighting the irrational side of Charles's character, his paranoid belief that he was being plotted against that was constantly revealed in his printed declarations that blamed 'a few factious spirits'. While there is little doubt that members of the Commons and representatives of the Covenanters maintained communication with each other, it is not clear why it would have been to Pym's advantage to derail the debate that would surely have resulted in declaring Ship Money illegal in favour of one whose outcome was far less certain.

There is little mystery in explaining the demise of the Short Parliament. The king had ventured every conceivable concession in every possible way. He promised a full session for grievances after a vote of supply and he promised to give joy in his reception of them. When the Commons rejected these promises, he offered to abandon Ship Money for any alternative preferred by parliament and he lowered his demands for funding. When the Commons refused this his thoughts naturally turned to dissolution. Instead he took the advice of his councillors to ask the Lords if they could use their influence to prevent an irreparable breach.[125] This resulted in nearly a week of further delay and additional provocation as the Commons conducted unruly debates on religious and fiscal grievances. The Lords were forced to conclude that they could not turn the direction of the Commons' proceedings. Now surely the king would end the fruitless session. Instead, he made yet one more direct appeal, in writing to avoid the ignominy of having the message rejected unheard.[126] This time the message was unequivocal: would the Commons supply the king or would they not? Still, no answer was forthcoming and this silence might well have been the death knell of parliament. But miraculously even in this void Charles thought there might be a ray

---

[121] Mark Fissel, 'Scottish War and English Money: The Short Parliament of 1640', in Mark Fissel (ed.), *War and Government in Britain 1598–1650* (Manchester, 1991), p. 200.

[122] Cust, *Charles I: A Political Life*, p. 5.

[123] Russell, *Fall of the British Monarchies*, pp. 122–3 valuably sifts the evidence.

[124] Gardiner, *History of England*, vol. IX, p. 116; Sharpe, *Personal Rule*, p. 873.

[125] Russell, using ambassadorial accounts, attributes this intervention to Strafford. Russell, *Fall of the British Monarchies*, p. 111.

[126] Cope, *Short Parliament*, p. 187.

of hope if he made one further concession. On 4 May he offered to relinquish all right to Ship Money in exchange for a vote of twelve subsidies. The Commons had driven a hard bargain. They had countered every proposal of the king with threats, provocations, or silence. Incredibly, they were still in session and had now received an offer so handsome that as one member observed 'within two months we would so gladly have embraced'.[127] Yet by the end of the day's debate they still had no answer to offer the king, no acceptance and no refusal.

It was not Charles I who ran out of patience on 4 May, it was Sir Henry Vane, senior, the king's Secretary and the queen's Treasurer. Vane had staved off one dissolution after another, had attempted in every debate to steer the House towards a positive outcome. It must be remembered that Vane was no radical. After his betrayal of Strafford it was easy for royalists to cast him as a villain but no one did more during the course of the Short Parliament to defend the king's position or advance his point of view. Indeed, he went further than his brief allowed on 2 May when he suggested that the king might be willing to abandon Ship Money altogether in return for supply. When some members of the Commons rose to that lure, Vane then had to persuade Charles to allow him to reel them in with a concrete offer. In the Banqueting House on 21 April the king had only offered to relinquish Ship Money in exchange for an equivalent sum to fund naval defence. He was willing to abandon the form but not the substance.

Those historians who stress 'the difficulty of trying to give Charles unwelcome advice' should consider Vane's position on 3 May when he had to explain to the king that he had inadvertently offered to relinquish the substance as well.[128] Nevertheless, he convinced the king to make a concrete offer that not only jeopardized his future solvency, but that for the first time constituted a royally initiated bargain.[129] It was Vane who proposed the deal and acted as its advocate, Vane who risked his reputation that he could get it done. Had there ever been a moment during that long day's disputation when he believed he could have clinched the bargain by lowering the price, why should anyone doubt that he would have leapt at it? The fact was that Vane was so overcommitted

---

[127] Maltby, *Aston's Diary*, p. 139.

[128] Cust, *Charles I: A Political Life*, p. 259. That Vane had exceeded his authority is clear from his statement late in the debate on 2 May, 'Would have the House clearly understand that nothing ever fell from him importing the clear taking away of Ship Money.' Maltby, *Aston's Diary*, p. 126.

[129] While it can be argued that Charles 'bargained' Buckingham's impeachment for subsidies in 1626 and the Petition of Right for subsidies in 1628 both were parliamentary rather than royal initiatives.

to the pact that he never noticed that while he was attempting to close a deal, his opponents were succeeding in closing a trap. Slowly it dawned upon Vane that he had been manoeuvred into the position that the Commons would not commit to trading for Ship Money whether it were declared legal or illegal, and they would not consider supply until parliament had made that determination.[130]

Those who were willing to bargain had raised the price considerably by insisting upon adding military charges and other non-parliamentary levies, those who were unwilling to bargain had won their point that the legality of Ship Money had to be determined first. Either way the deal was dead. Even if Vane had had authority to offer eight subsidies and close at six, if military charges were added to the equation the break-even point had probably been raised closer to twenty subsidies than to twelve. When he reported to the king that night and the Council the next morning it was with the sting of rejection. Hyde was told that he informed the king 'they would pass such a vote against ship money that would blast that revenue and other branches of the receipt'. Strafford remembered that he said, 'there was no hope that the Commons House of Parliament would give one penny'. When Charles was advised to dissolve the Short Parliament it was advice given by the single member of the Council who had gone the furthest to find a compromise. Throughout the three-week life of the Short Parliament, Sir Henry Vane, senior, had carried the water, now the well was truly dry.[131]

If Charles can no longer bear the blame for the dissolution of the Short Parliament what can be said of those members who came to Westminster determined that the parliament would fail? They have so escaped culpability that there is still no collective name for them. In recent studies not only are their ends justified, their means are admired. John Pym's ability to block compromises and turn debate away from productive channels has earned him accolades for 'the skills that made Pym such a successful Parliamentarian'.[132] One thing is certain, they were not risk averse. Even if it is true that their secret intelligence with the Scots removed their fear of an imminent invasion – the Covenanter leaders would later claim that they would never have entered England without an invitation – they had no way of predicting or controlling the outcome of the war. They could certainly make things harder on the king by denying him subsidies, but they must have known in the spring that

[130] Maltby, *Aston's Diary*, p. 142.
[131] *CHR*, vol. I, p. 182; T. D. Whitaker, *The life and original correspondence of Sir George Radcliffe* (1810), p. 235.
[132] Russell, *Fall of the British Monarchies*, p. 116.

he still had alternative sources of revenue sufficient to raise an army. Nor was the fruitless outcome of Charles's negotiations with European powers a foreseeable result. By doing everything in their power to wreck the Short Parliament, these members were risking the future of the institution itself. Maybe they believed that their situation was so hopeless that if they could not force the king to accept whole their view of his prerogatives in church and state and their vision of England's future then there was no hope that they could remain in their native land. We know of half-made plans to emigrate to America and if Hampden, Connecticut was a tribute of the future, Saybrook, Connecticut was not.

Even so, the stakes for which they played were truly breathtaking. Once the king publicly promised redress of grievances and another parliamentary session in the autumn they had no further need for the threat of a Scottish invasion. The king's offer to abandon Ship Money by a writ of reversal meant, *mutatis mutandis*, that impositions would be next to fall. Parliament's willingness to grant subsidies would ensure continued meetings, and continued meetings would ensure additional reforms. There was only one outcome to the Scottish crisis that could put these members of parliament in a marginally stronger position *vis-à-vis* the king than they were in now and that was the Scottish victory that did in fact transpire. To gamble everything on that was an incomparable and incomprehensible act of desperation. Against such men, Charles I never had a chance.

3 The Court and the emergence of a royalist party

Malcolm Smuts

This chapter begins with an obvious question that has never received a satisfactory answer: what role did the Court play in the emergence of a royalist party? To the extent that they have considered it at all, historians have usually taken one of two mutually incompatible positions with regard to this problem, neither entirely satisfactory. Some have treated the Court as the seedbed of royalism, an institution permeated by absolutist and crypto-Catholic values that provided the original core of the king's party and the ideology for which it fought.[1] Despite its superficial plausibility, this view must confront the serious problem that several leading courtiers supported parliament in 1641, while others avoided active commitment by departing for the continent. Since the parliamentarian courtiers included two successive Lord Chamberlains, the Groom of the Stool, the Captain of the Gentlemen Pensioners, the Lord Admiral and a Secretary of State[2] they cannot be considered a marginal group. Their existence lends substance to the rival hypothesis, lately favoured by revisionist historians, although its origins go back to Clarendon. This holds that the Court splintered and disintegrated in 1641, leaving Charles bereft of support until backbench MPs and conservative country gentry began rallying to him in reaction against the excesses of the parliamentary leadership, especially its attacks on episcopacy.[3]

Acknowledgements: The author wishes to thank J. S. A. Adamson, Caroline Hibbard and Jonathan Scott for helpful discussions related to this chapter.

[1] See, for example, H. R. Trevor-Roper, 'The General Crisis of the Seventeenth Century', in Trevor Aston (ed.), *Crisis in Europe 1550–1660* (1965); Perez Zagorin, *The Court and the Country: the Beginning of the English Revolution* (New York, 1969); Lawrence Stone, *Causes of the English Revolution* (New York, 1972), pp. 91–117; P. Thomas, 'Two Cultures? Court and Country under Charles I', in Conrad Russell (ed.), *Origins of the English Civil War* (New York, 1973) and, in a more plausible vein, Caroline Hibbard, *Charles I and the Popish Plot* (Chapel Hill, NC, 1983).

[2] The earls of Pembroke and Essex; the earl of Holland; the earl of Salisbury; the earl of Northumberland; and Henry Vane. I wish to thank John Adamson for reminding me of Salisbury's Court office.

[3] *HGR*, vol. I, p. 442.

Although at first glance more compatible with the evidence, this interpretation also creates difficulties, not least in explaining the roles of the king and queen in the formation of their own party. Even in normal times monarchs needed Courts to connect them to a wider political environment, but in a period of crisis this became doubly true. Without reliable allies in their own households, Charles and Henrietta Maria would have found themselves not merely psychologically isolated but bereft of means to obtain information, coordinate strategy and communicate with supporters in parliament and the provinces, without risking the immediate betrayal of their intentions to their adversaries. These were real problems in 1641. Although Clarendon exaggerated in claiming that the people the king trusted 'betrayed him every hour, insomuch as the whispers in his bedchamber were instantly conveyed to those against whom those whispers were',[4] confidential information leaked repeatedly, and many courtiers did cooperate with the parliamentary leadership. Having lost the confidence not only of the political nation but of many of his own servants, Charles found it difficult to know where to turn as he tried to regain the initiative. The story of his struggle to break out of this cage and of the people who helped him do so needs closer scrutiny.

This story, in turn, is intertwined with three others. One involves the relationship between policies of negotiation and policies of violence in royal councils. The new royalists of 1641 – men like Edward Hyde, Sir John Culpepper and Lord George Digby – were political moderates who believed that the parliamentary leadership had begun to pose a greater threat to traditional methods of governance than the king. They wanted to eliminate the contentious policies of the 1630s, while preserving an episcopal Church and traditional royal prerogatives, and believed that by following this prescription Charles would eventually rally enough support to defeat his adversaries through legal methods.[5] Although the king sometimes followed their advice, he also notoriously experimented with schemes for breaking the parliamentary opposition through force, notably the Army Plot of spring 1641. The courtiers who took part in this intrigue – who in several cases also figured prominently in later efforts to construct royalist armies – have elicited little sympathy from historians, perhaps reflecting a whiggish assumption that coups d'état and court conspiracies have no legitimate place in the modern English political tradition. But if we are to understand why a civil war took place and how the king acquired not just a political but a military

---

[4] *HGR*, vol. III, p. 202.
[5] David L. Smith, *Constitutional Royalism and the Search for Settlement, c. 1640–1649* (Cambridge, 1994).

following, their role needs to be understood. What sort of men became involved in royalist plotting and how did they differ in their previous background from courtiers who became anguished moderates or parliamentarians? Were the violent royalists of 1641 remnants of an absolutist coterie that had advocated force against Scotland and other harsh policies in the 1630s? Or was the situation more confused and fluid, so that political moderates became conspirators in response to changing circumstances?

A second, related, issue is the role of the queen and her entourage. Ever since the period itself, Henrietta Maria has been portrayed as an advocate of hard policies and patron of violent men.[6] But in earlier years she had been associated with anti-Spanish foreign policies favoured by courtiers like the earls of Holland and Northumberland, who became parliamentarians in 1642. According to the Tuscan ambassador, in 1635 she had even joined unnamed 'puritan' members of the Court in urging Charles to summon a new parliament.[7] What transformed the queen from a *politique* advocate of policies many puritans wanted into a polarizing symbol of popish malignancy? And what happened to her Court following as this transformation took place? These questions lead to the third issue: the international context of Caroline politics, especially the tangled connections between domestic religious conflicts and the context of the Thirty Years' War.[8]

We lack good answers to these questions because the internal history of the Stuart Court has received less attention than the debates of the Long Parliament and the histories of several counties. The remainder of this chapter is a preliminary attempt to redress this imbalance, by mapping some of the main lines of development from the mid-1630s, just before the eruption of serious trouble in Scotland, down to the spring of 1641. It examines how the political alignments of the earlier period developed in response to the widening crises of the following years, with a particular eye to explaining the emergence of a Court faction prepared to organize violent counter-strikes against the parliament.

The most significant disputes in Court politics during the early-to-mid-1630s centred on the question of whether Britain should re-enter the Thirty Years' War in alliance with Protestant states and France, or remain neutral while pursuing policies that benefited Habsburg interests.[9]

[6] The best modern treatment is Hibbard, *Popish Plot*.

[7] Malcolm Smuts, 'The Puritan Followers of Henrietta Maria in the 1630s', *EHR*, 93 (1978), 24–45.

[8] Jonathan Scott, *England's Troubles: Seventeenth-Century English Political Instability in European Context* (Cambridge, 2000).

[9] Kevin Sharpe, *The Personal Rule of Charles I* (New Haven, CT, 1992), pp. 507–36.

Courtiers favourable to Spain tended to have strongly anti-puritan views, and in some cases concealed Catholic sympathies, whereas those who favoured French and Protestant alliances were often more sympathetic to Calvinist values.[10] We might naturally expect the first group to become strong royalists in the Civil War and the second to evolve into parliamentarians, and in several conspicuous cases this happened.[11] Before assuming that earlier factional divisions determined how courtiers behaved in 1641, however, we need to enter a number of caveats. Several features of Court society worked to inhibit the emergence of sharp ideological partisanship, even when significant religious and political issues were at stake. The fact that courtiers needed to carry on the king's government fostered pragmatism and flexibility rather than rigid stands on principle. Everyone on the Council knew that European states often put secular interests ahead of religious convictions. Committed Protestants therefore sometimes expressed mistrust of Dutch or Swedish motives,[12] while crypto-Catholics who normally supported Spain sometimes changed their stance when convinced that the Habsburgs were unwilling to satisfy legitimate British demands. Despite his normal Habsburg sympathies the earl of Arundel began supporting a French alliance after returning from a diplomatic mission to Germany in 1637, during which he believed the Emperor had insulted English honour. Other courtiers, like Francis Lord Cottington, seem to have adjusted their views in response to changes in the king's attitude. In the early 1630s Cottington favoured Spanish interests during a period when Charles also tended to have a pro-Spanish orientation. He continued doing so in 1636, as Charles began to lose patience with Madrid, colluding with Secretary Windebank in allowing a ship carrying money for the Spanish Army of Flanders to leave an English port, when the king wanted it held as a bargaining chip. This led to an angry reprimand, a discussion by the Council of whether Cottington and Windebank should be punished and a brief night of house arrest, along with spluttering by the king about Spanish pensioners on his

---

[10] Examples of courtiers in the first category are Francis Cottington, Thomas Howard earl of Arundel, Francis Windebank, William Laud and Thomas Wentworth; the second is illustrated by Henry Rich earl of Holland (a patron of puritans, if not a particularly religious figure) and Philip Herbert earl of Pembroke. An exception is Walter (Wat) Montagu, a strong supporter of France in 1637 who had recently converted to Catholicism. We shall see, however, that Montagu became more sympathetic to Spain after about 1638.

[11] E.g. Pembroke and Holland (pro-French courtiers who supported Parliament); Wentworth, Laud and Windebank (pro-Spanish courtiers impeached by the Long Parliament); Cottington and Endymion Porter (pro-Spanish courtiers who became royalists).

[12] See, e.g., Leicester's analysis of Dutch and French motives in Arthur Collins (ed.), *Letters and Memorials of State* (1746), vol. II, p. 571.

own Council.[13] After these events Cottington started to ingratiate himself
with the French ambassador and pro-French courtiers like the earl of
Holland.[14] He may have come to share some of Charles's scepticism that
Madrid was bargaining in good faith; he may simply have been trying to
please the king; or he may have concluded, as the French ambassador
cynically remarked, that 'having drawn his share of Spanish silver it was
time to see what he could gain from France'.[15] Whatever his motives, he
showed more regard for expediency than rigid principle.

The political pragmatism of seasoned courtiers also affected their personal relationships. Although deep animosities did sometimes develop,
as with the simmering feud between Holland and Thomas Wentworth,
these were never simply products of religious or ideological differences.
The queen's ambiguous position, as a French Catholic who often supported Protestant alliances, helped to mitigate the divisive potential of
religion, but so did a simple recognition that people of different views
might prove useful allies in pursuing Court favour.[16] When the papal
agent, George Con, arrived in England in 1637 he received especially
warm welcomes from the earls of Pembroke and Holland, courtiers
known for supporting Protestant causes.[17] Two years later he was assid-
uously cultivated by the countess of Leicester, whose husband, the
king's ambassador to Paris, was reputed a puritan by many Court Catholics. Pembroke, Holland and Leicester knew Con had influence with
the queen and king and therefore made every effort to cultivate his
friendship, popery notwithstanding. This spirit of collegiality – kept
alive by exchanges of hospitality, gifts and small courtesies – provided
the glue that held this courtly and aristocratic society together, allowing
people of different views to find common interests and ways of working
together. So long as it persisted even bitter disagreements stood a fair
chance of peaceful resolution.

We therefore need to discover not just how disputes arose within the
Court but how they generated levels of animosity capable of dissolving
normal patterns of civility and pragmatism. Did Whitehall's factional

---

13 Archives du Ministère des Affaires Etrangères, Paris, Correspondance Politique
    Angleterre [hereafter AAE CPA], vol. 46, fo. 134r and 134v; TNA, SP16/330/1 and
    331/17; *CSPV*, vol. 24, p. 59.
14 TNA, 31/3/69; Sheffield Library Wentworth Woodhouse Muniments [hereafter
    Wentworth Papers] Str P7, fo. 55
15 Bibliothèque Nationale [BN], manuscrits français [mss. fr.] 15993, fo. 193; AAE CPA,
    vol. 47, fo. 626.
16 On this see Smuts, 'Puritan Followers' and 'Religion, European Politics and Henrietta
    Maria's Circle, 1625–1641', in Erin Griffey (ed.), *Henrietta Maria* (forthcoming,
    Manchester).
17 TNA, 31/9/124, Con dispatch of 25 July 1636.

conflicts escalate to a point at which colleagues found it impossible to cooperate with each other or did external events overwhelm courtiers' capacity to work out practical solutions to divisive problems? The answer is that we find evidence of both developments. As early as 1638 several convergent trends slowly redefined and sharpened the Court's factional alignments in ways that isolated several prominent figures. Over the preceding two years advocates of a French and Protestant alliance, who enjoyed the queen's support,[18] appeared to be gaining the upper hand. The French ambassador in London was busily distributing promises of French money and Henrietta Maria's favour to Madrid's traditional friends on the Council, like Cottington and William Laud, as inducements to support an offensive and defensive alliance against Spain.[19] That alliance would soon have come to include France's Protestant allies, Sweden and the Netherlands, pleasing not only the queen's circle but godly Protestants throughout England. Peers long disaffected from the Court, like the earl of Warwick, Lord Brooke and Viscount Saye and Sele, stood to benefit more directly, through royal support for the privateering campaign they had recently launched from their Caribbean colony of Providence Island.[20] Warwick sent a letter to Richelieu in early 1636, offering to put himself and his private fleet at the disposal of the French crown.[21] The following spring and summer the Council canvassed a scheme to lend fourteen royal ships to a fleet under the command of the Elector Palatine that would attack Spanish commerce. The Providence Island Company and a number of London merchants agreed to contribute to this venture, which promised to revive the partnership between the royal navy and English privateers that had flourished in the 1590s.[22] France lent diplomatic support to the scheme by including it in the draft treaty negotiated with Leicester.[23] A French and Protestant alliance would also have gratified Scottish Calvinists, not only for religious reasons but because the French wanted to recruit large numbers of Scots into their armies.[24]

---

[18] For the Queen's support of Richelieu's policies at this juncture see, e.g., BN, mss. fr. 15993, fos. 8v, 15, 32 and 52.

[19] In addition to references already cited see BN, mss. fr. 15915, fos. 9 and 78 and AAE CPA vol. 46, fo. 306.

[20] For the background see Karen Kupperman, *Providence Island, 1630–1641: The Other Puritan Colony* (Cambridge, 1993); Robert Brenner, *Merchants and Revolution: Commercial Change, Political Conflict and London's Overseas Traders, 1550–1653* (Princeton, NJ, 1993), pp. 300–3; Smuts, 'Henrietta Maria's Circle'.

[21] AAE CPA vol. 46, fos. 164–5v.

[22] AAE CPA vol. 46, fos. 188, 209, 306; TNA, C115/N8/8800.

[23] BN, mss fr. 15993, fo. 226.

[24] BL Add. MS 27,962 H, fo. 7; BN mss. fr. 15993, fo. 50; BN 15915, fo. 198.

But toward the end of 1637 the momentum for an alliance with France stalled, and shortly thereafter the first rumblings of a serious crisis in Scotland made Britain's re-entry into the Thirty Years' War appear increasingly unlikely. Several Protestant councillors – Henry Vane, John Coke and the earl of Northumberland – wanted a quick negotiated settlement with the Scots, whereas the normal hispanophiles, Windebank, Cottington and Arundel, were 'all earnest to put the King upon a war'.[25] As the king showed his preference for the second option, the Spanish party on the Council began to regain the ascendancy. Suspicions that the Scots had received secret encouragement from English puritans simultaneously encouraged Laud and Charles himself to see the conflict as a fateful showdown with the forces of Calvinist sedition.[26] By the winter of 1638–9 the Court was indeed preparing for war, but against Charles's own Calvinist subjects rather than Catholics in Germany, Spain and America.

These developments took place during a period when the queen, under Con's influence, had begun to take a more active role in encouraging Catholic proselytizing at Court. Con particularly targeted women courtiers in his efforts to win converts, scoring some notable successes. The queen became the leading patron and protector of a cohort of Catholic ladies that included the wives of two leading supporters of Spain: the earl of Arundel on the Council and Endymion Porter in the king's bedchamber. Con also recognized the Scots' rebellion as an opportunity to persuade the king that British Catholics were now more loyal to the crown than puritans, and therefore deserving of better treatment. Working with three Catholic courtiers close to the queen – her Secretary, John Winter, Wat Montagu, and Sir Kenelm Digby – he organized a voluntary contribution to the war effort by English recusants. Together with Arundel he devised a new version of the Oath of Allegiance that omitted all references to the Pope, instead condemning *any* attempt to use religion as a justification for disobedience. Along with the queen and a few other Court Catholics the Pope's representative began looking for ways to achieve full religious toleration. A hardening of anti-puritan sentiment therefore coincided ominously with the development of a much softer royal attitude toward Catholicism.[27] For those with long memories these developments must have seemed reminiscent of the situation

---

[25] Wentworth Papers Str P10b, 1 (Northumberland to Wentworth, 23 July 1638). Cottington and Arundel seem to have reverted to their usual pro-Spanish stance as Charles's interest in a French alliance waned.

[26] Wentworth Papers Str P7, 161 (letter of 11 February 1639).

[27] On this whole subject Hibbard, *Popish Plot* remains essential. See also my article on Con in the *Oxford DNB*.

during the Spanish Match negotiations of the early 1620s, when Arundel, Cottington and Porter had begun their rise in Court politics.

A more aggressive Catholic presence at Court would not, by itself, have prevented cooperation between the queen and solidly Protestant courtiers over foreign policy. But after 1638 Henrietta Maria's support for a French and Protestant alliance also began to weaken, for reasons having little immediately to do with British politics. Her relationship with the French government had long been complicated by Bourbon family quarrels that left her with divided loyalties between her brother, Louis XIII, and her mother, Marie de Medici, who had taken refuge in the Spanish Netherlands after being expelled from France in 1630. Henrietta Maria's cooperation with Richelieu in the mid-1630s stemmed from an uneasy compact, based partly on an understanding that if she helped him obtain an English alliance, he would forgive several of her close associates for plotting against him in the past. She may also have hoped that aiding the French crown's pursuit of an English alliance would strengthen her ability to negotiate her mother's return to France.[28] In any case, in late 1637 Marie de Medici enlisted her daughter's aid in efforts to persuade the French government to end her banishment.[29] This was something Louis XIII and his chief minister were not prepared to consider, but Henrietta Maria refused to accept their curt rejections of her pleas. She proposed to send Montagu to Paris as her personal representative until the French made it clear he was not welcome, whereupon she dispatched Jermyn instead, in early 1639. When he received polite but evasive responses she fumed that her brother had shown his disdain for England and herself, and threatened to seek revenge.[30] Although she continued to provide intermittent support for French interests for almost another year, her attitude toward the French government began to cool perceptibly, until in July the French ambassador reported that 'as best as one can judge' she had become 'an enemy'.[31]

This change in the queen's attitude owed something as well to the influence of an inveterate enemy of Richelieu, her childhood friend, Marie de Rohan, duchess of Chevreuse. In December 1637 Chevreuse fled France in disguise and took refuge at the Spanish Court. In April

---

[28] Smuts, 'Puritan Followers'; Victor Cousin, *Madame de Chevreuse: nouvelles études sur les femmes illustres et la société du XVIIe siècle* (Paris, 1862), pp. 354–68; BN, mss. fr. 15989, fos. 597–8; see BN, mss. fr. 15993, fos. 52 (Vantelet), 182 and 188 (de Jars) and 15915, fos. 47, 60v, 62, 70, 89 and 93 (de Jars), 262, 272 (Vantelet). More detail is provided in Smuts, 'Henrietta Maria's Circle'.

[29] The previous year Henrietta Maria's concern for her mother was said by the Venetian ambassador in London to be so intense as to affect her health, *CSPV*, 24, p. 264.

[30] AAE CPA vol. 47, fo. 421v.

[31] *Ibid.*, fo. 511v.

she sailed for England, carrying a proposal for a Habsburg – Stuart marriage alliance and plans for stirring up trouble for the Cardinal by working through discontented French noblemen living in London.[32] Chevreuse received a lavish welcome and over the next several months was constantly seen in the company of the queen and the king, to such an extent that several high-ranking English women began boycotting the Court from jealousy.[33] She arranged a private interview between Henrietta Maria and the Spanish ambassador, in which she acted as interpreter,[34] and in the opinion of both the French and Dutch ambassadors became the chief patron and manager of Spanish interests at the English Court, so that even pro-Spanish ministers on the Council became jealous of her influence.[35]

The duchess quickly set about drawing several of Henrietta Maria's associates into her intrigues. Sir Kenelm Digby and Henrietta Maria's confessor, Father Robert Philip, agreed to allow letters from Chevreuse's French friends to be addressed to them, to thwart Richelieu's efforts to intercept her correspondence.[36] Montagu, who had a long history of involvement in French plots, quickly became a close ally.[37] In May the Venetian ambassador reported that Chevreuse was 'trying to convert the Earl of Holland to the Roman faith and win him for the Spanish party. To please the queen, who is the principal instrument of this good work, he pretends not to be averse from it.'[38] When he ultimately declined to change his religion Holland saw his standing with Henrietta Maria deteriorate.[39]

It was now the turn of the French to see their supporters in London picked off by a pro-Spanish faction, which increasingly had the backing of Henrietta Maria. By December 1638 Louis XIII's Secretary for Foreign Affairs, Chavigny, was complaining that the money spent on pensions for the English queen's servants had failed to produce results.[40]

---

[32] Alnwick Castle MS 15, 83 (Northumberland to Leicester, 25 June 1640) on Library of Congress microfilms 041/aln7/1.

[33] *CSPV*, 24, pp. 366, 407; TNA, C115/109/N8.8819; BL, Add. MS 27,962H, fos. 134–5, 143, 150, 170, 177, 372; Wentworth Papers Str P7, fo. 100v; NAS, GD406/1/7543.

[34] BL, Add. MS 27962 H, 145 (Salvetti, 28 May 1638).

[35] TNA, 31/3/70, fo. 197; Groen van Prinsterer, *Archives ou Correspondance Inédite de La Maison D'Orange-Nassau*, vol. III (Utrecht, 1859), p. 157; AAE CPA vol. 47, fo. 626.

[36] AAE CPA vol. 47, fos. 137 (intercepted letter of Chevreuse to M. Guion), 163, 194.

[37] AAE CPA vol. 47, fos. 114 (intercepted letter of Windebank to Scudamore), 123, 129 (intercepted letters of Montagu to Kenelm Digby).

[38] *CSPV*, 24, p. 417 [28 May 1638].

[39] Wentworth papers Str P10(a) 171.

[40] BN, mss. fr. 15915, fo. 243 (Chavigny to Bellièvre, 31 December 1638).

The community of French malcontents hovering around the English Court had meanwhile grown exponentially with the arrival, in November, of Marie de Medici and her 600-strong Court-in-exile. Although it is difficult to establish whether this influx of French enemies of Richelieu had any discernible effect on English policy, France's ambassador, Bellièvre, believed that they were helping to push Charles into an alliance with Spain. These fears were reasonable, since the king had, in fact, begun to look to Spain for financial or military assistance against the Scots, canvassing schemes for obtaining 8,000 veterans from the Army of Flanders in return for allowing Spain to recruit twice as many fresh troops in Ireland, or for a substantial loan in return for a marriage alliance. In the winter of 1639–40, as Charles prepared for a second campaign against Scotland, reports of the successful conclusion of the second scheme circulated widely in both England and Europe.[41] The treaty ultimately failed, partly because Charles refused to meet Spanish terms, but also because French and Dutch advances and the revolt of the Catalans in June 1640 crippled Spain at the critical juncture. But for a time there appeared to be a real prospect that British puritanism might be forcefully suppressed with the aid of Spanish troops or money. Some of the rumours floating around the Court were even more inflammatory. Bellièvre heard the queen being told in March 1639 that the Imperial General Ottavio Piccolomini, whose army of German infantry and Polish, Hungarian and Croatian cavalry was fighting for Spain in Flanders, had offered to serve Charles I against the Covenanters.[42]

To be sure, the queen's party never 'became exclusively identified with Catholicism'[43] and Spanish interests, since she never completely abandoned her ties to France or her willingness to patronize Protestant courtiers. By exerting sufficient pressure Bellièvre managed to gain her assistance at critical junctures, especially on the eve of the Battle of the Dunes in October 1639, as Charles tried to decide whether to assist a Spanish fleet that faced imminent attack from a larger Dutch force in English waters.[44] She remained friendly with the earl of Northumberland, who had become Lord Admiral with her help in 1636, and she helped the future parliamentarian Henry Vane become Secretary of

---

[41] *CSPV 1640–1642*, pp. 31–2; Alnwick Castle MSS 15, 29 and 83; BN, Colbert MS 47 cited in Cousin, *Chevreuse*, p. 466; BN mss. fr. 15915, fo. 382. For background see Sharpe, *Personal Rule*, pp. 895–9; J. H. Elliott, 'The Year of the Three Ambassadors' in H. Lloyd-Jones, V. Pearl and B. Worden (eds.), *History and Imagination* (New York, 1981), pp. 165–81.

[42] AAE CPA vol. 47, fo. 431.

[43] As Kevin Sharpe asserts, *Personal Rule*, p. 839.

[44] AAE CPA vol. 47, fos. 558–60.

State in early 1640. But her increasingly frequent expressions of support for Spain, her enthusiastic backing for a marriage between her daughter Mary and the son of Philip IV, her more active advocacy of measures benefiting Catholics and her association with figures like Chevreuse, Montagu and Digby meant that she was now far from being a figure around whom supporters of a Protestant alliance could rally.[45] When Holland's enemy, Thomas Wentworth, earl of Strafford, arrived in London to join the council he quickly gained the support of Chevreuse, along with that of the countess of Carlisle, a veteran of English Court intrigues who formed an alliance with the duchess in early 1640.[46] Carlisle proceeded to attempt to strengthen Strafford's ties with her brother, Northumberland, and to recruit her brother-in-law, Leicester, to the anti-Scottish group on the Council that he and Laud headed, as the queen also drew closer to Strafford and his pro-Spanish policies.[47]

Several courtiers commented on the changing climate at Whitehall. Although Northumberland remained outwardly friendly to Strafford, who regarded him as an ally, he grumbled to sympathetic friends about the dominance of the Council by Laud, Hamilton and Strafford who 'are as much Spanish as Olivares', and complained that 'to think well of the reformed religion is cause enough to make the Archbishop one's enemy'.[48] In September 1639 the Venetian ambassador picked up a rumour that 'the Treasurer [Bishop Juxon], the Lord Keeper [Lord Coventry] and the Chamberlain [the earl of Pembroke], old but puritan ministers, will soon be changed ... in favour of persons entirely dependent on his Majesty, with the idea of cautiously weakening the puritan party'. Four months later he reported, 'they talk freely at the palace about replacing many ministers suspected of partiality towards the Scots and Dutch'.[49] Although the purges did not take place, the intended victims must have heard the same rumours. The fact that a bishop was included in the list of alleged 'puritan' ministers suggests how far the reaction against even moderate Protestantism had proceeded. Leicester was another target of such innuendoes. A report that Kenelm Digby had told the king he was

---

[45] For the queen's enthusiasm for a marriage alliance with Spain see van Prinsterer, *Correspondance*, p. 161. For examples of the queen's vocal support of Spain see Collins, *Letters and Memorials*, vol. II, p. 614 and HMC, *DeLisle and Dudley Manuscripts* (1966), p. 208.

[46] TNA, 31/3/72, fos. 46, 49.

[47] The earl's papers reveal his sympathy and respect for Spain, dislike for the Dutch and indifference to the fate of German Protestants from the early 1630s. Wentworth Papers Str P3, 5, 15; Str P8, 15; Str P9 17, 28, 39, 422; Str P10 *passim*; William Knowler, *The Earl of Strafford's Letters and Correspondence* (1735), vol. I, p. 299.

[48] Collins (ed.), *Letters and Memorials*, vol. II, pp. 617, 623.

[49] *CSPV*, 24, p. 581 and vol. 25, p. 12.

a puritan provoked him to write a letter of incandescent rage. Digby, Leicester fumed, was the son of an executed Catholic traitor, a man of 'jesuitical' views 'and scandalous life, shrewdly suspected of . . . poisoning his wife'. He then went on for more than a page arguing that the word puritan was 'bad English', an imprecise term that should have no place in discussions of a man's qualifications for office. In December 1639 Bellièvre wrote melodramatically that Holland had become such an object of obloquy within the Court because of his support for a French alliance that 'in my opinion they will cut off his head within twelve months'.[50]

This reaction against reputed puritans within the Court coincided with rumours that Charles might soon resort to authoritarian measures, possibly involving foreign troops, against members of the political nation who attempted to obstruct his policies. Bellièvre reported in December 1639 'that if they carry out that which they are proposing the King of England will be made absolute [*bien absolu*] and the resolution has been taken not to spare the heads of those who oppose him'. To this end, he continued, they were attempting to obtain loans that were thought to be for the purpose of raising troops before the upcoming session of parliament, 'to hold it in fear'.[51] There was talk of using Spanish troops, should Charles succeed in procuring them, to reinforce royal authority in England as well as Scotland. The following summer an Englishman reported that Charles was attempting to raise a force of 3,000 Danish soldiers to use against the Scots or, should the Covenanters come to terms, to 'bridle and bring under the stubborn dispositions of the Commons of this kingdom [England]'.[52] Whether or not these reports reflected the king's intentions, they attest to the confrontational atmosphere developing within the Court, and the desire of its more intransigent members to crush opposition by force. The presence of large numbers of French émigrés accustomed to a more violent style of politics, the arming of Irish Catholics for use against Scotland and the return of veteran officers and troops to participate in Britain's domestic wars must also have contributed to a climate in which the use of violence against English as well as Scottish dissent began to appear more plausible.[53]

---

[50] AAE CPA vol. 47, fo. 659v.

[51] AAE CPA vol. 47, fo. 652 (Dispatch of 22 December 1639).

[52] John Castle to the earl of Bridgewater, 1 July 1640, as quoted in Mark Fissel, *The Bishops' Wars: Charles I's Campaigns against Scotland 1638–1640* (Cambridge, 1994), p. 172. Cf. Steve Murdoch, *Britain, Denmark-Norway and the House of Stuart* (East Linton, 2003), chapter 4 and p. 95.

[53] AAE CPA vol. 47, fos. 550 (Bellièvre, November 1639); vol. 48, fo. 325 (Montreul, June 1641).

It is therefore clear that for some time before the summoning of the Long Parliament serious tensions had been developing between the dominant faction at Whitehall and courtiers like Holland, Pembroke, Northumberland, Leicester and Vane who disliked the direction of royal policies.[54] But this rift proves more useful in explaining why some courtiers deserted Charles than in tracing the origins of a royalist group. For the Scots victory at Newburn in August 1640, the summoning of the Long Parliament and the simultaneous near-collapse of the Spanish monarchy after the revolts of Catalonia and Portugal dealt devastating blows to the coalition that had dominated the Court during the previous year. By January 1641 the Spanish Match had been abandoned in favour of an alliance with the Dutch House of Orange. Strafford and Laud were in the Tower; Windebank, Finch and Kenelm Digby had retired to Paris; and rumours circulated that Cottington would soon become another target of parliament.[55] Although he managed to survive until after Strafford's execution he then resigned his offices and retired to his country house. By the following winter Arundel had also left for the continent, never to return to England. The pro-Spanish and strongly anti-puritan courtiers we might have expected to become hard-core royalists mostly abandoned the struggle before actual fighting broke out, with the exception of a few secondary figures, like Endymion Porter, and the two principal leaders, Charles I and Henrietta Maria.

Although the disintegration of the pro-Spanish group within the Court took several months to complete, it became evident very quickly that the king's defeat had initiated a struggle for power and office in which the Scots and parliament would attempt to play a leading role. As early as November, Northumberland confided to Leicester

that the King is in such a straight that I do not know how he will possibly avoid (without endangering the loss of the whole kingdom) the giving way to the remove of diverse persons, as well as other things that will be demanded by the Parliament.

In addition to the most obvious targets, like Laud and Strafford, he predicted that the earl of Newcastle, Jermyn and Wat Montagu would soon be displaced.[56] Northumberland himself, along with Holland, Pembroke and Henry Vane, began cooperating with the parliamentary

---

[54] It should be said that Northumberland and possibly Leicester were more willing to work with Strafford and other hispanophile courtiers until they saw how events would play out. Strafford liked and respected Northumberland and made every effort to win his support and Northumberland continued to serve competently, despite the misgivings about royal policies expressed in some of his letters.

[55] TNA, 31/3/72, fo. 361.

[56] Collins, *Letters and Memorials*, vol. II, p. 663.

leadership, hoping to remove rivals they disliked and extend their own power. Nearly all of this group had belonged to the queen's pro-French circle in the mid-1630s and Holland, in particular, continued to work closely with Bellièvre and Montreul, who shared his desire to remove not only Charles's pro-Spanish ministers but the English and Scottish Catholics in the queen's household, whose recent cooperation with Chevreuse and the Queen Mother had thoroughly antagonized Richelieu.[57] But some of the most virulent opposition to a negotiated settlement also came from within the queen's circle, from precisely those Catholics who feared becoming victims of parliamentary vendettas. On 13 December 1640 Montreul reported that Henrietta Maria had begun talking of leaving England for France, in hopes that by doing so she might frighten parliament 'to let her keep her English Catholics'.[58] The queen's French Almoner thought Montagu was probably behind this plan. A few weeks later Montagu pressed the queen to stiffen Charles's resolve to protect Strafford, no doubt because he feared that if the great minister were abandoned Catholics like himself might be next.[59] The queen's confessor, Father Philip, also seems to have opposed making concessions to parliament. Unfortunately this intransigence not only matched Henrietta Maria's own instincts but, to a considerable extent, her husband's views. Even at this late date both monarchs continued to toy with schemes for renewed military action. Holland told Montreul that Charles hoped marrying his daughter Mary to the Prince of Orange might allow him to obtain Dutch assistance.[60] The queen tried to negotiate a loan from the Pope that might be used to pay Irish or other troops to rescue the king from his predicament.

For a time both monarchs also dismissed reports of an imminent change in the great officers of state.[61] But in late December and early January reports began circulating that the king had at last decided to reverse course by taking parliamentary leaders into his Council.[62] This apparent change was due, in part, to increasing pressure from parliament, which impeached Secretary Windebank, Chief Justice John Finch and Wentworth's confidant in Ireland, Sir Thomas Radcliffe, and threatened to cut off the king's access to his last significant source of income,

---

[57] TNA, 31/3/72, fos. 345–6.
[58] TNA, 31/3/72, fo. 344.
[59] AAE CPA vol. 48, fo. 180 (Montreul, 3 January 1641, reporting information transmitted by Holland). A copy of this letter can be found in TNA, 31/3/72, fo. 368.
[60] TNA, 31/3/72, fo. 379.
[61] Collins, *Letters and Memorials*, vol. II, p. 664.
[62] These developments have now been clarified by John Adamson's *The Noble Revolt: The Overthrow of Charles I* (2007).

the customs duties. But it was also facilitated by courtiers who had remained close to the king and queen, but who now attempted to broker a compromise settlement with the parliamentary leadership. The most prominent of these figures was the king's cousin, James Hamilton, duke of Hamilton. Although he had not been enthusiastic about the campaigns against the Covenanters, Hamilton had become closely associated with them as the king's primary agent in Scotland during 1638 and 1639 and the commander of a naval squadron during the Bishops' Wars. As a result, by the autumn of 1640 Hamilton was often mentioned along with Laud and Strafford, as one of the great men most likely to be singled out for destruction when parliament met. He avoided this fate by contracting a marriage alliance with the Covenanter earl of Argyll and assisting the English parliamentary leadership by lobbying Charles to change the policies and personnel of his government.[63] But although Hamilton's moderation may have stemmed partly from a desire for survival, he appears also to have been acting from conviction. His letters throughout the Scottish crisis display a persistent fear that royal power might collapse, taking down with it traditions of deference to the peerage and gentry, and unleashing the fury of a violent popular party.[64] The king's defeat in the North further convinced Hamilton of the need to conciliate the aristocratic opposition, a goal he continued to pursue down to the summer of 1642 and in some respects thereafter, as leader of a moderate party in Scotland. Although Hamilton's moderation eventually cost him Charles's confidence, he remained close to the king in the early months of 1641, unlike Pembroke and Holland, who had already lost royal favour. This allowed him to act as a mediator.

The second courtier frequently mentioned by contemporaries as a promoter of 'bridge appointments' was the queen's favourite, Jermyn, a seasoned courtier of the second rank whose influence with both monarchs had grown during the previous year.[65] Known as a shrewd politician who planned his moves methodically before striking with decisive effect, he was also notoriously venal[66] and was one of the queen's courtiers rumoured to be most in danger of parliamentary attack in early December 1640. But he seems to have glimpsed an opportunity not only to protect himself but to advance his career by serving as a broker between Henrietta Maria and the parliamentary grandees. As Sir John Temple reported in early January, the queen 'hath now so great power as they

[63] HMC De L'Isle and Dudley, vol. VI, p. 389.
[64] E.g. NAS, GD406/1/553 (Hamilton to Laud, 7 June 1638).
[65] HMC De L'Isle and Dudley, vol. VI, p. 369.
[66] HMC De L'Isle and Dudley, vol. VI, pp. 362, 388, 394.

are fain to use some artifice to conceal it. And certainly all [officers], if [parliament] interpose not, will be made by [the queen] and [Henry Jermyn] must be solely employed in [treaty]'.[67] Jermyn was particularly active in promoting the interests of the earl of Leicester, coordinating his strategy with Leicester's relatives by marriage, Northumberland, Henry Percy and the countess of Carlisle.[68] It may be significant that every member of this family network except Leicester himself had at one time been close to Strafford, and that Carlisle in particular remained deeply committed to his preservation.[69] Jermyn and his royal patrons may have concluded that the support of Leicester and Northumberland might prove crucial in the king's campaign to spare Strafford's life.

But unlike Hamilton, who continued to support a negotiated settlement throughout 1641, eventually losing Charles's confidence as a result,[70] Jermyn soon reversed course again by involving himself in the first Army Plot. His co-conspirators included several other courtiers of the second and third rank with links to the queen: the poet Sir John Suckling, the playwright Sir William Davenant, Northumberland's brother Henry Percy, George Goring the younger, and (more peripherally) the earl of Newcastle. What distinguished this group from other courtiers? Despite their links to the queen, they were *not* men whose previous records and affiliations indicate pro-Catholic, pro-Spanish or absolutist sentiments. Jermyn, Goring and Percy had staged a petty demonstration during the first audience of an ambassador from the Emperor in 1636 when 'they stood in a door and laughed at him so openly as he saw it'.[71] Percy had thereafter worked closely with Northumberland and Leicester, both future parliamentarians. Suckling had seen action briefly in the Dutch army and had accompanied Henry Vane's embassy to Gustavus Adolphus in 1631, while Goring was a veteran officer in the Dutch army. With the exceptions of Newcastle, who had joined the Court too late to establish a record on foreign policy issues, and Davenant, whose views are unclear, they were all emphatically political Protestants, even if Suckling, Newcastle and probably the others held distinctly sceptical, rationalist and anti-clerical views.

Moreover Jermyn was not the only army plotter who had wanted an accommodation with the parliamentary leadership just a short time before. The fullest evidence for Suckling's attitude in early 1641 comes, unfortunately, from a document whose authenticity cannot be

---

67   *Ibid.*, p. 360. The bracketed words and names are in cipher in the original.
68   See *ibid.*, pp. 360, 362, 366–7, 387, 388, 394.
69   *Ibid.*, pp. 352, 374.
70   Richard Cust, *Charles I: A Political Life* (Harlow, 2005), p. 280.
71   BL, Add. MS 36448, fo. 52v, Walter Aston to Arthur Hopton.

proven: a letter attributed to him and addressed to Jermyn printed in early 1641. But since the views it states are consistent with other evidence of Suckling's beliefs, it has been accepted as genuine by the poet's modern editors, as well as by historians from S. R. Gardiner to Conrad Russell. The letter provides a remarkably cold-blooded assessment of the political situation. It warns Charles against relying on his 'party', since its members will be too concerned with saving themselves to take risks for him.[72] Instead he must realize that his 'great interest' lies in 'union with his people'. To achieve this goal he must abandon his servants to parliamentary justice while giving ground on other issues, even before being asked. Only in this way can he restore trust, so that 'the case will fall out to be no worse than when two duellists enter the field, where the worsted party (the other having no ill opinion of him) hath his sword given him again (without further hurt after he is in the other's power)'.[73] Davenant expressed similar views in an undoubtedly authentic verse epistle 'To the Queen' that must date from late 1640 or early 1641.[74] This calls upon her to become 'the people's advocate' by softening the 'extreme obdurateness' of the king's nature and teaching him that the prerogative, like gold, will be no less brilliant when made to 'yield'. No doubt with Strafford in mind, Davenant also hints that the queen must persuade Charles to allow a lethal act of justice: her 'triumphs' will be 'Esteem'd both just and mercifully good/Though what you gain with tears cost others blood'.

What turned these advocates of compromise into violent conspirators? Suckling's letter provides two hints. It especially stresses the need to involve the queen in bringing about a settlement, which is also, of course, the main theme of Davenant's epistle.[75] In addition Jermyn and Henry Percy were making it very clear to their parliamentary contacts that Henrietta Maria's support was crucial to their hopes of gaining office. Because of the army plotters' close relationships with Henrietta Maria, both personal loyalty and political interest dictated that they must re-establish her credibility as a *politique* figure eager to bridge confessional and political divisions, instead of a symbol of Catholicism

---

[72] I have used the version of this letter reprinted in *Fragmenta Aurea* (1658).

[73] *Fragmenta Aurea*, p. 110.

[74] William Davenant, *The Shorter Poems*, ed. A. M. Gibbs (Oxford, 1972), pp. 139–40. David Scott has discovered a manuscript letter of Davenant dated 19 January 1641 reporting the queen acting very much in the manner his verse epistle advocates (Staffordshire Record Office Dartmouth MS D(W)1778/I/i/12), which suggests a date for the poem of late January.

[75] *Fragmenta Aurea*, p. 111: 'For if she stand aloof there will still be suspicions: it being a received opinion in the world that she hath a great interest in the King's favour and power.'

and intransigence. But this must have proven extraordinarily difficult, both because the queen's record since 1638 cannot have inspired confidence among parliament's leaders and because she continued to regard them with mistrust and hostility. In addition she remained vulnerable to the pressures of associates like Father Philip and Montagu, to whom she felt intense loyalty.[76]

The scheme for 'bridge appointments' and a negotiated settlement therefore remained extremely fragile, the more so because both sides had become locked into a pattern of employing threats to strengthen their respective bargaining positions. The king and queen hoped that the prospect of office would moderate the demands of the parliamentary leadership but instead the Commons proceeded in January with the impeachments of Strafford and Finch, the Triennial Act, and the process of receiving county petitions against the bishops. On the 25 January 1641 Charles attempted to draw a line in the sand by delivering a speech to both Houses in which he made clear his refusal to agree to the abolition of bishops' votes in the Lords or to legislation empowering county officials to hold parliamentary elections in the absence of a royal command, as the Triennial Act provided.[77] In the same week he signalled his determination to save Strafford in a way that must have seemed particularly compelling to the queen and her Catholic circle: he pardoned a condemned priest named John Goodman. The Commons and its supporters in London immediately perceived that if Charles could spare Goodman he might also reprieve Laud and Strafford, and responded vigorously. The House not only called for increased surveillance of priests but initiated an investigation into the voluntary levy of Catholic contributions to the war against Scotland that Winter, Montagu, Digby and George Con had organized.[78]

In light of this background it is perhaps not surprising to find Henrietta Maria again attempting to frighten parliament. In mid-January 1641 she encouraged a false report that a new French ambassador hostile to parliament was on his way to England, privately telling the Court physician, Théodore Mayerne, that 'she wanted them to believe that I can make all France come here to avenge me if there is need'.[79] A short time later she and her servants spread another false rumour that Spain and France had concluded a truce so they could 'unite their forces to

---

[76]   See, for example, AAE CPA vol. 48, fo. 289.

[77]   Maija Jansson (ed.), *Proceedings in the Opening Session of the Long Parliament: House of Commons* (New Haven, CT, 2000), vol. II, p. 264.

[78]   *Ibid.*, pp. 290, 291 and 299.

[79]   TNA, 31/3/72, fo. 386 ('Et je veux bien qu'on sache que je puis faire venir toute la France pour me venger s'il est besoin').

defend and avenge Catholics'.[80] She also renewed her talk of going to Paris.[81] Montreul, who strongly disapproved, attributed her threats to leave the kingdom mainly to the influence of Montagu and Jermyn, 'because they fear that Parliament will attack them, the one because of religious affairs and the other because of the monopolies from which he has profited'.[82] Parliament had, in fact, broadened its enquiry into monopolies on 2 February, perhaps triggering Jermyn's fears.[83]

Even while the scheme for bridge appointments remained active, serious stresses had therefore appeared in relations between the parliamentary leadership and the queen's circle. Over the next several months these tensions must have grown exponentially as the atmosphere in London grew genuinely menacing, with the Commons leadership pushing ahead with the trial and then the attainder of Strafford, and crowds demonstrating in the streets against him, threatening bishops, Straffordian peers and obliquely the queen herself. Many observers feared an imminent outbreak of violence; even the Dutch representatives who had come to London to celebrate the wedding of the Prince of Orange's son to Princess Mary at the beginning of May felt unsafe in the British capital.[84] The earl of Warwick told Orange in the same period that he was immersed in 'affairs of state and Parliament, to remove the danger of civil war'.[85]

Fear of crowd violence and the parliamentary politicians who stood to benefit from it undoubtedly provided a second motivation behind the Army Plot. Suckling shared Hamilton's worries about violent popular insurrection:

For the people are naturally not valiant, and not much cavalier. Now it is the nature of cowards to hurt where they can receive none. They will not be content (while they fear and have the upper hand) to fetter only royalty but … will not think themselves safe while that is at all. And possibly this is the present state of things.[86]

It is therefore not entirely surprising that when an emissary from the English army arrived in London in late March 1641, conveying the soldiers' grievances over arrears in pay and other problems they blamed on parliament, Suckling and Jermyn saw an opportunity to respond to parliamentary and popular pressure with an opposing force. The

[80] AAE CPA vol. 48, fo. 231; for other examples see TNA, 31/3/72, fos. 386, 540v.
[81] TNA, 31/3/72, fos. 416, 423.
[82] TNA, 31/3/72, fo. 416.
[83] TNA, 31/3/72, fo. 428 (Montreul reporting information transmitted by Holland, 14 February 1641); Jansson, *Proceedings*, vol. II, p. 342.
[84] Van Prinsterer, *Correspondance*, vol. III, pp. 444, 466.
[85] *Ibid.*, p. 445.
[86] *Fragmenta Aurea*, p. 111.

protagonists behind the Army Plot appear to have fallen into two groups with somewhat different objectives. One, which included Henry Percy and several officers not closely affiliated with the Court, disclaimed any intention of using illegal violence, claiming only to want to make a show of solidarity with the king in defence of his legitimate rights, while asserting the grievances of the soldiery. Suckling, Jermyn and Goring, however, wanted to take control of the army by replacing its ailing commander, Northumberland, with the earl of Newcastle, while making Goring Lieutenant General. Having done this they proposed to move the army toward London. Even after these plans had been exposed Suckling continued with a plot to introduce enough soldiers into the Tower of London to overpower the Yeomen and release Strafford, enabling him to flee to an awaiting ship and refuge in France.[87] It is not entirely clear from the depositions taken after the Plot's collapse what the conspirators intended to do if their plans succeeded. But it is suggestive that in early May, just before the failure of Suckling's attempt to free Strafford, the queen's Almoner picked up a rumour that parliament would soon dissolve or adjourn until October. As soon as it 'breaks up Montagu will return [from Paris] close to the Queen, because the King now loves him as much as he previously hated him'.[88] With Cottington and Arundel still on the Council, the queen's Catholic circle still unrepentant, the king apparently more sympathetic than ever to figures like Montagu, and pragmatists like Jermyn now engaging in violent conspiracies, the party of force at Whitehall remained very much alive.

Several other traits of the army plotters stand out. They were all men who enjoyed close personal relationships with the queen, the king or Prince of Wales but lacked major political offices. Personal loyalty and service to the monarchs were central to their outlooks and career prospects. They also appear to have been especially interested in *military* service. There had been talk in 1638 of turning a few of the cavalry raised against the Scots into a permanent royal horse guard.[89] This makes it significant that Suckling and Percy both raised horse regiments for the Scottish wars at their own expense and that Percy engaged in Court lobbying to have his troop designated an honour guard to the Prince of Wales. Commissary Wilmot, a professional officer who had joined the plot, had also been given the command of a troop of horse to guard the king through the patronage of Hamilton,[90] while Newcastle, the

[87] The best summary is Conrad Russell, 'The First Army Plot of 1641', *TRHS,* 5th
      series, 38 (1988), 85–106.
[88] AAE CPA vol. 48, fo. 289 r/v.
[89] TNA, C115/N9/8854.
[90] Knowler, *Strafford,* vol. II, p. 181. I owe this point to David Scott.

Governor to the Prince of Wales, had contributed to the war effort from his own funds. Goring was an experienced officer. The plotters look like precisely the kind of men to whom the king would have turned to raise military forces without relying on normal legal methods. Their willingness to use violence stemmed from a sense of themselves as gentlemen soldiers, for whom honour, loyalty and valour were prime virtues.

The plot's aftermath reinforces the impression that its instigators were neither religious extremists nor natural enemies of parliament. Percy and Suckling fled to Paris. Since the earl of Leicester was now in London, seeking to advance his career by working with the parliamentary leadership, they were welcomed by the countess (Percy's sister), who presided over the English embassy in his absence. Her circle also included Secretary Windebank and Montagu. Even at this late date the customary rules of Court civility held, allowing the wife of a reputed puritan to extend her hospitality to royalist conspirators and exiled English Catholics. Goring managed to obtain parliament's forgiveness by furnishing evidence against the other conspirators, and by late summer Jermyn also hoped for a pardon through the queen's intercession with parliamentary leaders.[91] These men became royalist swordsmen not from extreme principles or an aversion to negotiated political settlements, but because the world they had known, in which personal friendships and pragmatic political alliances mattered more than ideology, had collapsed around them.

Yet on one level their choice did have significant ideological implications. In the 1630s courtly values of honour and loyalty had always seemed compatible with support for Protestant interests in Europe and Protestant unity within Britain. Many Caroline courtiers, especially those close to the queen, are best understood as men who combined a *political* commitment to Protestant causes with a cosmopolitan aristocratic culture stressing gallantry, courage, honour and disdain for religious bigotry. The vituperative politics of 1641 not only forced these courtiers to make difficult choices; it also gave rise to highly partisan polemical representations of their actions. Parliamentarian courtiers were alternatively stigmatized for deserting the king or praised for their commitment to the Protestant religion and the public cause of parliament and the subjects' liberties. By contrast the army plotters became identified with a Cavalier stereotype of courtly swordsmen imbued with an aristocratic sense of honour and personal loyalty to the king and queen, libertine morals, and contempt for puritan values.[92] It has been

[91]   HMC *De L'Isle and Dudley*, vol. VI, pp. 405, 409.
[92]   Suckling seems to have become a prominent model for this stereotype. See, e.g., *The Sucklington Faction or Suckling's Roaring Boys* (1642).

difficult ever since to appreciate the extent to which this contrast arose not from a clash of cultures but a division between men who shared a common culture.

If they resembled in outlook and background one group of parliamentarians, the army plotters differed significantly from other royalists. They had no deep commitment to the prayer book and episcopacy and they did not share the respect for the common law and the traditional forms of governance that historians have attributed to the 'constitutional royalists' who rallied around the king in 1641. In part the differences that separated the army plotters from a man like Edward Hyde derived from disparate experiences. A trained lawyer and judge's son, with limited experience of international affairs, Hyde instinctively tended to see the conflict of 1640–1 in terms of English precedents. By contrast Jermyn, Goring and Suckling – like their patron Henrietta Maria – were essentially European courtier politicians. Their cosmopolitan outlook helps to explain their willingness to resort to violence, since all the major western European monarchies – even the Dutch Stadtholders – had used soldiers in the recent past to suppress resistance to their authority. From a European perspective soldiers were ordinary instruments of power, especially in times of crisis. In that sense the movement toward greater uses of military force, in Scotland after 1638 and England in the 1640s, merely brought British politics closer to the European norm.

And yet the differences in outlook between the protagonists of the Army Plot and constitutional royalists like Hyde may ultimately have had more to do with tactics than fundamental principles. Throughout the early seventeenth century most Englishmen had continued to believe that the health of the body politic depended on maintaining or restoring a sense of unity between king and people, so that government might rest on 'love' or 'affection'. The letters during the Scottish crisis of courtiers who became parliamentarians, like Northumberland and Henry Vane, are full of anguished comments about the need to restore 'affection' and 'unity'. By contrast Wentworth had been openly sceptical of the value of 'love' as a political bond, emphasizing instead the importance of 'fear of punishment' and military power.[93] Suckling's letter to Jermyn and Davenant's epistle to the queen, written during the period when the scheme for 'bridge appointments' remained alive, also couched their pleas in terms of the need to nurture 'love' and 'affection'. But the Army Plot signalled at least a temporary break with this emphasis, in favour of

---

[93] I have discussed this topic in much fuller detail in 'Force, Love and Authority in Caroline Political Culture', in Ian Atherton and Julie Sanders (eds.), *The 1630s: Interdisciplinary Essays on Culture and Politics in the Caroline Era* (Manchester, 2006).

a raw assertion of military power. The plotters concluded that the political situation had deteriorated to a point that rendered efforts to regain 'affection' not only pointless but dangerous, obliging the king to recover his authority through coercive methods. Hyde's continuing commitment to 'constitutional' processes during the same period, by contrast, seems to have been motivated not simply by his respect for common law traditions, but his belief in the existence of a deep fund of loyalty to the king that might still turn the tide against the parliamentary junto.[94]

Historians have generally shown much more sympathy for Hyde's values than for the outlook of men like Jermyn, Suckling and Goring, who have been portrayed as not only irresponsible but out of touch with English values. This dismissive view needs reconsideration. Although very few English gentry had the deep experience of European politics of these courtiers, many had gone on the Grand Tour and a significant minority had seen service in European wars. They often displayed a keen appetite for European news. The courtly, cosmopolitan and soldierly values of the army plotters were not entirely alien to English landed society. It will take substantial additional research to determine how far the outlook of the army plotters was truly representative of a significant segment of the king's party. But the story told here should warn us against assuming that royalists as a body necessarily shared the 'common law mind' of their parliamentarian adversaries.

[94] I wish to thank David Scott for a helpful discussion of these issues.

4   Varieties of royalism

Barbara Donagan

I

A study of royalism necessarily entails a discussion not only of why some people unhesitatingly followed King Charles but also of what impelled erstwhile royalists to abandon the cause and others, who had once been parliamentarian or 'neuter', to become supporters of the House of Stuart. It requires attention to the 'middle', probably a majority of the population, who initially put peace and quiet above principle and hoped to evade choice between sides, and to some of the factors that nevertheless ultimately led many to become partisan, albeit often reluctantly. This chapter will look at some of the varieties of royalism that constituted its rainbow coalition, a coalition that included men and women of strikingly diverse personalities whose allegiance derived from a variety of considerations. It will also argue that convergences of opinion between many royalists and parliamentarians formed a common past and, together with links based on shared interest and social and economic connection, survived and helped to ameliorate the strains imposed by the killing, destruction, expropriation, violent polemic and disillusion of the Civil War. These convergences contributed to the survival of a society and constitution that retained enough of the elements familiar in the past to make the new states, both of commonwealth and Restoration, recognizably continuous with the old.

Two underlying assumptions cannot be explored in detail here. One is that, as already noted, most English men and women would, if they could, have remained 'neuters' in the struggle, and the other is that there is an important distinction between preferring one side to the other and active commitment, especially commitment that meant bearing arms against either the king or the parliament. Instead the argument will fall into three parts, the first of which will discuss the likeness of enemies. The second will deal with ways in which royalists made choices and with factors that led to support for one side or the other in the English Civil Wars. It will note some of the shared ground between royalists and parliamentarians that made choices difficult and sometimes surprising, as well as some of the factors that often rendered them less than pure and altruistic. A third section will suggest that despite this shared ground there are phenomena related to choice and conduct that seem to be specifically royalist and that reveal some significant divergences between royalists and parliamentarians.

II

The strident polemics of both parties tend to obscure their common ground, as does the temptation to present serried ranks of royalists confronting serried ranks of parliamentarians. Some examples, however, can tell us something about that common ground. The first relates to a flurry of letters from May to July 1642 exchanged between old friends and acquaintances in York and London. They were, for the most part, moderate men who as the Civil War progressed were marginalized by more radical colleagues. They were also the kind of men without whom there could have been no civil war or revolution in the first place. They hoped that reason and accommodation might avert catastrophe, although their hopes were fading fast. They sought 'a good understanding between the king & parliament' as what 'every good man did desire more than his own life'.[1] They were 'faithful & affectionate to his royal person' and condemned those who wished to divide the king from his parliament and people. They deplored those with 'disloyal hearts' to the king or 'turbulent hearts to this state', and those who wished to 'change the frame of government, to invade upon the king's just prerogative, or to leave him unprovided', and they proclaimed their 'loyalty & fidelity'.[2] One of them admitted to the 'hazards [he had] run' in incurring the king's anger for, he said, 'I ... adventured far to speak my mind freely according to my conscience', and had refused to condemn parliament's Militia Ordinance.[3] All conceived of the state as containing two legitimate institutions, crown and parliament.

For all their assertions of loyalty all but one of these correspondents were to support parliament. Only the last, Sir John Bankes, unhesitatingly

---

[1] Kingston Lacy, Bankes MSS, vol. 1 (unpaginated), Denzil Holles to Sir John Bankes, 21 May 1642.

[2] *Ibid.*, Lord Wharton to Bankes, 14 June 1642; the earl of Northumberland to Bankes, 9 May 1642; Lord Saye and Sele to Bankes, 8 June 1642.

[3] Despite a royal command 'on his allegiance' to declare the Militia Ordinance illegal Bankes had reiterated his refusal to meddle with matters voted by parliament. *Ibid.*, Bankes to Giles Greene, 21 May 1642. Greene, an MP, was a large tenant of Bankes and later, as an active parliamentarian, a faithful friend to the royalist Lady Bankes, who had commanded the defence of Corfe Castle against parliament.

followed the king to Oxford and died there. Bankes's correspondents, the earls of Northumberland and Essex, Lord Wharton, Denzil Holles and especially Lord Saye and Sele had mingled their declarations of loyalty to king and state with claims of the rights of parliament and the need for protection of laws, liberties and privileges. Yet even Say, it seems, did not foresee fundamental changes in the state: after a stiff summary of 'scornes to [the] authority of parliament' he still sought Bankes's intervention with the king to secure an office for a cousin who would use it for 'the king's service and profit'.[4] Bankes, for his part, was clearly unhappy with the king's course of action in the early summer of 1642. The exchange makes clear the determination of each party to the correspondence to defend a basic position that centred on the location of ultimate power in the state, but it also reveals a sense that men of good will could negotiate a reconciliation. As Northumberland wrote sadly on 29 June, 'we were growing into a very good temper and way of moderation', but events had overtaken their moderate and pacific hopes. Yet even at that late date he thought that 'an offer of an act of oblivion and general pardon ... would incline many to an accommodation'.[5] His opinion receives some support from Sir Hugh Cholmley's belief that if Sir John Hotham, a strong anti-Straffordian, had been granted a pardon and received into royal 'grace and favour' instead of being so coldly rebuffed that he feared to lose his head, he would have remained a 'faithfull and serviceable person' to the king. Instead Hotham deviated into parliamentarianism and refused to allow Charles I to enter Hull.[6] The need for oblivion and pardon, however, is in itself evidence of how positions had hardened; 'ways of force' could not long be postponed.[7]

The comments of members of the House of Commons as they promised contributions 'for defence of the parliament' on 10–11 June 1642 nevertheless provide further evidence of convergences between some at least of the parties to the war, in their use of constitutional formulae that moderate royalists would have found unexceptionable. A small but significant group of the members promising money, plate and horses in support of parliament hedged their offers with the cautious proviso that they were offered 'conjunctively for the defence of King, Kingdom & Parliament', or of 'the king & parliament conjunctively & not divided', or

---

[4]   *Ibid.*, Saye and Sele to Bankes, 8 June 1642.
[5]   *Ibid.*, Northumberland to Bankes, 29 June 1642.
[6]   Jack Binns (ed.), *The Memoirs and Memorials of Sir Hugh Cholmley of Whitby 1600–1657*, Yorkshire Archaeological Society, Record Series, 153 (1997–1998), p. 125; but see also Binns's sceptical note on this point.
[7]   Kingston Lacy, Bankes MSS, Bankes to Greene, 21 May 1642.

in one case 'for the preservation of the king & parliament according to his protestation, oath of supremacy & allegiance conjunctively & not [with] . . . other meaning'.[8] Sir John Holland's contribution of two fully equipped horses and £100 came on comprehensive terms: it was 'for maintenance of the true protestant religion the defence of the king's person his royal authority & dignity our laws liberties & privileges conjunctively'.[9] It was a position that could satisfy traditionalist parliamentarians, but it could also justify the actions of men who, like Hotham and Sir Hugh Cholmley, later left parliament's cause for the king's. Cholmley, for example, had originally fought for the parliament 'desir[ing] nothing but that the king should enjoy his iust rights as well as the subjects theirs', in the belief that such participation would quickly help to 'advance a treaty' between the two parties. Disillusion soon followed, but his change of allegiance did not require abandonment of his initial premise. By March 1643 Cholmley was a royalist and by the autumn of 1645 he had retired to the continent, whither Sir John Holland had preceded him by nearly two years.[10]

The frequent parliamentarian claims to be acting on behalf of the ancient constitution can be easily dismissed as a useful, soothing and hypocritical formula, but the considered provisos noted above are a reminder of the constitutional convergences that, as the war began, linked moderate royalists and moderate parliamentarians. They are also a reminder that the reservations implied in the statements of these moderate members of parliament could ease the way, intellectually and psychologically, for transference of allegiance, as in Cholmley's case, or retirement from the fray, as in Holland's.[11] Of the members of the Commons group discussed above only one, Edward Bagshaw (who had insisted on the oath of supremacy and allegiance), actually turned royalist, but it is not surprising to find that the remnant who remained in parliament were expelled in Pride's Purge.[12] As in most revolutions, conservative revolutionaries who were present at the creation were set aside or discredited if they did not adapt to new conditions and many, like Sir John Holland, joined moderate royalists and prudent neutrals on the continent.

---

[8] Bodl. MS Tanner 63, fos. 51, 53–9.
[9] *Ibid.*, fo. 57.
[10] Cholmley, *Memoirs*, pp. 104–5, 108, 143.
[11] An autobiographical apologia should always, of course, be treated with reserve, especially when, as in Cholmley's case, the actions recounted were controversial and widely condemned.
[12] D. Brunton and D. H. Pennington, *Members of the Long Parliament* (n.p., 1968), Appendix VI, pp. 225–45; Bodl. MS Tanner 63, fo. 57.

Attempts by moderates of both sides to find ways to a negotiated peace recurred, but as the polemics of the war became more strident and enmity became more rigorous similarities of constitutional formulae retreated as counters of discourse between opponents.

Common interests and shared local loyalties remained, however, and as armed confrontation began to seem inevitable in the summer of 1642 local leaders affiliated to opposing sides joined in efforts to keep 'the noise of the drum' from their counties. In Norfolk in July and August 1642, for example, the county's members of parliament dawdled over implementation of parliament's Militia Ordinance, preferring to keep it as a reserve power 'in case', and to preserve, in Sir John Holland's words, 'the peace of my country'.[13] In August the Lord Lieutenant Lord Mowbray, the earl of Arundel's son, arrived with orders to enforce the king's competing Commission of Array, but he left the county without doing so for 'the gentlemen of [his] side held it not serviceable'. Sir John Holland had called on Mowbray on his arrival, a courtesy demanded, he felt, by his long association with Arundel's family, and he successfully persuaded both Mowbray and his own potentially royalist friends that 'the suspension of the execution' of the Commission of Array was the only way to preserve the county's peace.[14] It became 'every honest man', Sir John wrote to his fellow Norfolk man and Member of Parliament Sir John Potts, 'to endeavour the peace of his country'; he should not 'depart from ... those principles that render a man faithful to his conscience and country'.[15]

Such complicity between opponents who were men of good will and who endeavoured to follow 'the command of reason signed by a good conscience' in the interests of local peace could not long withstand the extending demands of war.[16] By the twentieth of August Potts was already under pressure to provide soldiers for the earl of Manchester's force, and by February 1643 Norfolk troops were officially required to serve outside their own county. Meanwhile other Norfolk men began openly to support the king's cause.[17] The pretence that war could be localized, segregated and kept at a distance quickly grew hollow.

It had been unrealistic to hope that Norfolk could exclude violence from its border, but the county was not unique. In Yorkshire and

---

[13]   *Ibid.*, fos. 118, 121.

[14]   *Ibid.*, fos. 121, 126; Bodl. MS Tanner 64, fo. 145; Clive Holmes, *The Eastern Association in the English Civil War* (Cambridge, 1974), pp. 58 and 56–62; R. W. Ketton-Cremer, *Norfolk in the Civil War* (1969), pp. 145–7.

[15]   Bodl. MS Tanner 63, fos. 126, 120v.

[16]   *Ibid.*, fo. 116.

[17]   *Ibid.*, fos. 116, 130; Holmes, *Eastern Association*, pp. 60–2, 66; Ketton-Cremer, *Norfolk*, pp. 158–9.

Lancashire, for example, future royalists and future parliamentarians hoped that treaties of neutrality would effectively protect their counties. Such frail hopes had an early death, and those who had supported them were forced to decide how they would respond to openly warring sides. Some still hoped to avoid active choice, but most became partisan with varying degrees of enthusiasm. If Potts and Holland in Norfolk and the Fairfaxes in Yorkshire chose parliament, others who had initially supported its moderate programmes moved towards the king as the confrontation between royal and parliamentary power became starker and recourse to military and civil force metastasized.[18] Furthermore, the prospect of war did not always lead to a desire for peace. In some counties – notably Huntingdon – it offered prospects of pursuing ancient quarrels in the name of a higher cause. Nevertheless the linkages and likenesses seen in these fruitless efforts at neutralism serve to remind us that moderates of both sides had connived to subvert policies of 'central' authority and belligerent activists. Although they failed, they reveal shared interest and habits of county management and social intercourse as well as reconcilable constitutional principles, factors that helped to facilitate as well as to explain some of the shifts of allegiance that marked the Interregnum years.

III

These episodes in which future opponents cooperated to prevent war or to quarantine their counties from its contagion were marginal and ineffectual, but they raise a central question: how did men who had much in common, who sought a negotiated settlement, who abhorred the idea of civil war, and who bipartisanly argued in terms of conscience and principle, choose between king and parliament? The response of men like Essex, Saye and Bankes provides one answer. When choice was unavoidable they appear to have acted unhesitatingly and in accordance with their past positions; they had, in effect, already considered and identified their priorities. For many others, however, choices were surprising, or tortured, or fortuitous, or opportunist, or coerced. For yet others – especially royalists – choice seems to have been almost instinctive. We must also, of course, always remember that, as in the cases of Cholmley and Hotham, initial choice of allegiance was not necessarily a guarantee of permanent loyalty.

---

[18] Holmes, *Eastern Association*, pp. 60–2; Ketton-Cremer, *Norfolk*, pp. 149–56; D. Farr, 'The Shaping of John Lambert's Allegiance and the Outbreak of the Civil War', *Northern History*, 36 (2000), 260–5.

The processes by which seventeenth-century decisions were reached through appeals to conscience, casuistry and theoretical argument (whether religious or constitutional) have been extensively studied, but although they may seem more characteristic of puritan soul- and conscience-searching than of Cavalier insouciance, they were common to both sides; they could result in commitments that ran the gamut from wholehearted to reluctant or lukewarm, or indeed to neutralism. Nor were choices always predictable.[19] The story of the noble royalist Sir Edmund Verney, a pre-war critic of royal policies who died at Edgehill fighting for a cause he could not believe in and a king he could not desert, is well known. He had no illusions about the contradictory nature of his choice. He fought to 'preserve and defend those things, which are against my conscience to preserve and defend', because conscience also required that 'in honour and gratitude' he was bound to defend the master he had served and whose bread he had eaten for thirty years.[20] He envied Edward Hyde, the future earl of Clarendon, to whom he wrote, 'You have satisfaction in your conscience that you are in the right that the King ought not to grant what is required of him.' He himself had no such comfort and admitted, 'I do not like the quarrel.'[21] The royalist Lord Paget was equally aware of the conflicting demands of conscience and explicitly recognized the 'strangeness' of his choice. When the prospect of actually bearing arms against the king compelled him to leave London for York in June 1642, he acknowledged desertion of a valid cause:

It may seem strange, that I, who with all zeal & earnestness have prosecuted ... the reformation of all the disorders in Church & Commonwealth, should now ... desert the cause. Most true it is that my ends were the common good, & while it was prosecuted I was ready to lay down both life & fortune, but when I found a preparation of Arms against the King, under the shadow of Loyalty, I rather resolved to obey a good conscience than particular ends.[22]

The royalist allegiance of such men who had campaigned for reform in church and state can seem puzzling. For some, however, it is possible to identify a particular sticking-point, notably – as with Paget – the prospect of actually bearing arms against the king. Parliament's Militia

[19] G. E. Aylmer, 'Collective Mentalities in Mid Seventeenth-century England: II. Royalist Attitudes', *TRHS*, 5th ser., 37 (1987), 2–7; see also B. Donagan, 'Casuistry and Allegiance in the English Civil War', in Derek Hirst and Richard Strier (eds.), *Writing and Political Engagement in Seventeenth-century England* (Cambridge, 1999), pp. 89–111.

[20] Frances Parthenope Verney, *Memoirs of the Verney Family during the Civil War*, 2 vols. (1892), vol. II, p. 126.

[21] *Ibid.*

[22] Huntington Library, Ellesmere MS 7803; Bodl. MS Clarendon 21, fo. 89.

Ordinance and the king's competing Commission of Array presented many Englishmen with a stark and unwelcome choice, for they demanded commitment to one or other of the contending claimants to sovereign power in the state. The terms of opposition had moved from a condition that could, with some effort, be seen as a continuation of politics as usual, if in a particularly nasty and divisive form, to one of potential armed conflict between two agencies, each of which claimed primacy as the sovereign power. Subjects must now decide whether conscience and allegiance required that they bear arms (or pay for the bearers of arms) for the king, or legitimated armed service against him. For some of those who decided for the king on this and other grounds, it seems that the execution of Strafford had proved liberating, for it removed a barrier to their support.

One such royalist was Thomas Knyvett, who had previously opposed the king's policies and had detested Strafford: the 'bad cause' of 'so foul a man', he said in 1641, rendered him 'a satisfactory sacrifice'. Yet he was already deeply anxious about another accompaniment of parliament's reforms. In 1641 he had regretted the excesses of religious 'reformation' that went on 'as hot as toast', and feared that the violent turning of the tide would lead to future 'inundation'.[23] This fear that reform had gone too far and that religion, order, property and deference were endangered was a powerful argument for royalism at the beginning of the war. It also helps to explain some of the later defections by those who initially supported parliament as well as changes of heart by those who had initially wished to be neutral. There was much anxiety that the skin of order in society was thin and fragile, an anxiety that was compounded by the widely disseminated reports of the devastation and unbridled cruelties of the Thirty Years' War and, in 1641, of the Irish rebellion. Together they demonstrated, often in lurid detail, the chaos and dehumanization that could accompany war and the breakdown of civil and military authority. The disorders of both soldiers and civilians in the Scottish wars had brought home, on English soil, the weakness of authority in the face of ill-disciplined troops. The notorious events of the early months of the Civil War, such as the attack on Countess Rivers by an anti-popish mob in Essex, or the vandalizing incursion of raw and tumultuous London soldiers into Kent, where they offered violence to women, the weak and the old, and destroyed property indiscriminately, or the innumerable smaller incidents of the months before and after war formally began, all combined to persuade many, like Knyvett, that chaos could come

[23] Bertram Schofield (ed.), *The Knyvett Letters 1620–1644*, Norfolk Record Society, 20 (1949), pp. 30–1.

to England as it had to Germany and Ireland and that safety lay with the king and the preservation of ancient institutions and hierarchy. By September 1642 complaints of 'the insolencies of the soldiers' and of 'plundering multitudes of people tumultuously gathered together' had grown familiar.[24] As the war progressed the fear that the parliamentary cause was being hijacked by radicalism and an ordered society overturned was to lead many erstwhile parliamentarians to neutralism, exile, or the king.

These anxieties were not confined to a social or political elite. A 'Declaration ... of the County of Hereford' reflected at a more popular level the transition from consensual support for parliamentary reform to defence of the king. For many years, it said, the kingdom had suffered from

the dismal effects of an arbitrary government, & an high stretched prerogative; for the care of which distemper a parliament was believed by all men to be the only good old way of physic to cleanse the body politic.

Now, however, 'a worse disease threatened', and the kingdom was speeding 'to the other extreme, which portends ... ruin & destruction'. Not only was parliament rent by divisions, avarice and credulous acceptance of rumours against the king, but a 'whisper' from parliament was enough to raise 'the mutinous rabble'. A 'new and unheard of law & logic' was at work when a divided parliament was 'severed from the king the head thereof'. The king had been driven to act defensively by the 'insolencies' of the 'vulgar rabble', and in consequence the petitioners, as 'faithful subjects', were resolved to maintain the Protestant religion, the king's just power, the laws of the land, and the liberties of the subject.[25] The wheel had come full circle, and the reformers' catalogue of constitutional virtues was now deployed to support the king.

Some decisions thus had a clear pedigree in conscience and allegiance or in fear of social breakdown. Others were based on religion, an aspect of the problem that cannot be explored here other than to note that most Catholics were royalist, and that loyalty to a national, 'Anglican' church led many English men and women to defend it against Presbyterian, Independent or more radical assault. Less clear-cut are the kinds of cases in which external factors were at war with inclination. Sir John Reresby's 'principles lead him to be loyall' but he lived in the midst of parliamentarian neighbours and his royalism, when he finally acted, was cautious and calculatedly low profile.[26] Edward Pitt, an Exchequer official, retired

---

[24] Bodl. MS Tanner 63, fos. 149, 153; and see David Cressy, *England on Edge. Crisis and Revolution 1640–1642* (Oxford, 2006), chapters 16 and 17.

[25] Bodl. Add. MS c.132, fos. 35–6.

[26] Andrew Browning (ed.), *Memoirs of Sir John Reresby*, 2nd edn, in Mary K. Geiter and W. A. Speck (eds.) (1991), p. xliii.

to the country and hoped (vainly) to wait out the war unobserved and inactive. His inclinations were undoubtedly royalist, yet he was devastated when his eldest son secretly fled to Oxford to volunteer for the king's service. It was, he said, the boy's 'only inconsiderate act'.[27] Like many others, Pitt 'labour[ed] to tread that narrow path between his majesty and the parliament' but he was caught, in his words, 'between Scylla and Charybdis' – and to parliament he was a 'delinquent'.[28] He was typical of many who, notwithstanding inclination, wanted no part in the war. Closet royalists, like closet parliamentarians and the neuters who 'bug-beared' both sides, tried to negotiate an inactive passage between the combatants, but as the war lengthened it became harder to evade involvement.[29] Even so, Cliffe has estimated that 240, or just over 35 per cent, of the 679 Yorkshire gentry families that he studied managed to remain neutral.[30]

Not surprisingly pragmatism could also lead to prudential decisions that ran counter to inclination. Alice Thornton wrote of her brother that his 'affections and conscience carried him in judgement to serve his king, the church and state, by way of armes': his 'prudence for the preservation of his family', however, led him to 'sitt in quiet'. It was, he concluded, 'in vaine to strive against that impetuous streame, and involve himselfe in utter ruine willfully'. He offered instead the support of 'praiers and tears'.[31] Sometimes the convenience of the conclusion was veiled by a meticulous casuistical apparatus. The earl of Bridgewater's inclinations were clearly for the king, but he was threatened by the House of Lords, in fear of martial law, and too old and lame to flee. He persuaded himself that he could preserve the welfare of 'soul and body' by taking the Solemn League and Covenant in good conscience and without harming 'the Bird in the Breast' or 'infringing of . . . former oaths'. He left a record of a process of 'objections' and 'solutions' that was worthy of the most 'Jesuitical' casuist, although it was, he insisted, 'put into [his] mind' by God.[32] Evidence of complex ratiocination is not necessarily evidence of pure decision based on pure principle or pure logic, but the recurrence of appeals to conscience and judgment and of formal processes of argument

---

27 BL Add. MS 29974.2, fo. 381. In an incautious moment after he was imprisoned by parliament, Pitt wrote, 'I cannot suffer in a better cause', *ibid.*, fo. 365a. See B. Donagan, 'Family and Misfortune in the English Civil War: the Sad Case of Edward Pitt', *HLQ*, 61 (1998), 223–40.
28 BL Add. MS 29974.2, fos. 364a, 366, 368a.
29 Bodl. MS Tanner 63, fo. 116.
30 J. T. Cliffe, *The Yorkshire Gentry. From the Reformation to the Civil War* (1969), pp. 336, 338.
31 *Ibid.*, pp. 336–7.
32 Huntington Library, Ellesmere MSS 7772–7774.

is a further reminder of values and intellectual habits common to both parties to the war; they could be used to provide a decent cloak on occasions when men and women were nudged towards one side or the other by circumstances or interest.

A problem that has received relatively little attention except in the case of notorious side-changers is that of the volatility of allegiance. The circumstances of war could change mass loyalties, as in Cornwall: the county was famously loyal to the king in the early years of the war, but experience of the licence allowed to his troops by the younger Lord Goring later led it to welcome the parliamentary army. Such a change is unsurprising and indeed predictable (as Prince Charles and his council recognized when they vainly reproved Goring). On the national stage, the reasons behind defections by individuals and small groups were more diverse and more revealing. There were 'tergiversatious Bats' (in a contemporary's phrase) among the peerage, among all levels of the civilian population, and in the army. Richard Symonds wrote with disgust of one man, currently a royalist, 'first for the Parliament, then for the King, then theirs, then taken prisoner by us, and [with] much ado gott his pardon, and now *pro Rege*, God wott'.[33] We have already noted the cases of Sir Hugh Cholmley and Sir John Hotham, and the latter's execution in January 1645 by the parliament he had initially served illustrates the risks that renegades ran. The conventions of war and the formal articles of war issued by both sides mandated death for turncoat soldiers, while civilians were vulnerable to charges of treason. In practice, consequences varied. Unlike Hotham at Hull, Cholmley escaped after Scarborough Castle fell to parliamentary troops in July 1645, and after some years of exile on the continent he was able to return to England in 1649 and pick up the threads of his life again. His son, the younger Hugh, apparently suffered no reprisals while he remained at school in London. It may have helped that Cholmley's brother Henry had remained a parliamentarian.[34] Colonel Farr, a notorious turncoat who had defected to the royalists in 1648, was condemned to die with the royalist martyrs Sir Charles Lucas and Sir George Lisle but he too survived thanks to his old patron, the still influential earl of Warwick. Old patterns of influence survived in the war years, but even Warwick was unable to save the life of his brother, the multiple turncoat earl of Holland.[35]

---

[33]   Richard Symonds, *Diary of the Marches of the Royal Army*, ed. C. E. Long and Ian Roy (eds.) (Cambridge, 1997), p. 196; John Vicars, *Gods Arke Overtopping the Worlds Waves*, in *Magnalia Dei Anglicana* (1646), pp. 261–2.

[34]   Cholmley, *Memoirs*, p. 41. The younger Hugh was prudently too ill to join the royalist army in 1651.

[35]   *CJ*, vol. VI, p. 10.

Others did not change sides but simply left the fray for a variety of reasons. After defeat at Marston Moor in 1644 the earl of Newcastle retired to the continent; it was said that he could not abide 'the laughter of the court', but it was also reported that he resented being placed under Prince Rupert in command of his army and had 'before the battle ... resolved ... to quitt his imployment and the kingdome'.[36] Others, like John Evelyn, simply sought less stressful climes. It is noteworthy that Pitt's second son George left for the continent in 1644.[37] It seems too that some families continued to send their sons abroad not only for education and social polish but also in part to protect them from combat; Lady Norwich was 'troubled' when her husband recalled their second son from Paris to serve the king.[38]

Another point to consider is that armies were a good deal more volatile than their modern counterparts, although numbers are hard to come by. P. R. Newman estimated that only 24 of the king's 603 colonels changed sides between 1642 and 1646, of whom 15 went over from king to parliament and 9 from parliament to king.[39] At under 4 per cent this is not a very impressive figure, although colonels were less likely candidates for side-changing than, say, captains or corporals, while common soldiers ebbed and flowed between armies with notable volatility. A wider view indicates greater fluidity than Newman's figures suggest, although abandonment of the king's service did not necessarily mean a transfer of allegiance. The reasons for this instability were various. Both armies, for example, enlisted professionals from the continent, but this entailed risks. Many had returned home to England to take advantage of domestic employment opportunities, but some were more interested in the best offer than the cause, and some left the country when they tired of English service. Edward Massey entered parliament's service after he failed to secure attractive terms from the king, and later changed sides.[40] Another returning professional who served the king nonetheless pointedly noted, when his pay was in arrears, that he had *so far* loyally resisted tempting offers made by parliament.[41] General James King, created Baron Eythin late in 1643 by a grateful sovereign, had returned from

---

[36] Quoted in Austin Woolrych, *Battles of the English Civil War* (1966), p. 79; Cholmley, *Memoirs*, p. 138.

[37] Donagan, 'Family and Misfortune', 234.

[38] *CSPD 1644*, p. 110.

[39] P. R. Newman, *The Old Service. Royalist Regimental Colonels and the Civil War, 1642–46* (Manchester, 1993), pp. 119, 249; these totals cover England and Wales.

[40] P. R. Newman, *Royalist Officers in England and Wales, 1642–1660* (New York, 1981), p. 248; Gardiner, *HGCW*, vol. IV, pp. 196, 275. Gardiner suspected that Massey had already made approaches to the royalists in 1643.

[41] BL Harl. MS 6804, fo. 99.

the continent, partly at the queen's urging, and served under Newcastle, but by the spring of 1644 he was already restless. After the defeat at Marston Moor he 'conceiv[ed] the Kings affairs absolutelie destroyed' and reputedly was instrumental in persuading Newcastle to leave the country. General King himself, while protesting fervently that he would do nothing 'prejudiciall' to 'his sacred Ma[jes]tie', returned to Swedish service.[42] Furthermore, the death or defection of commanders could lead to the departure of their followers. Cholmley believed that, had Newcastle stayed, he could have rallied the broken royalist forces. Instead, 'upon his departure all most every one (especially such as had particular relation or affeccion to his person) quitt the Kings service and went to their own homes'.[43]

Some reasons for departure from service were personal. When Colonel Windebank, a member of a paradigmatically royalist family, was shot for cowardice after surrendering Bletchingdon House near Oxford his brother laid down his commission in protest.[44] Such changes of course naturally did not all run in one direction. One royalist turned parliamentarian because he feared retribution for speaking out against papists; on the other hand a parliamentarian turned royalist because he became enmeshed in the plottings of royalist cousins.[45] It is not surprising that in this environment it was tempting, and sometimes correct, to attribute defeats and setbacks to 'Infidelitie' like that of the royalist Scottish officer at Marston Moor who fled to parliament's forces with useful intelligence.[46]

Some careers still remain opaque. That of the future Viscount Ogle provides an extreme example of the desire both to be as inactive as possible and to keep open lines to both sides. He was appointed to command London's defences as the king approached Brentford late in 1642; he seems to have accepted the office without serious thought, seeing it as a routine duty for a member of parliament who was an ex-soldier. After a day of frantic activity setting up guards and defensive points, he retired for a few hours' rest and reflection on the situation in which he found himself. He slept little, but lay in his bed 'meditating with his self: that he was in rebellion: and what course he should take to

[42] Cholmley, *Memoirs*, pp. 136, 139; W. A. Day (ed.), *The Pythouse Papers* (1879), pp. 21–2; Newman, *Royalist Officers*, p. 215.

[43] Cholmley, *Memoirs*, p. 139.

[44] John Rushworth, *Historical Collections of Private Passages of State*, 8 vols. (1680–1701), vol. VI, p. 25. Windebank's brother was made a baronet six months later, which suggests some royal fence-mending.

[45] BL Add. MS 11,331, fo. 157; Jack Binns, 'Captain Browne Bushell: North Sea Adventurer and Pirate', *Northern History*, 27 (1991), 92–7.

[46] Cholmley, *Memoirs*, p. 137.

get out of it'. The next morning he set off by coach, nominally to inspect London's outer defence posts, but when he reached Knightsbridge he told the commander, Sir John Meldrum, that he felt unwell and would drive a little further to take the fresh air. Sir John 'bid God bless him', but once out of his sight Ogle whipped up his horses and ultimately reached his house near Winchester. From there he wrote to the House of Commons informing them that he had left London only because he had received news that his wife was dying but that he would return as soon as she recovered; at the same time, he offered his services to the king. The king – again according to Ogle's account – agreed that he should take no overt action but remain a 'sleeper' who would not act in the king's interest until specially called upon to do so. Having decamped from London, he hoped to mollify parliament with a persuasive if false excuse for his absence, and to be only an undercover royalist.[47]

Few allegiances were so deviously constructed, although Lord Herbert's negotiations with Edward Hyde in 1642 on behalf of himself and his father the earl of Pembroke displayed a similar slippery agility. In effect Herbert offered the king the opportunity to buy their loyalty in return for certain favours and a public apology to Pembroke for past slights. They declared their 'fervent zeal to the king's service' – if he met their terms. They seem to have felt that it was not prudent to remain in London while these negotiations continued, so Pembroke retired to the country while Herbert discovered a need to take the waters at Tunbridge Wells, but in the end nothing came of their proposals and they reverted to the opposition to the king for which Pembroke was already well known.[48]

Nor was Ogle the only 'sleeper'. With the king's approbation William St Leger 'entered deep into this rebellion'. The consequence was confusion among his officers and men, who had believed they were destined for politically neutral service in Ireland and now faced the prospect of fighting fellow Englishmen. Their commander's allegiance was clouded and their own uncertain, and they feared that the king would 'esteem [them] traitorous'. St Leger grew troubled at his double role and sought the king's permission to serve him openly, but he admitted that he could not be sure that all his men would follow him into royal service.[49]

---

[47] BL Add. MS 27,402, fos. 87v, 89–89v, and see fos. 86–99 for Ogle's account of his civil war career. Lady Ogle appears to have died shortly before the surrender of Winchester Castle in early October 1645.

[48] Bodl. MSS Clarendon 21, fos. 114, 118.

[49] Ibid., fos. 120–120v; Newman, Royalist Officers, p. 324. Newman believed that St Leger, a professional soldier, came to England in 1643, but he was at Brentford in August 1642.

These attempts to disguise affiliation or evade commitment – Ogle's efforts to retain a foot in both camps, Lord Herbert's attempts to sell allegiance, and St Leger's foray into undercover work – throw light on the confusion that could arise early in the war about the nature of a man's actions and on the temptation to keep lines of loyalty open to both parties. All three were shortly to espouse the king's cause or parliament's. In 1643 Ogle was finally forced into open defence of Winchester for the royalists, St Leger was killed at Newbury in 1644 fighting for the king, and Pembroke continued a parliamentarian until his death. Nevertheless they offer more evidence of the problems of securely identifying allegiance among fellow-countrymen, and of the kinds of dealings that contributed to the readiness to suspect the faithfulness of one's allies as well as the enemy.

Defections and departures frequently reflected the wider fortunes of war, from siege and starvation to defeat. Early in 1643 parliament's 'prosperous proceedings' in Lancashire attracted royalist defectors; in 1646, as the first war drew to its close, 120 royalist foot deserted from Pendennis Castle and offered to serve under Fairfax. Soldiers were also apt to follow the example of officers to whom they felt ties. We have already seen the effect of Newcastle's departure on his soldiers. If officers changed sides their men might well follow them, as did those who accompanied Major General James Chudleigh when he joined the royalists in 1643.[50] Side-changing could be easy – if also potentially dangerous – in the circumstances of civil war, and if we look beyond officers and the staunch and ideologically committed we become aware of a large-scale movement of soldiers between the parties. Not only did soldiers run from one army to another, but a standard way of handling the defeated was to 'entertain' them in one's own army. In such circumstances a loose and opportunistic allegiance was not unexpected, and such recruits tended to be flighty. In 1644 two troops of horse left Waller's army when its fortunes were at a low ebb; they 'were enterteyned by Lord Bernard [Stuart], and ... the next night ran away agen'.[51] Many soldiers who fought in the Civil War can only notionally be called either 'royalist' or 'parliamentarian', and their loyalty to individual officers or to company or regiment was often stronger than that to the cause.

[50]   Newman, *Royalist Officers*, p. 71; for a flattering account of Chudleigh's change of allegiance see Edward Hyde, *A History of the Rebellion and Civil Wars in England*, 3 vols. (Oxford, 1702–1704), vol. II, p. 210. Chudleigh had initially offered his services to the king but met with a cool reception. He thereupon took service in parliament's army, and later defected to the king's.

[51]   Symonds, *Diary*, p. 127.

IV

Much that has been discussed so far has bipartisan relevance, from the elements of constitutional arguments to modes of decision-making and problems of reliable loyalty. There are, however, some characteristics which, if not confined to royalists, yet seem distinctively their own. Two only can be described here; one reveals a royalist virtue, the other a royalist vice.

With the first of these topics, we return to the question of choice. If some royalists entered the king's service only after serious moral, intellectual and religious reflection of a kind that differed little in its processes from that of serious parliamentarians, and if the allegiance of others was volatile or a prey to circumstances, there were still others whose commitment was heartfelt but, it seems, largely unexamined. They introduce a new element into discussion of adherence to one side or the other, one that, because it is elusive and intangible, has rarely been seriously addressed, although it is a staple of the 'romantic royalist' tradition.[52] Where choice is in question, most attention has been paid to decisions that reflected a conclusion based on moral and religious principles and reached by familiar pastoral and casuistical methods of study, argument and advice as applied in each individual instance. Each case required a choice between right and wrong, and distinguishing between the two was often difficult. We have seen the process at work in the earl of Bridgewater's decision that he might in good conscience accept the Solemn League and Covenant. But I would suggest that another ethical strand was present, one that would now be described as 'virtue ethics'. In this scenario a good man (or woman) acts in accordance with his sense of his whole self, not in accordance with a particular set of arguments and judgment in an individual case. 'To act rightly is to do what a good person would do in these particular circumstances', according to one definition; such a criterion rejects 'conduct that would be seriously out of character for a virtuous person', according to another.[53] These, it can be argued, are question-begging definitions. Furthermore, decisions reached in this way will leave few records. Nonetheless 'virtue ethics' is a moral stance that can be observed among

[52] But see the valuable discussions in Aylmer, 'Royalist Attitudes', and P. R. Newman, 'The King's Servants: Conscience, Principle and Sacrifice in Armed Royalism', in John Morrill, Paul Slack and Daniel Woolf (eds.), *Public Duty and Private Conscience in Seventeenth-century England* (Oxford, 1993), pp. 225–41.

[53] Alasdair MacIntyre, 'Virtue Ethics', in Lawrence C. Becker (ed.), *Encyclopedia of Ethics*, 2 vols. (New York, 1992), vol. II, p. 1277; J. L. A. G[arcia], 'Virtue Ethics', in Robert Audi (ed.), *The Cambridge Dictionary of Philosophy* (Cambridge, 1995), p. 840.

royalists. The career of Lord Goring, later earl of Norwich, provides an example.[54]

The Gorings had been a Court family since the reign of Edward VI. Norwich rose under James I, who valued him for his 'peculiar jocularity of humour' – jokes at James's Court were not subtle – but also for his 'sagacity' and his diplomatic abilities. He continued to flourish under Charles I. He amassed profitable offices, but more important was his connection with Henrietta Maria; it began with the negotiations for her marriage, continued through the 1630s, when he displayed a kind of jovial, avuncular devotion to her welfare, and into the 1640s when he accompanied her to the continent in her quest for guns and money. He spent most of the 1640s and 1650s in Europe still serving the crown. Relations with the queen soured as she turned to new advisers, and Norwich grew old, poor and marginal, but his devotion to the Stuart cause never faltered and it remained essentially personal as Charles I's sons replaced their father and mother as the focus of his loyalty. The Prince of Wales was his 'sweet prince' and 'dear sweet young master', and as Charles II he retained Norwich's 'loyalty and passionate affection'.[55] Even in poverty and exile, when his 'fifty yeares service in [the] Royall Family' were little appreciated, Norwich still declared his loyalty to 'the last drop of my colde vaynes'.[56]

There are few signs of political reflection in his progress, although he was capable of rueful introspection about his own nature. On the other hand, he knew where he stood and what he was doing, and he did not sentimentalize. In 1633 he had written with a flourish to the king that he could not

> forget who made us of nothing, and who preserved us there ... Your service being by so long and sweet a custom now become a second nature, besides my obligation to address the whole course of my life to that only end where if I wittingly fail let me perish eternally.[57]

This proved to be no mere fair-weather flattery. In 1644 he wrote, 'I had all from his Majesty, and he hath all again', and he told his wife, '[H]ad I millions of crowns or scores of sons the King and his cause should have them all ... nor shall fear or loss of whatsoever ever change me therein.'[58]

[54] Lord Goring was created earl of Norwich in 1644. Here I will refer to him as Norwich, to distinguish him from his deplorable son Colonel (and after 1644 Lord) Goring.

[55] *CSPD 1663–1664*, p. 6; O. Ogle et al. (eds.), *Calendar of the Clarendon State Papers*, 5 vols. (1872–1970), vol. I, p. 284.

[56] *Nicholas*, vol. II, p. 259 and vol. III, p. 15. In 1655 Norwich wrote to Charles II, 'I will ever be within reach of your call, and noe more abandon my Allegiance to you then I will my Faith to God.' *Ibid.*, vol. II, p. 259.

[57] HMC, *Manuscripts of Earl Cowper* (1888), vol. II, pp. 22–3.

[58] *CSPD 1644*, pp. 110, 261.

Late in 1645, after offering advice that by then he did not really expect to be accepted, Norwich could still write, 'I have discharged my duty, and shall write on the gate as I pass by, that you can have no more of a cat than her skin.'[59] The essence of his stance was loyalty allied with good temper even in the worst disappointment and adversity. The key words are his own: loyalty had become 'a second nature' that shaped the 'whole course of his life'. He was a virtue ethicist ahead of his time. Like the French ideal of the *honnête homme*, a man who saw himself and his actions whole did not need to indulge in tortured choice.

There is no way of knowing the extent to which such loyalty was shared or extended beyond the Court. Simply being an old courtier was not enough – witness the side-changing earl of Holland. Others who were at times close to Charles I, like Digby or Wilmot, were more complex characters, though Ashburnham seemed to display a similar undemanding and personal allegiance. It cannot be described as a baronial or feudal phenomenon, nor does it have much in common with the martyrology and hagiography that followed regicide and the publication of *Eikon Basilike*. Yet it is a kind of royalism that would repay further exploration.

There is some evidence for such instinctive loyalty at more popular levels. It probably impelled some of those who, in the first rush of enthusiasm for the king and his cause, volunteered for his army. The scattered reports of dangerous words spoken against parliament in the summer of 1642 hint at an ingrained loyalty similar to Norwich's among at least some of the king's humbler subjects. In Salisbury Henry Whatly declared that the parliament was 'a company of rebels' and that 'they were all a company of fools that would not hold with the king'. In Leicester one man proclaimed, 'God bless the king and devil take the parliament', while at Daventry an ex-soldier named Norwood who had served briefly in the king's army was heard to say 'that he was only for the king with his life & estate'. These incidents, like other anti-parliamentarian outbursts, occurred on sociable occasions when tongues were almost certainly loosened by drink: Whatly's defence (for the offenders were promptly informed on and brought before the authorities) was that 'he was overtaken by drink when he spoke'.[60] If more venom was expressed against parliament than love for the king, the

---

[59]   Bodl. MS Clarendon 25, fo. 209.
[60]   Bodl. MS Tanner 63, fos. 66–7, 142v, 163, and see also fos. 40, 83, 147. The fact that informers reported their words, of course, suggests that not all their hearers agreed with the speakers.

reports nevertheless suggest that there was still a residue of instinctive loyalty to be tapped, even if it was hardly a manifestation of virtue ethics.

The second of the distinctive characteristics of royalism to be discussed here reveals an aspect that is rarely addressed by modern historians and that does not fit comfortably into any tidy explanatory framework: namely, the royalists' proneness to quarrels and violence. Of course parliamentarians too could be quarrelsome and violent. The story of the parliamentary cause in the 1640s is after all a story of quarrels that have been dignified into national history, and the violence of the language of sermons and pamphlets rules out any claims to conceptual moderation as a defining parliamentary characteristic. Their quarrels too could lead to physical violence in affrays and duels.[61] On the whole, however, their violence was directed against the enemy rather than each other.

It was otherwise with the royalists. Parliament's armies did not suffer to anything like the same degree from the endemic, disabling and sometimes lethal outbursts that characterized some royalist officers imbued with melodramatic habits of honour and the fast draw. The quarrels surrounding Charles I, as described by Sir Richard Bulstrode, are enough to make one sympathize with the king. On one occasion he was 'so much surprised at ... extravagant and insolent Discourses, that he rose from Dinner in great Disorder', and when one of the protagonists in the quarrel came close to demanding satisfaction from the king himself his 'Indignation' was so great that he dismissed them all from his presence.[62] The roster of feuds is notorious: it included Wilmot vs. Digby; Leveson vs. Bagot; Tuke vs. Porter; Washington vs. his officers; Rupert vs. The Rest.[63] Richard Symonds's diary of his marches with the king's army in 1644 and 1645 is dotted with references to affrays and duels; the problem extended far beyond the senior officers about the king.[64]

---

[61] For some examples of parliamentary quarrels, duels and violence, and their consequences see e.g. Bodl. MSS Tanner 61, fo. 106; 62/2A, fos. 420–1, 461; *CJ*, vol. III, p. 712; [John Washbourn], *Bibliotheca Gloucestrensis: A Collection of Scarce and Curious Tracts, Relating to the City and County of Gloucester* (Gloucester, 1825), pp. 100, 109; John Adair, 'The Court Martial Papers of Sir William Waller's Army 1644', *Journal of the Society for Army Historical Research*, 44 (1966), 210–11.

[62] Sir Richard Bulstrode, *Memoirs and Reflections upon the Reign and Government of King Charles the 1st* (1721), pp. 128–30, 142–7.

[63] William Salt Library, Salt MSS 481, 502, 550/22; 'Some Letters of the Civil War', *Collections for a History of Staffordshire*, Staffordshire Record Society (1941), pp. 142–4, 146; J. Willis Bund (ed.), *The Diary of Henry Townshend of Elmley Lovett, 1640–1663*, Worcestershire Historical Society (Series), vols. 61–3, 67 (1915–1920), [vol. I], pp. 151–2; Ian Roy, 'George Digby. Royalist Intrigue and the Collapse of the Cause', in Ian Gentles, John Morrill and Blair Worden (eds.), *Soldiers, Writers and Statesmen of the English Revolution* (Cambridge, 1998), pp. 84–9.

[64] E.g. Symonds, *Diary*, pp. 30, 36, 250, 261, 276.

The case of Lieutenant Colonel David Hyde is extreme but revealing. In the course of a drunken rampage in Worcester in January 1643 he beat women and other bystanders on the streets and threatened to 'pistol', cudgel and shoot his senior officers Sir William Russell and Sir James Hamilton, to throw his trencher at the mayor as he dined with him, and to burn the town and the mayor's house with it. He offered violence with sword, cane, pistols and knife as he ranged through the streets, and he challenged Russell's authority as governor of the city and abused Hamilton as a traitorous Scot and a papist. Only the notable tact and firmness of a junior officer ultimately persuaded him into a tavern and thence into custody. For this Hyde was briefly imprisoned and court-martialled, but by then his chief accuser was in action elsewhere and the case was dismissed. Two years later Hyde killed a fellow-royalist, Sir John Scudamore, in a duel. Six months after that he was still in Rupert's entourage.[65]

The episode offers many insights into both royalism and the Civil War more generally. It reveals, for example, sectarian divisions in royalist ranks between Protestants and Catholics and national divisions between English and Scots, and it tellingly demonstrates the integration of the civilian and military sides of the war and the vulnerability of civilians to soldiers' non-combat violence. Hyde was clearly fighting drunk, and a prime example of Ronald Hutton's 'English gentry turned feral' or Roger Manning's 'swordsmen'.[66] Nevertheless his case exemplifies both the royalist tendency to internecine violence and a debilitating degree of tolerance and ineffectualness in controlling it. All the armies of the Civil War were prey to internal violence – soldiers were not notably or naturally orderly – and all, in their articles of war, legislated against brawls, insubordination, striking an officer and duels. On these issues parliament's articles did not change in the course of the war, and courts martial dealt effectively with cases brought before them. From 1642, however, the royalists devoted five articles to prevention of duels to parliament's one, and their later, revised articles added further provisions – all to little effect – intended to prevent affronts to honour becoming the occasion for duels, while they mandated draconian punishment for drawing one's sword against a fellow royalist during battle or in a stronghold: the penalty for the former was to be 'shot to death', for the latter loss of

65 BL Harl. MSS 6851, fos. 72, 79, 81, 83–94, 108–9, 135; 6802, fo. 32(2); 6804, fo. 88; 6852, fo. 70; *CSPD 1645–1647*, p. 190; *Letters of the Lady Brilliana Harley*, T. T. Lewis, ed., Camden Soc., 58 (1854), 253.
66 Ronald Hutton, *The Royalist War Effort 1642–1646* (1984), p. 104, and see generally for the royalist command structure and commanders; Roger B. Manning, *Swordsmen. The Martial Ethos in the Three Kingdoms* (Oxford, 2003), especially chapters 6 and 7.

a hand and expulsion from the army.[67] Royalist articles of war overall were fussier and longer than parliament's, but these very specific and expanded clauses indicate an attempt to address a serious weakness in royalist armies.

Obviously not all royalists were, metaphorically, trigger-happy thugs. All quarrels did not end in violence, and the officer corps contained admirably cool, moral and professional men like Sir Henry Gage who saw quarrels as counter-productive. Nevertheless the febrile climate that surrounded much royalist decision-making and action – Court faction transferred to the conduct of war – cannot but have been a drain on the time, energy and judgment of senior commanders and a source of anxiety and frustration to civilian planners, who were themselves hardly free from feuds.

V

These strands in royalist conduct suggest significant differences between the parties that go beyond religious and constitutional ideologies; they reveal elements that were more damaging to relations *within* the royalist camp than to the enemy. They suggest weaknesses in the royalist 'state' that could profitably be explored and that go beyond Ronald Hutton's invaluable study. 'Instinctive' loyalty like Norwich's seems to reflect the legacy of a personal Court and 'familial' culture (in the seventeenth-century sense of an extended family) that is a recognizable survival from the reigns of James I and of Charles I in the 1630s. It did not provide a basis for an effective administrative system when the sovereign was forced to move from London to Oxford and lost control of the old government machinery. Men like Edward Hyde, the future earl of Clarendon, and Secretary Nicholas herald a transition to a new state order – they were, in a sense, professional ministers (although they too could not afford to lose royal support) rather than the favourites and faction leaders who had previously been able to conduct policy through the infrastructure of 'state's servants'. In the war years, however, Hyde and Nicholas and their ilk could not impose their new modes of conduct or thought on their party. Parliament in London had inherited the

---

[67] Compare *Lawes and Ordinances of Warre, Established for the better Conduct of the Army, By His Excellency the Earle of Essex* (1642), pp. [9–10, 12, 16,] 22–3 (p. 22, article 4, specifically relates to duels); and *Military Orders and Articles Established by His Majesty* (Oxford, 1642), pp. 4–5 and 6–7 (articles 47–51 specifically relate to duels); *Military Orders And Articles, Established by His Maiesty* (Oxford, 1643), pp. 6 (articles 27–33), 11 (article 73), 12 (articles 86–92; these are the expanded articles devoted to duels).

pre-existing machinery of government, the royalists in Oxford had to create a new one.

In the war years Charles and his advisers could draw on the personal loyalty of men like Norwich and Digby and at lower levels there were able and energetic officials like those who set up Oxford's hospital system, but in general the royalist cause lacked bureaucratic focus and cohesion, and it was weakened by divisions between regional commanders that frequently displayed the quarrelsome aggression already discussed. Parliament, on the other hand, by virtue of its base in London, retained the pre-war state bureaucracy, improved the existing administrative system and developed remarkably effective methods of oversight.[68] Nor did the royalist government have the will or the ability to control its rogue followers. Godly reformation may have been remarkably imperfect, but for many parliamentarians there was an internalized ethos and an acceptance of the kinds of moral choices that inhibited violent conduct against their own comrades (although it did not inhibit political and religious divisions). For the royalists neither the voices of moderation and reconciliation nor the strength of instinctive loyalty could overcome the weaknesses of their personal and somewhat *ad hoc* state system or suppress the debilitating violence of their quarrels.

This chapter began by noting the convergences between enemies, many of which survived the war and, in conjunction with familial, economic and social links, aided ultimate co-existence and even reconciliation. The Civil War also brought new feuds, however, like that preserved in local legend between the royalist Bankes family and the parliamentarian Erles. Yet many families with members on opposing sides retained ties of solidarity and affection – among them the Verneys, the Pitts and the Cholmleys. If in some families wartime divisions led to anger and lasting bitterness, in others surviving links of interest, kinship or affection helped defeated royalists to negotiate their way to reduced fines, recovery of property, or useful favours. Even during hostilities it had been possible to maintain social bonds between enemies, as correspondence during the siege of Boarstall between the besieged royalist Sir William Campion and besieging parliamentarian friends and well-wishers reveals.[69]

The end of the wars left royalists to face the consequences of defeat in lost or encumbered estates, debt, and plundered goods – Lady Bankes,

---

[68] See Ian Roy's suggestive comments on royalist structure of government and responsibility, in Roy, 'Digby', pp. 75–7, 89.

[69] See e.g. Cliffe, *Yorkshire Gentry*, p. 338, on the father who disinherited his son for choosing the wrong side, and East Sussex Record Office, Danny MSS *passim*, for the correspondence between Campion and his besiegers.

for example, spent years vainly trying to recover the contents of Corfe Castle, from tapestries to timber, and the family never returned to the slighted castle. Many families had been broken by death or separated by emigration: Campion was killed at Colchester, the Verneys were divided between England and the continent. In the 1650s old lines of social connection and interest survived and strengthened again. Most royalists showed considerable caution about committing themselves either to the brief and, from their point of view, disastrous third war of 1651 or the intermittent plots of the following years. This quiescence had its counterpart in the retirement from state affairs, often forced, of many of the parliamentarian leaders of the earlier war years. At the end of the 1650s they could again hope for a return to a shared moderate constitutionalism of the kind they had supported in 1642. The Restoration marked royalist victory after the years of defeat, but it came about with the support of old conservative parliamentarians like Lord Fairfax and the earl of Warwick's two sons-in-law, the earl of Manchester and Lord Robartes. The overthrow of monarchy as an institution had not been part of their programme, and they could find the Restoration settlement acceptable. What was restored, however, proved to be a new kind of monarchy, not the royalism of the 1640s. By 1660 each party knew what war entailed and each had experienced both victory and defeat. Few Englishmen were willing to face a return to hostilities, and the memory of war remained an inhibiting factor that worked against forcing constitutional or religious claims to the point of armed confrontation. The years after 1660 saw many acrimoniously contested issues, but they were fought out beneath the banner of dual loyalty to crown and parliament that the moderates of 1642 had vainly hoped to raise.

5 Royalist reputations: the Cavalier ideal and the reality

Ian Roy

I

Charles I began the Civil War at a grave disadvantage. Forced to leave his capital by the tumults around his Whitehall palace, and the hostility of the City, he had been deprived of the machinery of government, and the power to raise revenue. He lost the means to defend the realm; his castles, ports, arsenals, the navy, the lieutenancy and the county militias. A further blow was that, because of the political crisis that eventually brought down his regime, he was saddled with the evil reputation of those who had rallied to his protection when he was least popular, the army officers of 1640, the swordsmen. Many, having served abroad, had returned to England to command in the two Scots' Wars. The failure of his attempts to put down the Scottish Covenanters turned the tide against his government, and placed a mighty weapon in the hands of his critics in the Long Parliament. The means which had been created to fight the Scots, however, the forces then raised, the officers commissioned and the networks formed, were to be used by both sides in the summer of 1642. The Somerset infantry regiment under Colonel Thomas Lunsford, raised in 1640, was recreated two years later. Even the issues which dominated in 1642 had been stated earlier. The famous rallying cry of Sir Bevill Grenville is often quoted as an instance of the basic loyalty of the king's supporters at the start of the Civil War: 'I cannot contain myself within my doors when the King of England's standard waves in the field upon so just [an] occasion, the cause being such as must make all those that die in it little inferior to martyrs.' But it was actually made in April 1639, when it was much more 'political' and controversial, for what quarrel did a Cornish knight have with the distant Scots?[1]

Seeking support in summer 1642 the king had to rely on those swordsmen who had helped to put down the riots of the previous December.

---

[1] J. Stucley, *Sir Bevill Grenvile and his Times, 1596–1643* (1983), p. 78.

The king had the lion's share of these career soldiers, and would have had more except for a piece of good fortune for parliament. 'The darling of the Swordmen', the earl of Essex, a peer whose popularity far out-weighed his military experience and talents, had opted for their cause, more or less in a fit of pique after his dismissal from Court.[2] The Lord Generalship parliament bestowed on him, with its unprecedented wide powers of patronage, compensated for his loss, and he revelled in the title of 'His Excellency'. Of the fifty four who can be identified in a list of those returning from foreign parts, forty three can be found in the king's army by 1642. Of two hundred or so senior officers of the 1640 army who were recruited for the armies raised two years later, and who can be identified, over three quarters rallied to the king.[3] The political contro-versies of the intervening period had persuaded many military men that parliament could not be trusted. Fifty six had been cashiered on suspi-cion of Roman Catholicism. The leaders in the House of Commons were blamed for favouring, in payment of arrears, the invading Covenanters over the English army in the North. When the officers clamoured for their pay, and organized petitions, they were accused of complicity in the Army Plots of 1641, and were deemed unreliable. Others too were ex-cluded on political or religious grounds from the forces assembled for Irish service. The turbulence of the 'December Days' of 1641, when City apprentices and the disorderly poor clashed with armed courtiers and ex-officers, further helped to identify two competing parties in the state. The men-at-arms, associated in the popular mind with foreign service, were termed 'Cavaliers', their opponents 'Roundheads'. If one referred to the short hair worn by 'prentices', the other was descriptive of the swordsmen, 'men on horseback', the commanders recruited from Euro-pean armies: caballeros, chevaliers, cavalieri.[4]

The divisions of 1641–2, and the opprobrious terms employed, in-formed the debate that continued up to and beyond the outbreak of the war itself in summer 1642. This was another continuity with the recent past observable in those months. A fevered anti-popish panic gripped the nation, exacerbated by the news of the Ulster Rising, and the ensuing general alarm and distrust (the so-called 'fears and

---

[2] *CHR*, vol. II, pp. 14–16. His father (Elizabeth's Essex) had been 'a great darling of the people', especially Londoners, V. Snow, *Essex the Rebel* (1970), p. 310.

[3] NLW, Chirk Castle MS F 7442 (?1639); E. Peacock (ed.), *The Army Lists of Round-heads and Cavaliers* (1874); J. Rushworth (ed.), *Historical Collections of Private Passages of State, ...* (1680–1701), vol. III, p. 2.

[4] B. S. Manning, *The English People and the English Revolution* (1976), pp. 71–98. The most recent treatment of these events is David Cressy, *England on Edge. Crisis and Revolution 1640–1642* (Oxford, 2006).

jealousies'), made believable the wildest rumours of Irish invaders, Catholic plots and armed interventions.[5] The defenders of the Court were lampooned as men of violence, who beat up the young anti-Catholic protestors; some like Lunsford, a former outlaw and the king's short-lived candidate for the governorship of the Tower of London, were identified and their character blackened. The king responded with equal violence, denouncing the rioters and instructing the Lord Mayor to suppress them by 'shooting with bullets or otherwise to slay and kill such of them as shall persist in their tumultuary and seditious ways'.[6] In the febrile atmosphere generated by the failed attempt to arrest the Five Members, the flight of the king from London, his refusal of the Bills presented from parliament, and the assembling of a protective force in the North, his armed entourage became the target of an extraordinary outburst of black propaganda by the London press and pulpit. The best known was *Anti-Cavalierisme* by the notable London radical preacher John Goodwin, which set the tone for later squibs, verses and crude woodcuts, reviling 'the scum ... of the Land, that most accursed confederacy ... that bloody and butcherly Generation, commonly knowne by the name of Cavaliers', who, it was implied, surrounded the king.[7] Lunsford was depicted assaulting the citizens: he was later accused of eating babies. Another pamphlet showed the hungry monster, *The English-Irish Souldier* (April 1642), made up of the provisions he had stolen and 'who had rather Eate than Fight'. Before a shot had been fired Goodwin and others exclaimed of the Cavaliers 'what spoyle and rapine they make', and warned that they were already boasting of great rewards for their labours, out of their enemies' estates. It was a touchstone of parliamentarian propaganda that the royalists were beggarly ne'er-do-wells, hoping to enrich themselves by the sword.[8]

Charles's main task in the summer was to counter these allegations, and rescue if he could the good name of those who rallied to his standard, raised in August 1642. A pragmatic case had been made by a convert from the popular party in the Commons, Edward Hyde, arguing that the king had accepted the reforms presented to him in 1641, sacrificed erring ministers and bishops, but now held to the good old laws, the ancient rights of the monarchy and the established church. In the paper war which preceded the shooting war the defenders of monarchy gave as

[5] R. Clifton, 'The Popular Fear of Catholics', *P&P*, 52 (1971), 23–55.
[6] *CSPD, 1641–3*, p. 214.
[7] J. Goodwin, *Anti-Cavalierisme* ... ([21 Oct.] 1642), p. 2.
[8] *MPR*, vol. I, plate between pp. 428–9; Goodwin, *Anti-Cavalierisme*, p. 37; I. Roy, 'England turned Germany? The Aftermath of the Civil War in its European Context', *TRHS*, 5th series, 28 (1978), 127–8.

good as they got, helped by the access to provincial presses at York, then Shrewsbury, and, after July, Oxford. Hyde was so pleased by what a less literary and philosophical supporter called his 'fine writings', that he republished them in his later *History of the Rebellion*. So busy was the Oxford press with the printing of His Majesty's declarations that before long the capital 'H' had worn out and had to be replaced.[9]

In his speeches to the gentry and freeholders of the counties through which he passed the king reiterated the same simple message. 'A few discontented spirits' had hounded him from his capital, undermined the frame of government, so admirably founded and so long established, and now threatened to set the kingdom ablaze. They had unleashed schism in the church, and mob rule in the streets. Charles presented himself in person as the defender of the ancient constitution, the true reformed Protestant religion and the liberty and property of the subject, best protected by a strong king, whose indefeasible hereditary right, given by God's grace and sanctified by time, was the guarantor of every other property owner's inheritance. He had not previously been successful in projecting himself to his people – the Van Dyckian image was a formal, remote and chilly one – anxious as he was to steer clear of popery on one side and popularity on the other, but he surprised his courtiers by rising to the occasion now. He rode into the middle of the crowds assembled to hear him, and spoke confidently to them. He could not believe that his people had deserted him. It was a key element in royalist belief that the people were innocent but misled, even temporarily bewitched. The king's 'good subjects', 'the simple well meaning People', as the royal chaplain, Edward Symmons, called them, were basically loyal: could they be kept any longer deluded by a handful of ambitious politicians and hypocritical preachers, 'in this Trance'?[10] To give them the chance to repent he issued general pardons to over twenty counties, towns and professional groups, inviting those in arms to change sides. He would not start a war; the harvest had to be gathered; he had not laid siege to Hull, which had refused him entry. Whatever scandal had been 'cast upon the Cavaliers' no harm had come to any man from any member of his train. He would admit no popish recusant into his army. He would 'live and die' with his followers.[11]

---

[9] *CHR*, vol. II, bk v; F. Madan (ed.), *Oxford Books* (Oxford, 1912), vol. II, p. 162; W. K. Sessions, A *World of Mischiefe. The King's Printer – in York in 1642 and in Shrewsbury 1642–1643* (York, 1981).

[10] E. Symmons, *Scripture Vindicated from ... Mr Stephen Marshall* (1645), p. 11.

[11] *SRP*, nos. 344, 351–2, 355–64: no. 347 on recusants; E. Husbands, *An Exact Collection of all Remonstrances ...* (1643), pp. 488–90, 510–11, 514–64: 'our good subjects' mentioned pp. 515, 518, 521, 527, 546; *CHR*, vol. II, pp. 311–12.

This message was less complicated than his opponents' resort to the legal fiction that they fought for king and parliament, and to rescue the person of the king from his 'evil advisers'. Its appeal was potentially wide, and found a ready response. There has been 'a great alteration here', Henry Wilmot claimed in June 1642: the king is now 'the favourite of the kingdom'.[12] He could protect his servants. In manor houses up and down the land country gentlemen felt a basic instinct of loyalty to their sovereign lord, whatever their opinions on his previous policies. Kenelm Digby in Paris later confided that he could not lie idle 'while my sovereign is fighting for all that is his. My country is on fire, and all my friends engaged to the utmost in this unnatural war.'[13] In North Wales the minor poet and landowner, Sir Thomas Salusbury, was representative of these feelings. Consulting conscience and reason, he decided that to serve God he must serve God's anointed. He feared the multitude of schisms already plaguing the church, and pointed to the dreadful examples abroad of those who defied legitimate authority.[14] The mayor of Oxford was persuaded of the 'princely goodness' of the king, and the city's puritans began to feel the anger of 'Church and King' mobs.[15] For those in authority, who had taken the oaths of supremacy and allegiance to the crown, the plight of the king, 'my natural liege lord . . . hunted like a partridge', was an outrage.[16] The chief actors in this bloody tragedy, wrote William Chillingworth, have robbed our Sovereign Lord the King of 'his Forts, Townes, Treasure, Ammunition', and left him a helpless victim.[17] The homily on obedience was a more familiar text than any new-fangled resistance theory. It was the parliament which was seen as crushing the commonwealth with new taxes, making unprecedented claims to power, and dividing the nation.[18]

The embattled crown could also more easily represent its cause in visual terms than its opponents. Where most common soldiers were illiterate, and a substantial segment of the king's men, the Welsh and some Cornish, did not speak English, this was an essential means of communication. The royal standard raised was a declaration of war against his enemies, an invitation to the subjects of the king to rally to his cause. The banners made for the first regiments bore the emblems of

---

[12] *LJ*, vol. V, p. 167.
[13] Digby to Conway, 13 February 1645, *CSPD, 1644–5*, pp. 302–3.
[14] N. Tucker, *Denbighshire Officers in the Civil War* (1964), pp. 96–7.
[15] I. Roy, 'The City of Oxford 1640–1660', in R. C. Richardson (ed.), *Town and Countryside in the English Revolution* (1992), pp. 139–40.
[16] Symmons, *Scripture Vindicated*, p. 81.
[17] *The Life of William Chillingworth*, ed. Des Maizeaux (1725), p. 285.
[18] F. P. Verney (ed.), *Memoirs of the Verney Family During the Civil War* (1892), vol. I, p. 91.

monarchy (and its mottoes), the orb and sceptre, the throne in majesty, the order of the garter; they emphasized the union of the king and queen, some bearing their joint monogram. They would later refer to the heirs to the throne and so stress the hereditary succession, the fact that kingship never dies. Its sacred character had long been celebrated on the stage. 'Not all the water in the rough rude sea can wash the balm from an anointed king.' He is 'the deputy elected by the Lord', who cannot be deposed by weak human action, 'for heaven still guards the right'.[19] Biblical injunctions were popular. Proverbs, Romans and Psalms were quoted: 'touch not the Lord's anointed', and 'exurgat Deus dissipentur inimici' (let God arise and his enemies be scattered). A magical aura protected the king, who possessed the healing touch, inherited from his ancestors. When the Mint was set up at Oxford, the royal capital, the plain messages stated before his army, at Wellington in Shropshire on 19 September, were engraved on the coinage and on the first medals struck. The so-called 'Declaration' issues bore the legend 'Religio Protestantium Leges Angliae Libertas Parliamenti'.[20]

An important component of this display of loyalty might be termed anti-popularity. One way of defining a Cavalier was to depict its opposite in the harshest terms. The condemnation of the disorder and disobedience of the lower orders, the treacherous nature of the activity of the king's opponents (whose leaders had already been accused of high treason) was evident in regimental standards and pamphlet literature that emphasized aristocratic lineage, the existing social order, and the need to defend the nation against rising barbarism, novelty and chaos. The royalists' black propaganda pointed to the 'dismal inequality' of the coming struggle, with the prime nobility opposed by the urban poor (mechanic citizens) and their crafty masters (cheating merchants). With Londoners in the field, the campaign in the South will be fought 'pure Citizen to Cavalier without mixture', wrote one commentator in summer 1644.[21] Loyal verses and some banners contrasted pastoral images, a green and pleasant countryside, with the murky and pestilential air of towns, especially London, the overgrown and ungovernable hotbed of rebellion, commercial sharp practice and sexual licence.[22] In the simplest terms the

---

[19] Shakespeare, *Richard II*, Act 3, scene ii, 54–62.
[20] Ian Gentles, 'The Iconography of Revolution: England 1642–1649', in I. Gentles, J. Morrill and B. Worden (eds.), *Soldiers, Writers and Statesmen of the English Revolution* (Cambridge, 1998), pp. 99–101; DWL, MS F 12.7; F. Varley, *The Siege of Oxford* (1932), pp. 41–7; G. Boon, *Cardiganshire Silver and the Aberystwyth Mint in Peace and War* (1981), pp. 82–132. Charles, however, suspended the ceremony of touching for the King's Evil during the war.
[21] Carte (ed.), *Letters*, vol. I, p. 55.
[22] S. Porter (ed.), *London and the Civil War* (1996), pp. 149–74; *CHR*, vol. III, p. 20.

typical Cavalier was a bluff, honest countryman, untainted by city ways; his opponent a promiscuous – or cuckolded – cockney.[23]

At the popular level – no doubt not sanctioned by the king – there was a strain of low scurrility, sexual innuendo and obscene imagery which ridiculed his enemies. Several banners mocked Essex himself as a cuckold. While he headed the army which was to invest Oxford, his wife was living with her lover in the town. 'Cuckolds we come' was the motto of one standard that derided Essex's own banner with its slogan 'Beware, I am here'. He was addressed, in contempt of his grandiloquent title, and with a snide reference to his supposed impotency, as 'His Oxcellency'.[24] There were displays of horns incorporated in others. The subversive character of the parliamentary cause was represented by the cartoon of a Roundhead seizing the British imperial crown: he wears a jester's cap and bells, and a sword reaches from Heaven to strike him down. The caption, loosely translated, reads: 'You must be joking.'[25]

Despite this disdain for their opponents and these bold claims on their own part, there is a hint of fatalism in some royalist apologia; the king's person was sacred, his claims just, his loyal defenders virtuous, and his enemies vicious and unprincipled. But his cause was not necessarily popular; and it might not be successful.[26] The army chaplain, Symmons, who, as we shall see, had commended the name of Cavalier at the start of the war, regretted that two years later the king's followers were 'most like' the persecuted Early Christians.[27] There was a martyr-like quality to some of the heroic literature inspired by the war.

Two days after his speech in Shropshire it was reported that the king's army 'increases beyond imagination'.[28] His appeal had struck a chord, and the small band of ex-officers of 1640–1 was soon diluted by the volunteers who clamoured for commissions to raise men and horse, often at their own expense. Recruits were from all regions, for the army was a more national one, reflective of society as a whole, than that of their opponents, raised mainly in London and Essex.[29] The monstrous apparition identified as a Cavalier was replaced by a more complex image, because it was composed of many more numerous and varied elements. The majority of the English aristocracy supported the king, and he gave

23 The Parliamentarian forces were often described as cockneys, intent on 'King-catching', in 1643–4, Carte, Letters, vol. I, pp. 58–60; HMC, 1st Report, p. 8.
24 Snow, Essex the Rebel, p. 343.
25 Ian Gentles, 'The Iconography of Revolution', p. 101; DWL, MS F 12.7.
26 Secretary Nicholas's letters hint at this, CSPD, 1641–3, pp. 389–90.
27 Symmons, Scripture Vindicated, p. 70.
28 Nicholas to Boswell, HMC, 10th Report, vol. VI, pp. 86–7; CSPD, 1641–3, p. 389.
29 P. Young, Edgehill 1642. The Campaign and the Battle (Kineton, 1967), chapters xi and xii.

commands accordingly. His own family was involved. Three of his Stuart cousins were to die in the cause. He made his nephews, Rupert and Maurice, leading generals. His initial weakness, deprived of his revenues and military and naval establishments, meant that he had to depend on his wealthiest supporters and reward them appropriately. The earl of Newcastle, although a great courtier, a poet and dramatist with no military experience, was given command of the North. Politically influential figures, such as lords Hertford, Worcester and Winchester – the last two despite their Catholicism – made vital contributions in money, men and prestige. Within six weeks of his ban on recusant recruits the king had asked Newcastle to enlist them, and they proved to be important in the Northern counties.[30]

At the regimental and troop level the typical senior officer was an amateur in military terms but usually a prominent local figure. In most counties beyond the reach of London, East Anglia and the South East the majority of the leading gentry, of greatest wealth and highest status, who customarily filled the bench of justices, and were deputies to the Lord Lieutenant, were sympathetic to the royal cause. It has been roughly calculated that of 1,630 field officers who had served in the royal armies, and claimed benefit of a reward in 1663, a thousand were of armigerous family. They included forty-four peers, fifty-six baronets and seventy-two knights. Thirteen peers and forty-two baronets and knights died in his cause.[31] Such men were experienced administrators, and able to persuade tenants and servants to take up arms. Salusbury was 'elected' Colonel of the Regiment of Foot in Denbighshire.[32] The typical Cavalier officer needed guidance in arms, however, and was often advised by one of the swordsmen from foreign parts, or with at least Scots' Wars experience.

The latter category of veterans had a crucial part to play in the compiling of the *Military Orders* by which the army being raised was to be regulated. These, consisting of eighty-two articles, were first printed at York in August, a whole month before those of the earl of Essex, perhaps reflecting the greater doubt in the minds of the parliamentarian leaders about their legal status, a matter that had lessened the generals' authority in the Scots' Wars. The *Orders* were read to the troops first mustered in Shropshire, and the king solemnly promised that he would severely punish any who disobeyed them. An oath of allegiance was then taken

---

[30]   *MPR*, vol. I, p. 317.
[31]   P. Newman, 'The 1663 List of Indigent Royalist Officers', *HJ*, 30 (1987), 885–904; J. Prestwich, *Respublica* (1787), pp. 131–49. Unfortunately Dr Newman's figures cannot be relied on in detail.
[32]   Tucker, *Denbighshire Officers*, pp. 98–104.

by all, no doubt designed to counter the Protestation oath that parliament had asked all adult males to subscribe to in early 1642.[33]

Like many of the swordsmen, the key articles of the *Orders* bore the
stamp of earlier campaigns. They were based on the code produced for
the army of 1640: some articles even possessed an Elizabethan ancestry.
Machinery was created to enforce the orders, under a Provost Marshal
General; every regiment was to have its own provost to punish and
imprison as required. On the march in this first campaign of the war it
is not known how effective this code was: if Hyde can be believed there
was little indiscipline, and punishment was severe and exemplary when
it occurred. The inhabitants of the country through which the king's
men passed, who hid their goods and were ready to resist – having
believed the black propaganda of the London press, that the Cavaliers
were 'fierce, bloody and licentious' – were evidently surprised at their
good order. The king could afford to be merciful, resisting calls for the
notoriously disobedient town of Birmingham to be punished.[34] If the
letters of Sergeant Wharton of Essex's army are any guide it was
the Roundhead forces which robbed and desecrated their way through
the Midlands. Summer 1642 was a bad season for the deer of any 'ma-
lignant' landowners in the path of the army. It was obvious too that the
parliamentarians had their fair share of the rogue element among the
career soldiers employed as officers for this expedition.[35]

It was not too farfetched to believe that, in their own eyes, with the
ideals eloquently set forth, and the restraint displayed, the reputation of
the king's followers would be transformed. Certainly Edward Symmons,
addressing the troops, claimed that the term Cavalier could be rescued
from its ill fame. 'A complete Cavalier is a child of honour ... the only
reserve of English gentility and ancient valour, and [he] hath rather
chosen to bury himself in the tomb of honour, than to see the nobility
of his nation vassalised'.[36] Under its royal and noble leadership the army
could not fail to be imbued with aristocratic values of generosity, un-
selfishness and mercy, and Christian virtue.

In the maintenance of these high standards, and the improvement of
morals among his followers, royalist army chaplains would have a vital
part to play. Those of the king's officers who had served abroad in the
Swedish forces knew the contribution made by Lutheran ministers to
the Protestant crusade of the great Gustavus Adolphus. Charles had, as

---

[33]   *Military Orders and Articles* (Oxford, 1643), Falconer Madan, *Oxford Books* (2 vols.,
       Oxford, 1912–31), no. 1211; *CSPD, 1641–3*, p. 381.
[34]   *CHR*, vol. II, p. 359.
[35]   *CSPD, 1641–43*, pp. 371–3, 379–80 and following.
[36]   *MPR*, vol. I, pp. 414–15.

we have seen, an equal sense of the goodness of his mission, and its sacred character: his quarters would be a strong bulwark against the persecution of his loyal clergy. Oxford, as royal capital, welcomed 'many great bishops, and learned doctors, and grave divines'.[37] The king appreciated that recruiting active and eloquent clerics into his army would benefit his cause. He created a hierarchy of chaplaincy, headed by two Chaplains General, and required every regiment to appoint and pay for a suitably qualified person. The revised *Military Orders* included the daily reading of prayers for units not in the field, with compulsory attendance. The use of the Book of Common Prayer was enjoined. A special *Soldiers' Catechism* was published in 1645, a direct response to that of Parliament, and several chaplains evidently worked hard at the improvement of their flocks.[38]

But if a crusade was envisaged the flower of the Caroline clergy was conspicuous by its absence. The king's choice of Chaplains General was uninspired; few clergymen of distinction willingly joined his forces in the field. Only seven of 228 Oxford Fellows became army chaplains. While Charles imitated his opponents by instituting Fast days, and several monthly sermons then delivered were printed, their impact was limited. The regimental chaplains spent much of their time inveighing against the sins of their own soldiers, attending Court, or lobbying for their pay at HQ. The prominent Laudians at Oxford were active as propagandists, editing the royalist newspaper for example, rather than as preachers. Edward Symmons, himself a conscientious minister, was forced to admit that the days of fasting appointed by the king were 'much neglected in His Quarters'.[39]

The rather lame efforts of the royalist clergy contrasted with the fervour, enthusiasm and drive for reform of their opponents. Parliament's religious leaders had no doubts in urging their supporters to extreme measures. Chillingworth, who had given up his Oxford post to join Hopton's army, and whose writings on Christian moderation were well known, condemned the popular and respected London preachers as 'the loudest Trumpets of Warre'.[40] Symmons attacked their uncharitable, indeed bloodthirsty, utterances which derided half measures (the celebrated 'Curse ye Meroz' sermon of Stephen Marshall, condemning neutrality), and approved genocidal policies in Ireland. Their exhortations

---

[37]   *The Burdens of England* (1646), sig. A2v.
[38]   Madan, no. 1210. The first eleven articles relate to religious duties, *ibid.*, no. 1788.
[39]   I. Roy and D. Reinhart, 'Oxford and the Civil Wars', in N. Tyacke (ed.), *The History of the University of Oxford*, vol. IV, *Seventeenth-Century Oxford* (Oxford, 1997); Symmons, *Scripture Vindicated*, sig. A2v.
[40]   'William Chillingworth', in *Oxford DNB* (2004).

reeked of hypocrisy, damning those sins they most enjoyed themselves, rather than 'those they have no mind to', as *Hudibras* was later to note in a famous phrase.[41] This argument was echoed later in the popular view that while the Cavaliers had the sins of men, their opponents had the sins of the Devil. Chillingworth, serving as a chaplain, and very aware of his charges' human failings, as we shall see, viewed the struggle pessimistically as prophaneness contending with hypocrisy: 'on the one side horrible oaths, curses and blasphemies; On the other pestilent lyes, calumnies, and perjury'. 'Publicans and sinners', he wrote, contended with 'Scribes and Pharisees'.[42]

II

But the plans of war rarely survive first contact with the enemy, and the idealized behaviour depicted – or hoped for – in the earliest sermons and speeches soon came adrift. The high command, after the first battle, Edgehill, was forced to publish royal proclamations to prohibit plundering by their troops. The printed *Orders* had forbidden it, but they had been ignored. The first real encounter of the war unhinged and dismayed many of the participants, not least the political leaders of parliament. No doubt surprised by the strong showing of the royalists, and horrified by the ensuing carnage, few had acquitted themselves well: they blamed their followers for desertion and cowardice. Lord Wharton acquired his nickname, it was alleged, by hiding in a sawpit.[43] When Denzil Holles's regiment was destroyed in the sudden and bloody attack on Old Brentford, the true nature of warfare was revealed. It confirmed their view, already formed, that they should retire from the fray and that 'Scotch commanders' would be more useful.[44]

On the king's side too many of the untrained, poorly armed and badly led infantry ran away, leaving their squires-in-arms disheartened. Salusbury's Foot, for example, may initially have shared their colonel's high hopes, but at Edgehill they were largely unprotected – having only pikes and agricultural implements, few muskets – and were severely mauled. It must have been plain to the king and his generals that part-time soldiers could not be relied on, and that the work would have to be done by the experienced officers. The swordsmen were 'a generation of men much cried up and of great worth', and honoured among the king's

[41] Symmons, *Scripture Vindicated*, pp. 11, 68; S. Butler, *Hudibras*, part I, c. i, 213.
[42] W. Chillingworth, *A Sermon Preached at the Publike Fast* (Oxford, 1644), p. 13.
[43] G. P. T. Jones, *Sawpit Wharton* (1967): although there is no contemporary evidence of this.
[44] *CSPD, 1641–3*, pp. 367, 401; HMC, 10th *Report*, vol. VI, p. 37.

followers: they were men of 'great esteem'.[45] The leadership had to be strengthened, as well as the code of war. There was considerable doubt as to what was legitimate spoil following a successful encounter with the enemy, or the occupation of a hostile town. In early November, as his forces passed through the Thames valley – an area considered disloyal – his men took the law into their own hands. A prominent courtier thought that if the king's orders were disobeyed, and essential supplies withheld, they could be forcibly distrained.[46] This may explain, though not excuse, the action of an equally senior officer, Lunsford's brother, on first entering Oxford, now the royal capital. With another field officer of the Lord General's Foot, an elite regiment, and a file of musketeers, he threatened to blow up the house of a wealthy citizen, privileged of the university, unless he paid them all he had. He did so, and died three years later lamenting the fact. This theft took place within 400 yards of the royal apartments.[47]

The lack of any punishment for such actions indicated that the king's much advertised mercifulness to his recalcitrant subjects might not survive exposure to the harsh realities of the war. It would not be long before Birmingham was visited by fire and sword. And, on the other hand, his dependence on the military would make it difficult for him to punish severely, as he had promised, those of his followers who transgressed his orders. The earliest code was, however, strengthened and made more complete with the addition of a further seventy articles. The input of the foreign service professionals was plain in the borrowings from the military laws promulgated over ten years before by Gustavus Adolphus himself. The new commander-in-chief, Forth, and Rupert were 'both strangers to the government and manners of the kingdom', as Hyde said, but were trained in Swedish methods.[48] There was in the revised orders a more frank admission of the evils associated with camp life; they addressed for the first time such matters as the problem of shortage of pay, the question of booty, and the position of women camp followers. Many of the crimes specified carried the death penalty. As previously, all new recruits were to take the oath of allegiance adjoined to the *Orders* and the articles were to be read to them.[49]

---

[45]   Ludlow so described them, C. Firth (ed.), *Memoirs of Edmund Ludlow* (1894), vol. I, p. 38.

[46]   Killigrew at Reading, 7 Nov. 1642, Appendix ii, in J. P. V. Motten, *Sir William Killigrew* (1980).

[47]   M. Toynbee and P. Young, *Strangers in Oxford* (1973), pp. 208–9.

[48]   *CHR*, vol. III, p. 224.

[49]   *Military Orders and Articles Established by His Majesty* (Oxford, 1643), Madan, no. 1210.

To supplement and keep these regulations up to date the high command issued a stream of royal proclamations over the course of the war. Examined in detail they form a running commentary on the conduct of the king's men. The breakdown of discipline and order which battles entail led not only to plunder but desertion: settlement into winter quarters led to many taking unauthorized leave, and this was addressed. There were special problems with the occupation of Oxford by the army, as we shall see, and its new role as royal HQ, prison, garrison and Court. More than twenty proclamations and orders attempted to regulate civil – military relations in the overcrowded town, and keep good order within the verge of the Court.[50]

The main problem for the royalists was that their share of the resources of the kingdom, to maintain armies in the field, and a host of garrisons, was woefully inadequate. Even their smaller base area, from which they exacted their main military income, the Contribution, was not free of enemy incursions, unlike London and most of the South East for parliament. Oxford was one thirtieth the size, and an even lesser proportion of the wealth, of London. From the start the king could not pay his troops adequately, and had to accept that they would to some extent live off the land. The level of Contribution was based on the number of troops quartered, and the crucial separation between the taxpayer and the soldier recipient, maintained – more or less – by parliament, could not be long sustained by the king. Where the soldiery depended for their survival on exacting money, goods and free quarter from the civilian population, whatever ticket system might be devised, abuses would follow.[51] Once the Contribution fell into arrears the soldiers had to become tax collectors. This situation fatally weakened the high command's ability to command obedience. In far-flung garrisons and units in the field little could be expected from the central stores, and little heed need be paid to the orders of the distant HQ. As an agent of the Oxford arsenal wrote, 'the Governors heere in the west [are] all Like kings'.[52]

A further difficulty was that for much of the conflict the War Council of ministers and generals created by the king, to advise him on policy and supervise its execution in the field, was flawed. Consisting of up to

---

[50]   168 proclamations were issued between June 1642 and Feb. 1646: *SRP*, nos. 345–519. See especially nos. 367 (25 Nov. 1642), 370 (28 Nov. 1642); on Oxford see nos. 388–9, 420, 447, 470, 473, 519.

[51]   *CHR*, vol. III, pp. 79, 88, 107, 167. See also *SRP*, vol. II, nos. 439–42 (August 1643), and I. Roy, 'The English Civil War and English Society', in B. Bond and I. Roy (eds.), *War and Society. A Yearbook of Military History* (1975).

[52]   I. Roy (ed.), *Royalist Ordnance Papers*, vol. II, p. 385.

twenty members, and embracing all arms and departments of state, it should have acted as an impartial forum for debate; and for a time it worked well. But as setbacks occurred divisions in its ranks began to appear. Rival factions emerged in the course of the campaigning season of 1643, and in the following year the courtiers of the queen, those close to Charles's nephews Rupert and Maurice, and leading office-holders such as Culpepper and George Digby, as well as resentful English aristocratic generals such as Lords Wilmot and Percy, quarrelled over the direction of the war and the share of resources. It was soon known in royalist quarters that the orders from the Court were the product of bitter wrangles, or only half-heartedly agreed by one faction or another, and were likely to be changed arbitrarily. The authority of the high command was severely weakened as a result.[53]

When regular pay failed men under command had to fend for themselves, more or less with the connivance of their captains. While the rank and file would desert the service if not given at least a proportion of their pay, those commissioned by the king himself, presumed to be committed to his cause and serving for other than material rewards, were having to survive for long periods on their own resources. In May 1643 a petition from his infantry officers in camp at Culham near Oxford reminded the king that they had long subsisted without pay.[54] It was hardly surprising that absenteeism among regimental officers was common. The initial idealism of Sir Thomas Salusbury sank in the mud of Culham camp, from where his chaplain lamented his absence from his woebegone infantry: the colonel had preferred to ride with Prince Maurice's cavalry in another more glamorous action.[55] At key points in the campaigns of 1643 and 1644 even the officers of the admirable Sir Ralph Hopton, who unusually combined political and military authority, as a leading MP converted to the king's cause, and the career soldier who had rescued the Queen of Bohemia after the battle of the White Mountain, had to be recalled to the colours.[56] A common feature of long-fought-over areas, such as Somerset, Dorset and Wiltshire in 1644 and 1645, were the disorderly units of cavalry, detached from regular forces and garrisons, which terrorized the local population in their search for quarters, food and clothing. Royalist 'Straggling Horse' were the subject of several proclamations at Oxford, and special county

[53]   The case of Sir William Vavasour, who complained of 'the variety of orders from court', is instructive. BL, Add. MS 18981, fos. 76, 155, 157; R. Hutton, *The Royalist War Effort, 1642–1646* (1982), pp. 112–19.

[54]   BL, Harleian MS 6804, fo. 92.

[55]   Tucker, *Denbighshire Officers*, pp. 110–11.

[56]   Proclamations issued for this purpose, *SRP*, nos. 443, 460, 475.

marshals, armed with a guard of twenty men, were appointed to deal with the problem.[57]

Among the most openly rapacious and merciless commanders were those hardened in the Irish wars. The expression 'Trim law', the harsh subjugation of the countryside to the needs of a garrison, on the model of the area round Trim in County Meath, became common. Any other code of conduct, such as the chivalric, was a joke to Col. Edmund Verney, the younger son of Sir Edmund, the king's standard bearer, who wrote from Trim that, at the taking of a nearby castle, 'we put some four score men to the sword, but like valiant knights errant, gave quarter and liberty to all the women'.[58] Another harsh practitioner was the soldier of fortune who cared nothing about local reactions to his behaviour, for he was 'here today and God knows where tomorrow'.[59] These commanders were not necessarily the worst for their men: they had greater assurance of being paid. As Sir Richard Grenville, a prime example, was to say, he could not and would not command unpaid soldiers. He made himself unpopular with local officials and landlords, rival generals and politicians in the West, by his insistence on paying his men at whatever cost to the host population.[60]

'Obedience and Money' were indissolubly linked. Foreign service professionals were dismayed by the behaviour of their troops in England. Sir Arthur Aston, a Catholic swordsman who had served in Muscovy, Poland and Germany, despised the common soldiers he found under his command at Reading, 'so poore and base' he could do nothing with them. What they needed was German discipline. He was forced to take harsh measures, executing two mutineers.[61] Sir Jacob Astley, a highly regarded officer – he had supposedly trained Prince Rupert himself while in the service of the Palatinate – and a much less violent character, was obliged to do the same later.[62]

That the royalists were not alone in tackling these problems is shown by the events at Bristol in early 1643. There an old soldier, Colonel Thomas Essex, appointed by parliament to the important post of governor of England's second port, was faced with a delegation of his men politely asking to be paid. 'Noble governor, give me leave to speak a word or two with you', said one. Essex shot him dead. He then organized a party in his quarters at which the guests had to step over the dead

---

57   *SRP*, nos. 404, 461, 471, 505; BL, Harleian MSS 6802, fo. 44; 6804, fos. 104–6.
58   *Verney Memoirs*, vol. II, p. 135.
59   The earl of Glamorgan's comment on Forth in HMC, 12th *Report*, pp. 56–63.
60   'Sir Richard Grenville', in *Oxford DNB*.
61   Charles I to Aston, Oxford, Dec. 1642, Belvoir Castle, Lindsay Papers, QZ 22, fo. 40; W. Day (ed.), *The Pythouse Papers* (1870), pp. 12–13; *MPR*, vol. II, pp. 175–6.
62   *MPR*, vol. I, p. 491; Bodl. MS Firth C 6, fos. 45, 48.

body. Essex was exceptional in a 'puritan' cause, a roistering blade, accused of luxurious living – 'feasting, gaming and drinking' – while his soldiers starved, and he was shortly afterwards replaced.[63] But the protection which their superior knowledge and supposed indispensability gave the swordsmen, and the consequent toleration of bad behaviour by the rogue element amongst them, was not confined to the king's men.

Not all disorder was concerned with pay. The equivalent of Colonel Essex was Lieutenant Colonel David Hyde on the king's side. He was a marked man after he had belaboured the rioters at Whitehall, cocked his pistol in the House of Commons and threatened those within while the king attempted to arrest the Five Members. At a New Year's Eve dinner hosted by the mayor and governor of Worcester he ran amok, insulted his hosts, quarrelled with fellow soldiers over some previous service at Bergen-op-Zoom, and assaulted 'in a most furious manner' a woman in the street, who protested that she was 'the mother of fower poore children'. Despite the *Military Orders* of the king Hyde was not brought to court till four months later; and he was not condemned. He was causing trouble in the garrison of Bristol later in the war.[64]

If there were extreme examples of bad behaviour there were others of good conduct and even an instance of the nobility to which the king had aspired in his opening addresses to his troops. From the same military background came Sir Henry Gage, of a Sussex Catholic gentry family, whose adherence to his religion (and a decayed inheritance) had forced him to seek his fortune abroad, in the Spanish army of Flanders. This was one of the finest schools of arms in Europe, but it set him off from the majority of his fellow countrymen; when the king contemplated importing 'German Horse' to strengthen his hand in the political difficulties of 1628, he had had Gage in mind. Before the Civil War Gage had powerfully and secretly assisted his sovereign with men and arms from the Low Countries, by arranging loans from Spain.[65]

All of this could not recommend him to the king's enemies, nor indeed some of his friends, to whom the cause of the Protestant Netherlands and the Swedish king was a noble one. Gage's loyalty was not to the state but to his sovereign, and his Jesuit training, and service with a hostile foreign

---

[63] S. Seyer, *Memoirs . . . of Bristol and its neighbourhood* (1821–3), vol. I, pp. 326–7; TNA, HCA, 30. 855, nos. 563–6, letters of Thomas Chambers (March–April 1643). I owe this reference to Dr Andrew Thrush, History of Parliament Trust.

[64] Manning, *English People*, pp. 77, 96; BL, Harleian MS 6851, fos. 72–3, 79–94, 102–3, 118–19, 122, 135; MS 6852, fo. 70; MS 6804, fo. 88; William Salt Library, Stafford, S.MS.45, 21 March 1645.

[65] 'Sir Henry Gage', in *Oxford DNB*; [E.Walsingham], *Alter Britanniae Heros* (Oxford, 1645); Gardiner, *History of England*, vol. VI, p. 224.

power (though not when Spain was at war with England), would set him
apart. But he was a superb soldier, and there was relief when he replaced
the unpopular and dictatorial Arthur Aston as governor of Oxford late in
1644. His predecessor tried to discredit him to the king: Gage was, he
claimed, 'the most Jesuited Papist alive'. According to his biographer,
admittedly a most biased source, he was the pattern of English gentility
and the possessor of every military virtue. He was governor for less than
a month, however, killed in a skirmish in February 1645. How his reputation would have fared in the disorderly closing months of the royalist
occupation can only be a matter of speculation. He was certainly admired
by all, Catholic or Protestant, military or civilian.[66]

What commended Gage and other Catholic soldier-martyrs to their
hagiographer, George Digby's secretary and spy, Edward Walsingham,
was their noble character, their 'honourable extraction', and their
European education – acquiring linguistic skills which would allow them
to command multi-national forces. Their rule was marked by 'civility
and gentilenesse'; they kept firm discipline by 'gentle admonition' rather
than 'menacing words, fearfull oaths and often severe blows', and protected the civilian population. It may be that their Catholic background,
some tainted by association with treason (the case of the sons, Kenelm
and John, of the Gunpowder Plotter, Everard Digby), required them to
be of especially good behaviour. They abhorred the main vices of the
camp, swearing, lust and drinking. There was no prejudice in their
favour, and, debarred by their religion, they had no hope of future reward in England. They could not refuse any task, however unpleasant,
'in point of honour'. While observant in their religious duties they had to
play down their beliefs, and their service with the champions of the
Counter-Reformation on the Continent. Their exploits became famous.
John Smith, the brother of Lord Carrington, rescued the royal standard
at Edgehill and was knighted on the field. He was, wrote Walsingham, 'a
most valiant, loyall, and Christian knight'. John Digby was 'a civill,
courteous and well bred Cavalier'. Both died in the cause; Smith (and
Gage after him) given full military honours at their burial in Christ
Church.[67]

The besetting sin of the foreign-trained career soldiers was their
proneness to duelling. Their off-centre position, set apart from civilian,
and, if they were Catholic, Protestant society, their overseas experience

---

[66]   CHR, vol. III, pp. 407–8, 442–3.
[67]   [E. Walsingham], *Britannicae Virtutis Imago* (Oxford 1644); 'The Life of Sir John
      Digby', in *Camden Miscellany*, xii (1910), pp. 59–149. It is probable that George
      Digby, Walsingham's employer and patron, was the driving force behind this heroic
      literature, in a time of paper shortage at Oxford.

among many foreign and competing elements, made them very conscious of supposed slights. The 'nice and jealous profession' of arms, as Hyde described it, was beyond his civilian lawyerly experience and imagination and he puzzled over the behaviour of the royalist officers in the West, who could agree with nobody who crossed their paths. Both Kenelm and John Digby were famous for fighting duels and taking part in street brawls. The peacetime Court of the king had been little better, and several leading courtiers, including those closest to the queen – whose brother, Louis XIII, in France, had prohibited duelling among the nobility and courtiers, and famously made an example of some of the most notorious – were involved in duels to defend their honour. After the war they resumed this practice, with a whole new set of grievances to be fought over.[68]

Men of great virtue and integrity, and unspotted conduct, were exceptional, as comparisons with other officers conceded. Among the inveterate sins of the camp just mentioned was swearing, and the London newsbooks had long fixed upon this as characteristic of the Cavaliers. The mythic Agamemnon Shaglock van Dammee appeared early on in print; thereafter the royalists were the 'damn mes' in popular parlance. That this was not just enemy propaganda was admitted in a proclamation of June 1643, which stated that 'a general liberty [had been] taken by all sorts [of] using unchristian and new coyned oaths and execrations, prophanities, drunkenness and whoredom'.[69] These moral sins, viewed by the king and others as disfiguring his cause and bringing down a judgment from heaven, were best remedied by the army chaplains admonishing their flocks and adhering strictly to their duty of taking divine service and reading the catechism to the troops. As we have seen, Chillingworth, in a fast sermon of October 1643, had condemned the horrible oaths of the king's men. They made him share the fear, with his sovereign, that 'the goodnesse of our cause may sink under the burthen of our sinns'.[70] Charles repeated the injunctions of his father, James VI and I, and fixed penalties. In April 1644 a further attempt was made to curb 'execrable oaths', part of the general reformation of manners initiated by the Oxford Parliament, and the sermons preached before that assembly deplored that and other wicked practices.[71]

---

[68] [Walsingham], 'Life of Digby'; *CHR*, vol. III, p. 30; I. Roy, 'George Digby, Royalist Intrigue and the Collapse of the Cause', in Gentles, Morrill and Worden (eds.), *Soldiers, Writers and Statesmen*, pp. 68–90.

[69] *The Speech of a Cavaleere to his Comrades* ... (1642), *A Perfect Declaration of the Barbarous and Cruell practises* ... (1642). This was among the first to make the claim, later repeated, that the Cavaliers offered rewards for new-coined oaths; *SRP*, no. 424.

[70] Chillingworth, *A Sermon Preached at the Publike Fast*, p. 13.

[71] *SRP*, nos. 424, 484; Madan, no. 1590.

A more personal concern was revealed in the MS draft of the June 1643 proclamation. As well as swearing, cross-dressing was abhorrent to nature, heaven, and the monarch, and a clerk drew up an additional clause condemning those impudent women who, to follow the drum, had counterfeited their sex by wearing men's apparel. This particular censure of what must have been a minor and rare offence, and its prissy tone, may well be that of the king himself, but if so it is curious that it was not incorporated in the printed version. Did Charles have second thoughts; or was he dissuaded by wiser heads; or was the shortage of printing paper at Oxford to blame?[72]

The calling of the Oxford Parliament, designed to show the extent of the support the king had from peers and MPs, provided a reality check on the performance of his troops in the provinces. While those most heavily engaged in his service were excused attendance, those who could be spared in these winter months flocked to Oxford to give advice and – the Court hoped – aid the war effort by voting more taxes. But they also came to complain about the defects of royalist organization, as they saw it, and hold to account the regional generals and the forces under their command, whose depredations they deplored. Charles, who liked to appear a knowing king, addressed the assembly in Christ Church Hall in January 1644. Warding off criticism, he said that he was not so ill a soldier as not to foresee how difficult it was to keep a strict discipline. 'The sense I have of their sufferings, who deserve well of me, by my Forces, hath been a greater grief to me than anything of my own particular.'[73] The MPs were not deterred. They were reinforced in their views by the Friday Fast sermons they heard at the University Church. That of 8 March 1644 condemned 'execrable oaths, Riot, all manner of luxury, pride, rapine, oppression, incontinence &c'.[74]

Several leading officers were hauled over the coals for their maladministration and waste; sensible suggestions were made for the strengthening of existing regiments and disbanding weaker ones; and there was general condemnation of the lawless activities of some commanders. The 'Oxford jailer', Provost Marshal General William Smith, who had acquired an evil reputation for his cruel treatment in Oxford Castle of high profile prisoners such as John Lilburne, Edmund Ludlow and other leading Roundhead officers – given maximum publicity in the London press – was arrested and imprisoned.[75] Lord Loughborough, who

---

[72] BL, Harleian MS 6804, fos. 75–6. The fair copy, omitting this clause, is Harleian MS 6802, fo. 215; *SRP*, no. 424.
[73] J. Rushworth, *Historical Collections*, vol. V, pp. 560–1.
[74] Madan, no. 1590: Henry Vaughan, *A Sermon Preached* (Oxford, 1644).
[75] W. Scott (ed.), *A Collection of ... Tracts ... of Lord Somers*, 2nd edn (1810), vol. IV, pp. 502–19; *CSPD, 1644*, p. 57.

dominated the area round his HQ at Ashby-de-la-Zouch, was censured by local MPs as a notorious 'rob-carrier', whose men were out of control.[76] The conduct of Colonel Thomas Blagge, governor of Wallingford, was examined and held to be both illegal and insupportable by the country people. He had seized clothiers on their way to market and gone so far as to ransom the mayor of Reading on one occasion.[77]

The MPs at Oxford had no need to look further than the state of the city itself to see the weaknesses in royalist administration, the conditions under which their soldiery lived, the frequent breaches of the code of conduct, the king's regulations governing the garrison, which they were attempting to remedy. With the meeting of the assembly itself the city was grossly overcrowded. The natural desire of the king to reproduce in his capital the full panoply of government and to display the grandeur of his Court, had appalling consequences. There was a constantly shifting population of temporary migrants, and hot competition for billets for men and stabling for horses, which led to quarrels and in some cases duels. Living conditions, already difficult in pre-war Oxford, worsened, with the slums of west Oxford receiving the largest number of impoverished, often Welsh or Irish, troops. The city became pestilential, with the constant passage of lousy soldiers spreading disease: firstly and most fatally, 'the disease of the camp', no doubt a form of typhus; and then in 1644 the plague itself. A fifth of the population succumbed in the war years.[78]

To combat these problems life in the garrison was increasingly regulated, not only to reduce swearing. Excess and luxury in apparel was forbidden; the strength of the beer brewed was reduced; access to the royal apartments at Christ Church restricted; admission of the king's followers to the city belatedly curbed. A curfew was enforced, and eventually martial law was applied to citizens as well as soldiers.[79] The preamble to the last proclamation issued at Oxford, in February 1646, tells it all. 'That many and great Disorders have been, and are frequently Committed in this Garrison of Oxford, both in the Evenings, and in the Night time.' The Oxford Parliament ordered all colleges and householders to light their passages between dusk and the sounding of the tattoo to mark the night-time curfew. All taverns were then to be shut.[80]

---

[76] HMC, *Hastings*, vol. II, p. 121; *CSPD, 1644*, p. 20.
[77] BL, Add. MS 18981, fo. 57; *MPR*, vol. II, p. 330; *CSPD, 1644*, pp. 50–1; TNA, SP 16/501, fos. 48–50.
[78] I. Roy, 'The City of Oxford 1640–1660', in Richardson, *Town and Countryside*.
[79] BL, Harleian MS 6804, fos. 28–9.
[80] Proclamation, 3 February 1646, *SRP*, no. 519; Madan, no. 1838.

The city had by then long been notorious for assaults, murders, duels (largely unpunished, as the king's Secretary, Edward Nicholas, complained as early as 1643), and general mayhem. Even the godly Richard Atkins, the 'Praying Captain' in Prince Maurice's Horse, had been forced into issuing a challenge to a fellow officer.[81] The diaries of resident Oxford scholars, a herald, and an observant guardsman, testify to the frequency of duels, indulged in by even the most senior courtiers and officers.[82] Where the officers at HQ led, the soldiers followed. At Burford, famous for the three New Model Army mutineers shot there in 1649, the burial registers reveal an equally poignant tale from the years of civil war: five men killed by their fellow soldiers, in the months between November 1644 and May 1645.[83] At the same time that parliament was at last creating a national, non-regional army, well paid, disciplined and, as a result, obedient to its orders, the Cavaliers were drifting to disaster. Hyde, horrified at the disorders and disobedience he witnessed in the king's Western forces, came to a grim conclusion. 'As, many times, men in a scuffle lose their weapons, and light upon those which belonged to the others ... such ... had been the fortune of the King's armies in the encounters with the enemy.' The royalist commanders

grew insensibly into all the license, disorder and impiety, with which they had reproached the rebels; and they, again, into great discipline, diligence, and sobriety ... Insomuch as one side seemed to fight for monarchy with the weapons of confusion, and the other to destroy the King and government with all the principles and regularity of monarchy.[84]

In other words, and in the last analysis, the king had the better cause, parliament the better men.

In the last years of the war the Cavaliers were hated and feared throughout the length and breadth of the land. The defeat of the king's main armies in 1644 and 1645 saw the war collapse into an intolerable small scale 'war of posts', which unleashed numerous straggling, unofficered bands of reformadoes, intent on pillaging the remaining resources of the countryside. The surviving royalist garrisons filled with

---

[81] *MPR*, vol. II, p. 189 (Nicholas in May 1643); P. Young (ed.), *Military Memoirs of the Civil War: Richard Atkyns* (1967), pp. 31–2.

[82] A. Clark (ed.), *The Life and Times of Anthony Wood* (Oxford Hist. Soc., 1891), vol. I, p. 91; A. Clark (ed.), A. Wood, *Survey of the City of Oxford* (Oxford Hist. Soc., 1889), vol. III, p. 245; W. Hamper (ed.), *The Life, Diary ... of Sir William Dugdale* (1827), p. 56; C. Long and I. Roy (eds.), *Richard Symonds's Diary of the Marches of the Royal Army* (1997), pp. 30, 36, 250, 261, 276.

[83] R. Gretton, *The Burford Records* (1920), p. 206.

[84] *CHR*, vol. III, p. 222.

ungovernable troops; many governors tried where possible to forbid them entry. Even close to Oxford, and as early as February 1644, mounted hangers-on of the main army stole horses, trampled the growing corn and became highwaymen. It was easy enough for the Dorset parliamentary committee, headed by that notable turncoat Anthony Ashley Cooper, to make use of the stereotypes drawn from the Black Legend (first applied to Spain in its long war with the Netherlands) of atrocities of all kinds committed on the continent, or in Ireland, to blacken the reputation of the royalist forces there.[85] When the citizens of Birmingham, with 'mettle equal to their malice', had shot at Rupert's troops, he took his revenge, and accidental fire did the rest. He could be depicted thereafter in the London newsbooks as 'The Bloody Prince', whose love for England could be discovered in Birmingham's flames.[86] This was, however, as his Roundhead captors discovered on the surrender of Bristol, a case of mistaken identity. After Marston Moor and Naseby the prince shared with the New Model Army's high command – whose professional conduct and military skills he had seen and admired – a distrust of the king, his Court, his leading ministers, and his potential allies, the French and the Scots. The most notorious name was acquired by the disorderly troops under Lord Goring in the West, whose evil memory, as 'Goring's crew', lasted for over a century. In North Wales one of the most rapacious commanders, hardened in the Irish wars, Sir William Vaughan, nicknamed 'the Devil of Shrawardine', harried the land without mercy.[87]

The ideals set out by the king four years before were a distant memory. His brave attempts to discipline his men were unlikely to be successful unless he could solve the problems he had inherited at the start of the war. He had been denied his revenues and warlike materials; he had to raise an army from scratch, with the aid mainly of swordsmen, who wielded a double-edged weapon: they were militarily effective but never ceased to be unpopular. With skilful propaganda and a broad-based political and religious appeal he had recruited half the nation, and maintained a war effort for three campaigning seasons against all the odds. His men had battled against the overwhelmingly unfavourable picture painted by the London press and pulpit, which could find enough

[85] B. Donagan, 'Codes and Conduct in the English Civil War', *P&P*, 118 (1988), 65–95.

[86] *CHR*, vol. III, pp. 19–20; *Prince Ruperts Burning Love to England: Discovered in Birminghams Flames* ... (1643); *The Bloody Prince, or a Declaration of the Most Cruell Practices of Prince Rupert* (1643).

[87] Gardiner, *Civil War* (1910), vol. II, p. 317; D. Underdown, *Somerset in the Civil War and Interregnum* (1973), pp. 105–20; *Symonds's Diary of the Marches* (1997), pp. xxiv–xxviii.

examples of royalist barbarity and bad behaviour to sustain parliament's cause. 'The wicked ways of the cruel Cavaliers' was a well-worn cliché before the end of the war. But the London newsbooks suppressed the even more lurid tale of the governor of Bristol, who had murdered one of his own soldiers and feasted over his body. One or two individual examples – ironically enough, best shown in the case of some Catholic foreign service swordsmen – had given reality to the picture of the idealized Cavalier. To set beside the cruelty of a Lunsford, a David Hyde or a Richard Grenville there was the integrity of an Astley, a Hopton and a Gage. But the mutually destructive end game played by the last remnants of his armies fixed in the popular mind, for many years, the worst aspects of royalist conduct.

6   Counsel and cabal in the king's party, 1642–1646

David Scott

Late in 1643, with the royalist war effort faltering, Charles's bedchamber man Endymion Porter identified two evils that had 'much slubbered the Kings affaiers'. The first was 'the manie mistakes wch have lately hapned in his Ma^{ts} councells'; the second was the fractious state of royalist politics – 'wee have such a seminarie of faction both in the courte and Armie, as God must worke miracles if the King bee well served'.[1] Porter's belief that the ills afflicting the king's cause were essentially political in nature fits well with the findings of the latest military history of the English Civil War.[2] If the king did not lose the war through lack of resources, as now seems clear, then the answer would seem to lie with the problems of counsel and factionalism that Porter highlighted. Unfortunately, these are precisely the aspects of the king's party that have most successfully defied analysis. For all the recent work on the Caroline Court, Ian Roy's observation, forty years ago, that the whereabouts of power and influence at Oxford (the king's wartime headquarters) remains largely obscure is still true today.[3]

   The dynamics of counsel – how and from whom the king took advice – and the formation of Court factions were of course intimately linked. Courtiers with easy access to the king, and therefore to the royal ear, were likely to attract supporters eager for preferment or to advance particular policies. At the same time, factions tended to form in opposition to those who were thought to monopolize counsel or to exercise an undue influence upon the monarch. Lord Digby's emergence in 1645 as the king's principal adviser was a powerful stimulus to Court factionalism, just as Buckingham's ascendancy had been in the 1620s. My aim here is to develop a better understanding of which individuals and groups dominated

Acknowledgements: I am grateful to John Adamson, Sean Kelsey, Anthony Milton, Sarah Mortimer, Paul Seaward and Malcolm Smuts for commenting on earlier drafts of this chapter.
[1] Bodl., MS Carte 7, fos. 341r, v.
[2] Malcolm Wanklyn and Frank Jones, *A Military History of the English Civil War* (Harlow, 2005).
[3] Ian Roy, 'The Royalist Council of War, 1642–6', *BIHR*, 35 (1962), 168.

royalist counsels, and of the political structures – institutional and factional – by which policy was formed, mediated or resisted. As I have argued elsewhere, recent accounts of the structure of royalist politics are merely variations on the essentially Whig theme of a contest between 'constitutionalists' and 'absolutists'.[4] This chapter will advance a new model of royalist factionalism, abandoning the anachronistic and misleading notion of a struggle for or over 'the constitution', and highlighting instead the 'British' and European context of divisions in the king's party.

Casting royalist factionalism into a new mould will necessarily involve some attempt to explore the ideological differences that underlay these divisions. Much of the work on royalist political thought has focused on the king's apologists in the propaganda war against parliament. But it is the political assumptions of the Court grandees that require investigating if we are to learn more about the factional forces at work within the king's party and their ideological underpinnings. One of the key unanswered questions here is to what extent Court divisions during the Personal Rule carried through to the 1640s. Malcolm Smuts has suggested that political disagreement among the king's leading councillors in the 1630s was less about differences over constitutional principle than practical statecraft; and that this debate in Court circles was shaped by the humanist *topos* of whether political authority should rest ultimately on force or love.[5] On the face of it, questions of this sort would have become even more relevant after 1640, and it seems worth asking how much impact they had upon royalist counsels and divisions during the Civil War.

I

The search for sources of power and influence in the king's party has tended to focus on either particular individuals or the institutional apparatus created to manage the war effort. Charles's most favoured adviser for the first two years of the war was undoubtedly the queen, even though she was away from Court for much of that time.[6] Her influence was greatest in foreign policy matters, especially diplomatic affairs and efforts to secure overseas aid. She also took a particular interest in Irish

---

[4] See David Scott, 'Rethinking Royalist Politics: Faction and Ideology, 1642–49', in John Adamson (ed.), *The Civil Wars: Rebellion and Revolution in the Kingdoms of Charles I* (forthcoming).

[5] Malcolm Smuts, 'Political Thought in Early Stuart Britain', in Barry Coward (ed.), *A Companion to Stuart Britain* (Oxford, 2003), pp. 285–8; 'Force, Love and Authority in Caroline Political Culture', in Ian Atherton and Julie Sanders (eds), *The 1630s: Interdisciplinary Essays on Culture and Politics in the Caroline Era* (Manchester, 2006), pp. 28–49. I am grateful to Professor Smuts for allowing me to read this essay prior to publication.

[6] Richard Cust, *Charles I: A Political Life* (Harlow, 2005), pp. 361, 369–70, 385.

policy.[7] Oblique references in her correspondence suggest that she was involved in the planning stages of the king's cessation of arms with the Catholic confederates of Ireland in September 1643.[8] And after her return to France in 1644, her Court became a focal point for a variety of schemes and intrigues intended to further a military alliance with the Irish confederates. She had less clout, however, when it came to domestic affairs. The king's decision to besiege Gloucester in August 1643 and to summon the Oxford Parliament were evidently taken against her advice.[9] Nor was she entirely successful after 1643 in keeping Charles to her own hard-line agenda in treaty negotiations.

The king's preference for personal counsel also extended to matters military. The most powerful of the executive agencies created at the wartime Court was the Council of War, which was up and running by late 1642. Ian Roy, in his study of the Council, concluded that it functioned successfully as an administrative organ, but that its role as an advisory body was largely confined to immediate military business.[10] The king took counsel on strategic matters mainly from Prince Rupert, the earl of Forth, Henry Wilmot and other senior officers. At times he seems to have relied almost wholly on Rupert for tactical advice.[11] Even at the height of the Council's influence, during the 1644 campaigning season, the king tended to conduct operations on the basis of informal discussions with his field commanders and a few favoured courtiers (especially Digby and Sir John Culpeper). The Council's Secretary, Sir Edward Walker, thought that its 'mixt' membership – part civilian, part military – had fostered 'Animosities ... betweene the interests' that had compromised the war effort.[12] Charles can be forgiven therefore if he often sought guidance on military matters from elsewhere.

The Council of War's obvious institutional rival was the Privy Council and its administrative cousin the 'sitting council at Oxford' or Lords Commissioners.[13] The importance of the Privy Council in the decade or

---

[7]   LQHM, pp. 234–5; Edward, earl of Clarendon, *The Life of Edward Earl of Clarendon*, 2 vols. (Oxford, 1857), vol. I, p. 178; Cust, *Charles I*, pp. 386–7.

[8]   LQHM, pp. 66, 149, 156.

[9]   *Ibid.*, pp. 225, 285; *CHR*, vol. III, pp. 145, 149.

[10] Roy, 'Council of War', 161–3.

[11] Bodl., MS Carte 5, fos. 40r–v; BL, Reserved Photocopy 1998 (vi), 2095; *CHR*, vol. II, p. 351; vol. III, pp. 344, 345–6; Roy, 'Council of War', 163, 166.

[12] Parliamentary Archives, WAL/2, fo. 109.

[13] Jerome de Groot has argued that the 'Council of Oxford' established in May 1645 effectively replaced the Court as the 'focus of power politics': Jerome de Groot, 'Space, Patronage, Procedure: The Court at Oxford, 1642–46', *EHR*, 117 (2002), 1223. In fact, this body was simply the sitting Council at Oxford that had been set up in 1643 and whose commission was renewed and enlarged from year to year: W. H. Black (ed.), *Docquets of Letters Patent ... 1642–6* (1837), pp. 30–1, 220, 269–70; Roy, 'Council of War', 160.

so preceding the Civil War is a matter of some contention. Kevin Sharpe maintains that the 1630s witnessed a revival of the Council as the 'principal organ of influence and government'.[14] L. J. Reeve, on the other hand, insists the Council was eclipsed as a policy-making body early in the Personal Rule by a compliant Court clique.[15] The Council's influence and input seems to have varied according to the issue in question. But certainly with the outbreak of the Scottish Prayerbook Rebellion in 1637 the balance of power in the 'bi-polar' politics of the Caroline Court tipped perceptibly from the Privy Council to the entourage.[16] The earl of Dorset, a Court insider during the 1620s, was not alone in feeling that he had been excluded from the king's inner counsels by the later 1630s.[17] Those advising the king and shaping policy during the Scottish crisis were either trusted members of his household or the 'Committee of State' – comprising Laud, Cottington and a few other leading courtiers – 'which was reproachfully after called *the Juncto*, and enviously then in the Court *the Cabinet Council*'.[18] At least privy councillors were strongly represented in the junto. But with the removal, flight, or estrangement of the king's principal ministers in 1640–1, his recourse to 'unsworn counsellors' (the queen above all) became a practical necessity. Every major design of 1641–2 to restore a personal monarchy – the Army Plots, the Incident, and the attempted arrest of the Five Members – emanated from the inner recesses of the king's and queen's households.[19] This reliance upon cabinet counsels continued during the Civil War. Marchamont Nedham (aka *Mercurius Britanicus*) pronounced the Oxford Parliament a futile exercise on the grounds that there was a 'darke Iunto' of courtiers and clerics with access to the king and queen in their private apartments 'that unyeas all, and unnayes all'.[20] This was

14 Kevin Sharpe, *The Personal Rule of Charles I* (New Haven and London, 1992), p. 268.
15 L. J. Reeve, *Charles I and the Road to Personal Rule* (Cambridge, 1989), pp. 198–9, 226–7.
16 John Adamson, 'The Tudor and Stuart Courts 1509–1714', in Adamson (ed.), *The Princely Courts of Europe: Ritual, Politics and Culture under the Ancien Régime 1500–1750* (1999), p. 113; Neil Cuddy, 'Reinventing a Monarchy: The Changing Structure and Political Function of the Stuart Court, 1603–88', in Eveline Cruickshanks (ed.), *The Stuart Courts* (Stroud, 2000), p. 72.
17 David L. Smith, 'The Fourth Earl of Dorset and the Personal Rule of Charles I', *JBS*, 30 (1991), 279, 283–4.
18 *CHR*, vol. I, pp. 195–6; BL, Add. MS 15567, fo. 30v; William Knowler (ed.), *The Earl of Strafforde's Letters and Dispatches*, 2 vols. (1739), vol. II, pp. 181, 186; Peter Donald, *An Uncounselled King: Charles I and the Scottish Troubles, 1637–1641* (Cambridge, 1990), pp. 52–3, 55, 58, 89, 108, 321.
19 James Greenrod, ' "Conceived to give Dangerous Counsel"': William Murray, Endymion Porter, the Caroline Bedchamber and the Outbreak of Civil War, March 1641–June 1642', unpublished MPhil. thesis, University of Sheffield (2003), pp. 2–3, 76–8, 134.
20 *Mercurius Britanicus* (26 Feb.–6 Mar. 1644), p. 196.

sensationalism, to be sure. But as we shall see, such tales of bedchamber politicking were not confined to the parliamentarian press.

Royal efforts in 1642 to revive the prestige and authority of the privy council – part of Charles's campaign to reinvent himself as a law-abiding monarch – were to some extent successful. The Privy Council's impact on royalist counsels was apparently at its greatest during the first year of the war, prompting Richard Cust to argue that it 'remained a powerful presence at the heart of government'.[21] Leaving aside whether the Council had been a powerful anything since the late 1630s, there is certainly evidence that it acted, or attempted to act, as a brake on royal initiatives. It tried (unsuccessfully) to prevent Charles receiving the earls of Bedford, Clare and Holland after they deserted parliament in August 1643.[22] And in the spring of 1644 it managed to block, at least until 1645, a scheme promoted by Digby to set up a Council in the West under the Prince of Wales.[23] The Privy Council also served as a powerbase for those seeking some kind of negotiated settlement, and as such helped to advance both the Oxford and Uxbridge treaties.

The most sustained bid to promote a political solution to the war was the series of royal manifestos in 1642–3, portraying the king as a constitutional monarch and designed to detach moderate elements at Westminster from the 'fiery spirits'. Sir Edward Hyde was one of the architects of this policy, but for all his eulogies on the virtues of conciliar government he seems to have used 'private conferences' with Charles rather than the Council to get his message across.[24] Overall, there is little to suggest that the Privy Council made a positive contribution to royalist policy-making. Indeed, at times the king seems to have regarded it more as a hindrance than a help, authorizing a series of 'close' committees to pre-empt its discussions. The best known of these bodies was the 'junto' established in the autumn of 1643, consisting of the duke of Richmond, Lords Cottington and Digby, and Culpeper, Hyde and Nicholas.[25] Richmond, Digby and probably several other members of this group were impatient with or distrustful of the 'cowardly fools and knaves' on the Council.[26] Nor was the Council's reputation improved by its refusal to grasp the nettle of negotiating a treaty with the Irish confederate commissioners in the spring of 1644. Commenting on these

21   Cust, *Charles I*, pp. 362, 368.
22   *CHR*, vol. III, pp. 146–7, 150–2.
23   TNA, PC 2/53, p. 227; *MPR*, vol. II, pp. 412–13.
24   *CHR*, vol. I, p. 261; vol. III, pp. 224–5; *Life*, vol. I, pp. 179–81, 183, 190; vol. II, p. 297;
       E. I. Carlyle, 'Clarendon and the Privy Council, 1660–1667', *EHR*, 27 (1912), 251–3.
25   Clarendon, *Life*, vol. I, p. 177.
26   BL, Add. MS 29570, fo. 89; *Nicholas*, vol. XL, pp. 157–8.

negotiations, one of Ormond's correspondents observed 'that the king had fools enough of his privy councell allready; and that, I believe, your lordship findes true'.[27]

If certain privy councillors came to assume a 'powerful presence' at Oxford during the war it was more in spite of the king than because of him. In June 1645 the lords commissioners (who were mostly privy councillors), attempted to recall the king's field army for the defence of Oxford. Amazed at their temerity, Charles reminded Nicholas

that the Councell was never wont to debaite upon any matter not propounded to them by the King: & certainley it were a strange thing if my marching Army (espetially I being at the head of them...) should be governed by my sitting Councell at Oxon: when it is scarce fitt for my selfe at such a distance to give any positive Order.[28]

By late 1645 the leading lords at Oxford were pursuing what amounted to their own policy with respect to parliament, and were not so much counselling the king as trying to pressure him into making peace. Charles complained to the queen early in 1646 that

there is none doth assist me heartily in my steady resolutions [not to forsake the church, his friends, 'foundations'] but Sr Edw. Nicholas and [John] Ashburnham; all the rest are very inclinable to most flexible councels, yet grumbling when they are not employed, and, when they are, do rather hinder than further business.[29]

The most important piece of business – Charles's flight from Oxford in April 1646 – was effected in defiance of every one of his privy councillors.

The pattern of royal counsel-taking and policy-making established during the later 1630s continued into the 1640s. At times of crisis, the king turned instinctively to his circle of confidants; and the separation he had maintained for much of the 1630s between his 'proper Ministers' (i.e. those who transacted affairs of state) and his entourage – the often good-looking and stylish men with whom he liked to spend his lighter hours – began to break down. Counsel and influence in the wartime Court ran largely through 'cabinet counsels' and 'juntos' or through trusted intimates. It was the frequent complaint of those trying to advise Charles that 'the orator convinces sooner than the argument', and that even when decisions were taken in Council, the king would often change

---

[27] Carte, *Life*, vol. VI, pp. 84, 198.
[28] Henry B. Wheatley (ed.), *The Diary and Correspondence of John Evelyn*, 4 vols. (1906), vol. IV, pp. 161–2.
[29] John Bruce (ed.), *Charles I in 1646: Letters of King Charles the First to Henrietta Maria* Camden Society, LXIII (1856), pp. 11–12.

them after informal consultation with individual courtiers.[30] Charles might urge the Prince of Wales 'never to repose so much upon any mans single counsell, fidelity, and discretion, in managing affaires of the first magnitude', but it was advice that he had often failed to take himself.[31]

If there was one institution that informed contemporaries assumed was the seat of policy-making at Oxford it was not any of Charles's formal councils but his bedchamber.[32] Set up by James I in 1603, the bedchamber constituted the heart of the king's private apartments, and was off-limits to all but his bedchamber men and princes of the blood. As Neil Cuddy and Kevin Sharpe have shown, the early Stuart bedchamber men were both an important medium of counsel and a key instrument in the crown's exploitation of its prerogative powers.[33] Much of their influence died with the duke of Buckingham in 1628, but began to revive a decade later. Some of Charles's principal advisers during the 1637–40 Scottish crisis were bedchamber men.[34] Indeed, several royalists later claimed that members of the bedchamber, 'men most endeared to the King of all the world', had betrayed his 'most secret counsels [to the Covenanters], of which they themselves onely were either authors or partakers'.[35] This view of the bedchamber as both influential and treacherous was shared by Hyde.[36] It was possibly Hyde who briefed Matthew Wren (son of the Laudian bishop) on the wartime bedchamber.[37] Wren alleged that there were many instances when 'they who at night have pulled off his doublet or stockings, have at once divested him of the resolutions of the preceding day'.[38] Bulstrode Whitelocke made a similar claim. When at one point during the Oxford treaty negotiations in 1643

---

[30] BL, Add. MS 18981, fo. 82; Carte, *Life*, vol. VI, p. 50; *CHR*, vol. III, pp. 344, 347; John Gutch (ed.), *Collectanea Curiosa*, 2 vols. (Oxford, 1781), vol. I, pp. 244–5.

[31] *Eikon Basilike* (1649), p. 240. Wing E270.

[32] For the bedchamber's role, and its composition during the 1640s, see Neil Cuddy, 'The Revival of the Entourage: The Bedchamber of James I, 1603–1625', in David Starkey (ed.), *The English Court from the Wars of the Roses to the Civil War* (1987), pp. 173–225; TNA, LC 3/1, fo. 1.

[33] Cuddy, 'Revival of the Entourage'; 'Reinventing a Monarchy', pp. 70–3; Kevin Sharpe, 'The Image of Virtue: The Court and Household of Charles I, 1625–1642', in Starkey (ed.), *The English Court*, pp. 234–5, 244–57; Adamson, 'Tudor and Stuart Courts', pp. 110–13.

[34] Sharpe, 'The Image of Virtue', p. 251; Donald, *An Uncounselled King*, pp. 52–3, 55, 58, 89, 108, 321.

[35] George Wishart, *The History of the Kings Majesties Affairs in Scotland* (1647), p. 4; James Howell, *The True Informer* (1643), p. 15.

[36] *CHR*, vol. I, pp. 340, 555.

[37] Martin Dzelzainis, 'Edward Hyde and Thomas Hobbes's *Elements of Law, Natural and Politic*', *HJ*, 32 (1989), 306.

[38] Gutch (ed.), *Collectanea*, vol. I, p. 244.

the king changed his mind overnight, the parliamentary commissioners (of whom Whitelocke was one) were informed that

after we were gone from the king, and that his council were also gone away, some of his bedchamber (and they went higher) hearing from him what answer he had promised us, and doubting that it would tend to such an issue of the treaty as they did not wish; they being rather for the continuance of the war, never left pressing and persuading of the king, till they prevailed with him to change his former resolutions.[39]

The fierce competition among leading royalists for a place in the bedchamber says much about its ranking in the hierarchy of Court office. Charles was even more careful than James had been to preserve the exclusivity of the bedchamber:

the privilege and dignity of which room was then [during the Civil War] so punctually preserved, that the king very rarely called any privy counsellor to confer with him there, who was not of the bedchamber: which maintained a just reverence to the place, and an esteem of those who were admitted to attend there.[40]

Money was certainly one incentive for seeking entry to this royal inner sanctum. Because of their intimacy with the king, bedchamber men enjoyed a privileged, and potentially highly lucrative, position either to move their own suits or as patronage-brokers. This was particularly true of the grooms of the bedchamber (usually minor gentry), whose duties were more practical than those of the gentlemen of the bedchamber (usually peers), and therefore required a more familiar and regular attendance upon the king. It was said of Daniel O'Neill's appointment as a groom in 1644 that 'He cannot fayle there of makinge a fortune.'[41]

But it was not only money that fuelled the competition for places in the bedchamber. Political influence at Court depended in large part on access and proximity to the king; and the bedchamber was the surest way of obtaining both. Of the five men named by one of Ormond's Court correspondents in April 1643 as 'most powerfull about the King', none was a privy councillor, and two – Ashburnham and Porter – were grooms of the bedchamber.[42] And of these five men it was Ashburnham who 'for matter and familiaritye' was regarded as 'the favorite'. Many at Court would have agreed with Hyde that Ashburnham had 'so great an interest in the affections of his master, and so great an influence upon his counsels

[39] Bulstrode Whitelocke, *Memorials of the English Affairs*, 4 vols. (Oxford, 1853), vol. I, p. 200.
[40] Clarendon, *Life*, vol. I, pp. 191–2.
[41] Carte, *Life*, vol. VI, p. 116.
[42] Bodl., MS Carte 5, fo. 40v. The other three men were Rupert, Wilmot and Digby.

and resolutions, that he could not be ignorant of any thing that moved him'.[43] Secure in the king's favour, Ashburnham used his position as treasurer-at-war and *de facto* treasurer of the chamber to encroach on Hyde's territory as Chancellor of the Exchequer – a good illustration of the gains the entourage made at Oxford at the expense of ministerial officeholders.[44]

As for Porter, he professed to have little power at Court: 'I am no statesman', he informed Ormond, 'my cource is in a lower sphere'.[45] Yet the fact that he corresponded with Ormond, and was recommended by the marquess's agents as a man worth cultivating, is significant in itself. Although not as influential as Ashburnham, he clearly enjoyed the king's trust and favour; and in one key area of policy – Irish affairs – may have been privy to Charles's most secret counsels. The king entrusted the great seal to Porter during the royal visit to Scotland in 1641, and it was alleged that he had custody of it again when Ormond's commission to negotiate the Irish cessation was issued in April 1643.[46] Porter's correspondence seems to betray knowledge of plans for a cessation months in advance of Ormond's commission.[47] And he certainly had a hand in the king's most clandestine Irish design, the earl of Glamorgan's mission in 1645 to negotiate a peace treaty cum military alliance with the Irish confederates. Glamorgan confided to Hyde after the Restoration that his commission from the king to treat with the Confederates had not been 'inrolled or assented unto by his Council, nor indeed the seal to be put unto it in an ordinary manner, but as Mr. Endymion Porter and I could perform it, with rollers and no screw-press'.[48]

Even the most favoured of the royalist grandees found it prudent to insert their own men into the bedchamber. The elaborate, almost farcical, lengths that Digby went to in order to get his 'dear friend' Daniel O'Neill made a groom were matched by Rupert's dogged persistence in securing a groomship for his 'creature' William Legge.[49] It is also plausible to suggest that Cottington's and Culpeper's influence at Court owed at least something to their friendship with Porter and Ashburnham

[43]   *CHR*, vol. IV, pp. 183, 267; *Life*, vol. I, pp. 88, 173, 194; Carte, *Life*, vol. VI, p. 147; Sir Edward Walker, *Historical Discourses* (1705), p. 129.
[44]   Jens Engberg, 'Royalist Finances during the English Civil War 1642–1646', *The Scandinavian Economic History Review*, 14 (1966), 83–4, 86.
[45]   Carte, *Life*, vol. V, p. 256.
[46]   *The Kingdomes Weekly Intelligencer* (12–19 Dec. 1643), p. 276 [recte 278]; (30 Jan.–7 Feb. 1644), p. 325.
[47]   Bodl., MS Carte 4, fo. 358.
[48]   *CSP*, vol. II, p. 202.
[49]   *CHR*, vol. III, pp. 514–21; BL, Add. MS 18981, fo. 39; *MPR*, vol. II, p. 406; *LQHM*, p. 296.

respectively. Hyde claimed that Culpeper 'had an entire confidence and friendship with Mr. John Ashburnham, whom the king loved, and trusted very much; and who always imprinted that advice in the king's mind, which the other [i.e. Culpeper] had infused'.[50]

The very nature of the bedchamber's function – to administer the king's private life – makes its political role during the Civil War impossible to reconstruct. Nevertheless, it is clear that Richmond, Ashburnham, Porter and Will Morray dispensed of large amounts of patronage and revenue, and wielded great influence, on the strength of little more than their intimacy with the king as bedchamber men.[51] At the same time, the triumph of access over high office was not confined to the bedchamber. The clerk of the closet (the cleric who controlled the king's private chapel, or 'closet'), Richard Steward, and favoured royal chaplains could sway the king more effectively, because of their close attendance upon him, than could any Court bishop.[52] The queen's favourite Henry Jermyn also punched well above his weight in Court offices. It was reported from Oxford in 1644 that neither 'prince Rupert, nor all the numbers in arithmeticke have any efficacy, but are cyphers, without lord Jermine'.[53]

The bedchamber was probably not the power behind the throne that contemporaries sometimes imagined. The courtier who came closest to monopolizing counsel, if only briefly in 1645, was Secretary of State Lord Digby – though his office gave him excellent access to the king, and he himself was exceptionally well connected in the bedchamber. Nor did the closet-councillors at Oxford form the 'darke Iunto' of parliamentarian propaganda. Factions at Court often cut across the council-entourage divide rather than reinforcing it. Moreover, a serious rift developed in the bedchamber during the course of the war. In April 1643 Ashburnham (with Porter as his second) fought a duel with Richmond's younger brother – 'yett encreases more and more in fav[ou]r every day' – and by 1645 Richmond clearly resented his bedchamber rival, and probably *vice versa*.[54] The king himself became embroiled in this quarrel, and would end the Civil War politically estranged from his senior bedchamber men. These two developments – the rise of Digby

50　Clarendon, *Life*, vol. I, p. 88.
51　BL, Add. MS 29570, fo. 89; *CHR*, vol. I, p. 207; *Life*, vol. I, pp. 194–6; Malcolm Smuts, 'William Murray', *Oxford DNB*; History of Parliament Trust, London, unpublished articles on John Ashburnham and Endymion Porter for the 1640–60 Section.
52　Anthony Milton, 'Anglicanism and Royalism in the 1640s', in Adamson (ed.), *The Civil Wars*.
53　Carte, *Life*, vol. VI, p. 38.
54　Bodl., MS Carte 5, fo. 40r; Clarendon, *Life*, vol. I, pp. 192–7.

and the fracturing of the entourage – were closely linked to the subject of the next section of this chapter: factional politics in the wartime Court.

II

Perhaps the most striking feature of the reconstructed Court at the outbreak of civil war was its heterogeneity.[55] The leadership of the king's fledgling party in England comprised several very different groups in terms of Court experience and political background. Exquisite courtiers such as the duke of Richmond rubbed shoulders with swaggering military men (the true 'Cavaliers' or 'swordsmen') and boorish country peers such as the marquess of Hertford. Running through and across these structural divisions was a whole complex of friendships and enmities. The personal feud between Prince Rupert and Lord Digby, for example, was notorious, and did great harm to the royalist cause. It began in the summer of 1643, and by 1645 had assumed definite political overtones. But there was also no love lost between Rupert and two other Court heavyweights, Wilmot and Ashburnham. On the other hand, one of the most enduring friendships at Court was that between Rupert and Richmond. Some of these attachments and animosities had a political dimension, but not all. Hyde and Digby, for example, remained fast friends even when their political views grew 'diametrically contrary'.

The antagonism between the swordsmen and leading civilian councillors was the most damaging of the structural tensions within the king's party. The rivalry between these two constituencies was at its most intense during the first year of the war, when it broadly corresponded with a significant political split within the royalist leadership. The swordsmen and the circle of courtiers who looked principally to the queen for advancement (there was considerable overlap between the two groups in 1642–3) were generally eager to settle the war solely by the sword. Many of these men, and indeed the queen herself, had been implicated in the 1641 Army Plots, or had otherwise incurred charges of treason against them at Westminster. A negotiated settlement threatened to leave them at the mercy of parliament, and therefore an absolute victory seemed their safest option. For most of those associated with this royalist war party the fear of parliamentarian vengeance proved relatively short-lived, and several, including Rupert, would emerge as advocates of a negotiated settlement well before the king's prospects had become militarily hopeless. But before 1644 a gung-ho attitude generally prevailed among the king's leading officers.

[55] For this section, see Scott, 'Rethinking Royalist Politics'.

The swordsmen's hatred of the Roundheads was matched by their contempt for many of the king's civilian councillors. A parliamentarian officer sent to Rupert's headquarters in October 1642 with a letter to promote a treaty was allegedly told by Wilmot, O'Neill and other Cavaliers that they had 'lockt up his Majesties eares and tongue from the Lords at Court, who they ... said were both treacherous and cowardly ... but now of late hee had learnt to keepe his Councels from them'.[56] By the treacherous and cowardly 'Lords at Court' the swordsmen were referring to what might be termed the peace interest at Oxford. This was a group of courtiers, strongly represented on the Privy Council, whose conception of what constituted an acceptable settlement was close enough to that of moderate parliamentarians to make them willing to countenance major royal concessions. The earl of Dorset – the earl of Essex's 'confidant' at Court – was part of this group, as it seems was the king's Secretary of State Viscount Falkland. Hyde insisted that his 'dear friend' Falkland had not been 'so much enamoured on peace that he would have been glad the King should have bought it at any price'.[57] But there is every sign that given the opportunity Falkland was prepared to barter on issues that Hyde regarded as non-negotiable.[58]

Between the stark alternatives of an absolute victory and peace at any price lay a third option – a political coup organized in conjunction with parliamentarian moderates against the fiery spirits at Westminster. Hyde's role in the Oxford peace treaty in the spring of 1643 is a good example of this stratagem in action. Hyde rejected any idea of a settlement on the basis of parliament's official peace propositions. Instead, he favoured the secret and far more lenient terms being offered to the king by the earl of Northumberland – one of the leaders of the peace party in the two Houses. Hyde was confident that if the king conferred office and favour on the earl it would create such a majority for peace at Westminster that further parliamentarian resistance would collapse. Charles, however, was not persuaded that any concession on his part would enable Northumberland to master the earl of Essex and the more fiery spirits in parliament, and the negotiations came to nothing.

An even more ambitious design to build upon the middle ground in English politics was attempted early in August 1643. Royalist gains in the North and West during the summer of 1643 threatened to bring an absolute victory within the king's grasp, with the expected result that the swordsmen (in particular the circle around Prince Rupert) would prevail

[56]   *A Letter sent from a Gentleman to Mr. Henry Martin* (1642), pp. 3–5.
[57]   *CHR*, vol. III, p. 189.
[58]   BL, Harl. MS 1901, fos. 64r-v, 74–5; *CSPD 1641–3*, p. 457.

in the post-Restoration Court at the expense of the lords at Oxford. Anxious to pre-empt a military victory, Rupert's enemies at court – who included several of his erstwhile allies, notably Digby – attempted to bring the war to a swift and politically engineered conclusion. The series of vaguely worded peace propositions that Northumberland and the peace party grandees at Westminster drew up in July and presented to the Commons in August were almost certainly part of this design. The intention, it seems, was to use Essex's army, and possibly elements loyal to the marquess of Hertford (Rupert's principal enemy at Court and the nominal commander of the king's army in the West), to underwrite the peace propositions, and if necessary to quash opposition to them by force. With the swordsmen and fiery spirits neutralized, it was thought that the king could be restored to power on the very softest of terms. In the event, this projected settlement quickly collapsed. Hertford and Essex proved poor foundations on which to build a bi-partisan peace coalition; and Rupert's victory at Bristol, and the fiery spirits' control of the London mob and militia, ensured that the militants at Westminster and Oxford retained the upper hand.

Victory for the hawks in the summer of 1643 ended any prospect of an exclusively English settlement of the war, and ushered in a new phase in the conflict. Until the second half of 1643 the wars and unrest in all three Stuart kingdoms had consisted of a series of largely discrete, if causally interlinked, conflicts. But all this began to change in September 1643 following the king's cessation with the Irish confederates and the negotiation of the Solemn League and Covenant between the English and Scottish parliaments. Under the impact of the cessation and the Covenant, England became the main theatre in something not far short of a single war. And as the nature of the conflict in England changed, so too did factional alignments at Oxford.

There had been a fault-line within the king's party from its very inception over the propriety of deploying Irish Catholic troops in Britain. Digby and several other members of the queen's circle had been contemplating pitting Irish 'rebels' against English 'rebels' well before the actual outbreak of the Civil War. Yet there were also senior royalists, including Ashburnham and other figures close to the queen and committed to the vigorous prosecution of the war, who were distinctly unhappy at the prospect of importing Catholic troops. So long as victory by English force of arms, whether on the battlefield or in support of a political coup, seemed within reach, then there was no need to confront this potentially divisive issue. But it was becoming clear by early 1644 that the king would be hard pushed to defeat both the English parliamentarians and the Scottish Covenanters unless he brought over Catholic as well as Protestant troops from Ireland, and that this would entail making significant political and religious concessions to the Irish confederates. Rupert's defeat at Marston Moor in July 1644 forced the royalist grandees to confront the question of foreign intervention head on. Victory for the king now looked increasingly unlikely without such outside assistance – most obviously in the form of an Irish Catholic army. Marston Moor – and still more the king's defeat at Naseby a year later – left the grandees with only two real choices: either they must bring in foreign troops or they must seek a genuine accommodation with parliament. And already by early 1645 rival factions were forming around these stark alternatives.

As the structure of royalist factionalism changed, so the personal feud between Rupert and Digby became more ideological in nature. Digby's capture of the king's Irish policy during 1644 may well have increased tension between the two men. One of the few issues on which Rupert's thinking seems to have moved beyond personal pique was that of making significant concessions to the Confederates. His ultimate ambition was to lead a Protestant Anglo-Scottish expedition to recover his family's patrimony in the Rhineland from its Catholic conquerors – which sat uneasily with plans to restore royal authority in Britain by means of an Irish Catholic army. Although Digby supported Rupert's appointment as commander-in-chief of the royal army in November 1644, it was, as the prince quickly discovered, merely a precursor to the creation of a rival command under Digby's friend Lord Goring to 'counterpoise' his own. It was reported from Oxford in December that 'our soldiers are most for peace, Prince Rupert first of all'.[59] Rupert's friend the duke of Richmond was one of the architects of the Uxbridge treaty, and also attempted to persuade the king to go to London to treat in person. Within a few months of the collapse of the treaty in February 1645 – which the pro-accommodation faction blamed on Digby – Richmond was involved in secret negotiations with the Independent grandees to surrender Oxford to the New Model Army.

By the summer of 1645 the factional battle-lines among the grandees were beginning to harden. The heads of the foreign-alliance faction were Digby, Jermyn, Culpeper and possibly Cottington; shortly to be joined by Ashburnham. In the pro-accommodation camp were Rupert, Richmond, Rupert's old enemy the marquess of Hertford, and a majority of the lords at Oxford, including the earls of Dorset, Lindsey, Southampton and Portland. The defeats of English royalism at Naseby (June 1645) and of Scottish royalism at Philiphaugh (September 1645), and Ormond's snail-like progress in negotiating an Irish treaty, seemingly

[59]   BL, Harl. MS 166, fo. 135.

left the royalists little option but to sue for peace. Digby and Jermyn were determined to fight on, however, and began to explore the possibility of a military alliance with the king's ostensible enemies, the Scottish Covenanters. Their prospects of detaching the Scots from their parliamentarian allies were improved by the growing power of the anti-Scottish, Independent faction at Westminster. By the autumn of 1645 a number of leading Covenanters were beginning to question whether Scotland's interests might not be better served in alliance with a defeated and, they hoped, chastened king rather than with the English parliament. Just as the Irish option seemed to be foreclosed, this development opened up a series of new military and diplomatic possibilities for the foreign-alliance faction, now dispersed between Paris and Oxford.

The king's willingness to allow Digby and Jermyn to make overtures to the Covenanters widened the breach among leading royalists. Ashburnham and Culpeper had been reluctant to seek military assistance from Irish Catholics, but were happy to do so from Scottish Protestants, and threw their support behind Digby and Jermyn. Yet to Richmond, Hertford and their circle, the idea of a restoration by means of a Covenanter army represented an even more flagrant encroachment on English sovereignty than bringing in confederate Catholic troops. From the autumn of 1645, the Richmond–Hertford group was defined largely by its conviction that a negotiated settlement with parliament was preferable to a rapprochement with the Covenanters. To this end it attempted to push the king into talks with the Independents at Westminster, who were themselves resolutely opposed to further Scottish intervention in English affairs.

The first round in this new contest to shape royal policy was won by the foreign-alliance faction. With Ashburnham as their point-man in the bedchamber, the queen, Digby, Jermyn and Culpeper persuaded the king to surrender himself to the Scottish army at Newark in May 1646. The following month, largely the same group cajoled the Prince of Wales into leaving Jersey – where he and his Council had taken refuge after the collapse of the royalist war effort in the West – and joining his mother in Paris. His removal to France, and the royalist–Covenanter alliance it supposedly underpinned, were denounced by Hyde and most of the prince's other councillors. When the prince left for Paris – accompanied by Jermyn, Digby and Culpeper – Hyde and his friends disdained to follow, and from that point onwards were broadly aligned with Richmond, Hertford and their circle back in England.

With the king and prince safely out of the Independents' clutches, Jermyn, Culpeper and Ashburnham wrote a series of letters to Charles, begging him to take the Covenant and endorse a Presbyterian church settlement – the minimum terms on which the Scots would engage for him. The three men calculated that an agreement with the Scots would provoke a new civil war, and that a restoration of monarchy by means of an Anglo-Scottish Presbyterian army, backed by the French, would give Charles the power, somewhere down the line, to recoup his lost sovereignty. Theirs, however, was not the only royalist counsel the king was receiving during his Scottish captivity. In September 1646, Richmond collaborated with the younger Vane, Cromwell and other Independent grandees to present their own terms to the king. If Charles agreed to wash his hands of presbyterianism and allow limited religious toleration, Richmond and his Independent allies offered to restore him to 'the full execution of his regal authority', and to establish a 'moderated Episcopacy'. These terms probably formed the basis of the *Heads of Proposals* that the army, the Independent grandees, and the Richmond–Hertford group presented to the king the following year. Charles, however, would neither take the Covenant nor trust his sovereignty to the Independents, and the upshot was that early in 1647 the Scots surrendered him to the English parliament. For Ashburnham and his friend Nicholas this was one betrayal too many by the Scots, and they made common cause with the Richmond–Hertford group. Cottington and Porter also moved closer to the pro-accommodation faction. They could stomach the idea of the confederates as saviours of 'a tottering monarkie', but not the Covenanters.

The power struggle within the king's party, like that at Westminster, thus had a strongly 'British' dimension; and in the case of the royalists the divisions that emerged in the mid-1640s would persist more or less until the Restoration. The London newsbooks often depicted the infighting at Oxford in terms of the 1630s Court rivalry between pro-Spanish and pro-French interests. But by 1642 these divisions had been superseded by a new set of alignments. Royal policy, and perforce royalist politics, was strung out between two differing agendas – on the one hand, absolute victory and securing foreign aid; on the other, political coup and accommodation. The question of what these shifts of policy have to tell us about the intellectual context of royalist counsels is the theme to which we now turn.

III

The Court in 1650 was a breeding ground for 'statists' and 'atheists' – or so it appeared to the out-of-favour Sir Edward Nicholas.[60] If their counsels prevailed then he feared the king's party would succumb to 'the Doctrine of the tymes', putting 'the Rules of Necessity and Prudence'

[60]   *Nicholas*, vol. XL, pp. 172, 186, 188; *CSP*, vol. II, p. 286.

before the dictates of 'Iustice, Religion and Conscience'.[61] This was highly charged language. Terms such as 'statists', 'atheists' and 'prudence', used in a political context, were closely associated in the minds of contemporaries with Machiavellian and Tacitist ideas on statecraft: in particular, the ruthless pursuit of power in the name of reason of state, and the ready resort to extra-legal force to achieve political goals.[62] The strategy of the Jermyn–Culpeper grandees, with their unscrupulous quest for an alliance with the Covenanters, seemed to Nicholas redolent of these pernicious Tacitist doctrines. The king, wrote Jermyn, must 'goe to the utmost length he can possibly for suche a satisfaction of Scotland as may beget an unanimous engagement of the nation for his interests'.[63] Necessity demanded such an engagement, which in turn required dissimulation with regard to the Scots and a relaxation of royal commitments to uphold the Church of England and the 'known laws'. And lurking in the background was the idea that force (in this case, in the form of a Scottish army) was a surer foundation on which to rebuild monarchy than the affection of the king's subjects. If Nicholas did indeed perceive his Court opponents as Machiavellian or Tacitist, or perhaps even Hobbesian reason-of-statists, it would raise interesting questions about the nature of royalist factionalism. Were these courtiers using the language of necessity in a programmatic fashion – that is, to advance a coherent theory of royal power and government? And if so, from where did they draw their inspiration?

Reason of state was by no means an unfamiliar Court maxim before the 1650s. The first two Stuart kings and their ministers regularly invoked the law of necessity to justify measures that went beyond the ordinary remit of the prerogative.[64] According to Geoff Baldwin, reason of state provided Charles I with a 'potent set of ideological resources'. It also gave practical and moral force to 'absolutist' elements within Caroline political thought; the tenets, for example, that the crown was the sole arbiter of what constituted necessity, and that there were no enforceable limits upon royal authority.[65] Nevertheless, reason of state

[61] Surrey History Centre, Nicholas papers relating to Scottish affairs, G1287/35.
[62] P. Burke, 'Tacitism', in T. A. Dorey (ed.), *Tacitus* (1969), pp. 165, 166; Burke, 'Tacitism, Scepticism, and Reason of State', in J. H. Burns and Mark Goldie (eds.), *The Cambridge History of Political Thought 1450–1700* (Cambridge, 1991), p. 482; J. H. M. Salmon, 'Stoicism and Roman Example: Seneca and Tacitus in Jacobean England', *Journal of the History of Ideas*, 50 (1989), 204, 217.
[63] NAS, Hamilton manuscripts, GD 406/1/2119.
[64] G. Baldwin, 'Reason of State and English Parliaments, 1610–42', *History of Political Thought*, 25 (2004), 620–41.
[65] Anthony Milton, 'Thomas Wentworth and the Political Thought of the Personal Rule', in J. F. Merritt (ed.), *The Political World of Thomas Wentworth Earl of Strafford 1621–1641* (Cambridge, 1996), p. 153.

under the early Stuarts failed to develop the scope and cogency it did in
contemporary France and Spain – largely, it seems, because 'political
neostoicism' (the vogue for using Roman political parallels as a guide to
statecraft) never caught on in England to the extent that it did on the
continent.[66] It was not that English scholars and politicians were indif-
ferent to the revival of interest in Tacitus and other Roman imperial
historians in the late sixteenth century; but that they tended to read
Tacitus in ways critical of prudential statesmanship and princely
power-politics. One of the hallmarks of the evil courtier, according to
a treatise on the Court dedicated to the duke of Lennox (the future duke
of Richmond) in 1633, was a propensity to 'reade Tacitus Guichardine
[Guicciardini] Thusidides [Thucydides] and others, to make the plotts
of such as are of the same Batch with Seianus'.[67] Charles, like his father,
was apparently suspicious of scholars who adapted Tacitus for 'statist'
purposes. Yet as Malcolm Smuts has suggested, the ideas of Tacitist
writers such as the celebrated Flemish neostoic Justus Lipsius may at
least have helped to shape the conceptual framework within which
Caroline policy was formulated.

Lipsius's most influential work, his *Politicorum Libri Sex* (published
in an English translation in 1594), has been aptly described as a 'handbook for princes and their advisers'.[68] Although Lipsius acknowledged
that the 'chiefest strength and charge of principalitie' consisted in the
love that rulers fostered in their subjects, he and his many imitators
expended considerably more ink in advising princes to master the arts
of force and dissimulation as the surest means of retaining power and
enhancing the *grandezza* (might and majesty) of their state.[69] Princely
authority was more likely to prosper 'being slightly watered with the
dewe of evill'.[70]

The possibility that some of Charles's ministers were applying Tacitist precepts to the business of government is not entirely implausible.
Viscount Wentworth, Deputy and later Lord Lieutenant of Ireland, is

---

[66]   Salmon, 'Seneca and Tacitus', 202, 209, 223–4. For 'political neostoicism', see Ger-
        hard Oestreich, *Neostoicism and the Early Modern State*, transl. David McLintock
        (Cambridge, 1982).
[67]   Beinecke Library, Osborn shelves b 165, fo. 40. I am grateful to Diane Ducharme for
        discussion on this manuscript.
[68]   Justus Lipsius, *Sixe Bookes of Politickes*, transl. William Jones (1594), p. 74; Mark
        Morford, 'Tacitean *Prudentia* and the Doctrines of Justus Lipsius', in T. J. Luce and
        A. J. Woodman (eds.), *Tacitus and the Tacitean Tradition* (Princeton, NJ, 1993), pp.
        132, 139.
[69]   Lipsius, *Sixe Bookes*, p. 74; Oestreich, *Neostoicism*, p. 71; Salmon, 'Seneca and Tac-
        itus', 204, 216–17.
[70]   Lipsius, *Sixe Bookes*, p. 115.

known to have read works by Tacitus and several neostoic writers, including Lipsius, and certainly pursued policies consistent with the ethos of Lipsian Tacitism.[71] More specifically, he exhibited a number of traits central to the Lipsian model of prudential statecraft – a deep-seated aversion to mass politics ('popularity'); an intolerance of religious dissent; a willingness to use extra-legal force in cases of necessity; a conviction that a disciplined standing army was essential to political control; and an appreciation of the role of money in enhancing power.[72] During the Second Bishops' War of 1640 it was the newly created earl of Strafford who emerged as the leading Court advocate of using force to resolve the crisis, urging Charles to 'Goe on with a vigorous warr, as you first designed, loose[d] and absolved from all rules of government, beinge reduced to extreame necessitie, everything is to be done that power might admit.'[73]

Of course Strafford's brusque style of government had been evident before he went over to Ireland. But his time in Dublin in the 1630s gave him greater licence to develop and apply his ideas, and also brought him into contact with an older and more virulent strain of 'Thorough' than any he was likely to have encountered in domestic politics. Since the late sixteenth century, English political thought about Ireland had differed significantly from English political thought about England. It had been more open to schemes for uprooting ancient customs, more comfortable with the use of extra-legal force, and more willing to use Tacitus, Machiavelli and other 'statist' writers as positive models.[74] When Englishmen applied Tacitus to England they tended to think, like Ben Jonson, of Sejanus, the wicked favourite of Emperor Tiberius – or in other words, of virtue corrupted by power and Court vices.[75] But when Englishmen applied Tacitus to Ireland they would be more likely to think of how Agricola, the first-century Roman governor of Britain (and Tacitus's father-in-law), had tamed the barbaric Britons by forcing them to adopt Roman customs.[76] A number of late Elizabethan English writers on Ireland employed Tacitus, Machiavelli, Guicciardini and

[71] Milton, 'Wentworth', pp. 133–56.
[72] Richard Tuck, *Philosophy and Government 1572–1651* (Cambridge, 1993), pp. 58, 61–3, 80, 109–10, 223–4.
[73] HMC 3rd *Report*, p. 3.
[74] Ciarán Brady, 'Spenser's Irish Crisis: Humanism and Experience in the 1590s', *P&P*, 111 (1986), 17–49; Nicholas Canny, 'Debate. Spenser's Irish Crisis: Humanism and Experience in the 1590s', *P&P*, 120 (1988), 201–9; Andrew Hadfield, 'Tacitus and the Reform of Ireland in the 1590s', in Jennifer Richards (ed.), *Early Modern Civil Discourses* (Basingstoke, 2003), pp. 115–26.
[75] Salmon, 'Seneca and Tacitus', 219–20, 224–5.
[76] Hadfield, 'Reform of Ireland', pp. 117, 123–4.

other sources closely associated with political neostoicism to address the problems that Ireland posed to its English governors.[77] The possibility that these writers in turn influenced Irish policy and its exponents such as Strafford is worth further investigation.

Strafford was in some ways the political godfather to the foreign-alliance faction in the wartime Court. His friend the earl of Newcastle was a member of this group and a patron of the Personal Rule's most formidable apologist, Thomas Hobbes. Hobbes's first major philosophical work, *The Elements of Law* (completed by May 1640), was dedicated to Newcastle, although its main target audience was evidently the king and his ministers, and probably Strafford above all.[78] Part of Hobbes's purpose in writing the *Elements* was to lend weight to the Straffordian position that the king had propriety in his subjects' goods. One of the reasons Hobbes fled abroad in November 1640 was the fear that he and his treatise might become part of the Long Parliament's investigation into Strafford's 'arbitrary and tyrannical government'. Hobbes's political thought had already moved well beyond the intellectual boundaries of Tacitism in any generally accepted sense of that term. But in his emphasis on discipline and force as the building blocks of a stable regime – ideas he developed in his later writings – he owed much to the work of Lipsius and the neostoic movement in general.[79]

To what extent did Hobbes exert an influence on the hardline foreign-alliance faction at Court during the Civil War? The evidence is circumstantial, but nevertheless suggestive. In exile in Paris, Hobbes remained on friendly terms with Newcastle and other members of the queen's circle; and he was certainly well insinuated at the Court of Henrietta Maria by 1646, when Jermyn secured his appointment as tutor of mathematics to the Prince of Wales.[80] Hobbes's links with the Jermyn–Culpeper group were apparently at their closest during the second half

[77] Sydney Anglo, 'A Machiavellian Solution to the Irish Problem: Richard Beacon's *Solon his Follie* (1594)', in Edward Chaney and Peter Mack (eds.), *England and the Continental Renaissance: Essays in Honour of J. B. Trapp* (Woodbridge, 1990), pp. 153–64; Lisa Jardine, 'Mastering the Uncouth: Gabriel Harvey, Edmund Spenser and the English Experience in Ireland', in John Henry and Sarah Hutton (eds.), *New Perspectives in Renaissance Thought: Essays in the History of Science, Education and Philosophy* (1990), pp. 68–82; Lisa Jardine and Anthony Grafton, '"Studied for Action": How Gabriel Harvey read his Livy', *P&P*, 129 (1990), 30–78; Hadfield, 'Reform of Ireland', pp. 115–26.

[78] Thomas Hobbes, *The Elements of Law Natural and Politic*, ed. J. C. A. Gaskin (Oxford, 1994), pp. 19–20; Milton, 'Wentworth', p. 154.

[79] David Burchell, 'The Disciplined Citizen: Thomas Hobbes, Neostoicism and the Critique of Classical Citizenship', *Australian Journal of Politics and History*, 45 (1999), 506–24.

[80] BL, Add. MS 4278, fos. 263, 265v; Bodl., MS Clarendon 29, fos. 40r-v.

of 1646, at precisely the time when its leading members were trying to persuade the king of the decidedly Hobbesian proposition that the sword was 'the only engine able to doe your business'.[81] And just as a strong military party was the only means to restore the king, so force was necessary to maintain 'the power and dignity of ... the Crown' thereafter.[82] Without 'the power of the sword', Jermyn and Culpeper told the king, 'the Kingly office signefyes very litle'.[83] Significantly, they and Ashburnham drew a distinction between conscience and 'the prudentiall part of any consideration'. The king's conscience in respect of maintaining episcopacy must be set aside where necessity demanded. 'All that they [the Scottish Covenanters] can ask', thought Culpeper, 'or the King part with, is a trifle in respect of the price of a Crown.'[84] A measure of dissimulation was also required on Charles's part, for 'the only way to destroy this wicked government [Presbyterianism] is to establishe it for the present'.[85] In emphasizing the military component of royal authority, separating prudence and conscience (and prioritizing the former), advising dissimulation where necessary, and treating the monarchy as just one among several competing political interests, the Jermyn–Culpeper grandees demonstrated more than a hint of the Tacitist approach to statecraft that Strafford had shown. These courtiers had apparently absorbed the key lesson of the Personal Rule (and particularly Strafford's lieutenancy of Ireland) and the Civil War for governing the three kingdoms – that 'Majestie without force is unassured'.[86] And like Strafford, they were primarily interested in ways of enabling Charles to get things done, not in advancing theories of his legal and constitutional position. A resort to Irish, Scottish, or continental troops to redress the king's defeat in England – 'the Seat and Center of his Empire' – was a natural consequence of such an approach.

The usefulness of the neostoic legacy in shaping royalist policy was also appreciated by the opponents of the foreign-alliance faction. Hyde's role as both politician and historian was heavily influenced by his engagement with Tacitus and other Roman writers.[87] But Hyde read these sources in a different moral and philosophical light from that of Lipsius and his followers, and with reference to contemporary works that were critical of

[81] *CSP*, vol. II, p. 261.
[82] *Ibid.*, p. 264.
[83] *Ibid.*, p. 301.
[84] *Ibid.*, p. 207.
[85] *Ibid.*, p. 274.
[86] Lipsius, *Sixe Bookes*, p. 82; Oestreich, *Neostoicism*, p. 70.
[87] Paul Seaward, 'Clarendon, Tacitism, and the Civil Wars of Europe', *HLQ*, 68 (2005), 289–310; Martine Watson Brownley, *Clarendon and the Rhetoric of Historical Form* (Philadelphia, PA, 1985), pp. 136, 148–9.

Lipsian Tacitism. Hyde was also an exceptional figure within the king's party, and cannot easily be assigned to any royalist faction. Even so, by 1646 he seems to have been fundamentally in accord with the Richmond–Hertford group; he certainly found the counsels of the Jermyn–Culpeper grandees deeply repugnant. Taking Hyde and his friends as broadly representative of the Richmond–Hertford group, we encounter a very different conception of the monarchy from that of the queen's circle. Royal authority, in Hyde's reckoning, derived ultimately not from the sword but the affections of the English people, 'without which he hath no hope of reigning'.[88] Nicholas took a similar view, urging Charles to cultivate the 'esteeme & affecc'on of yor people, whose love I humbly conceave to be soe much yor Maties interest, as that it ought to be preserved & reteyned by yor Matie by all possible means'.[89] Hyde and Nicholas regarded the monarchy not simply as a political phenomenon therefore – as Jermyn and Culpeper did – but also as a moral force, rooted in a reciprocal relationship of trust and loyalty between king and people, and indivisible from the honour of the English nation. Despite his legal training, Hyde envisioned the government of England as essentially a moral construct, that depended for success more on personal integrity than constitutional checks and balances. His insistence that the king's party adhere to 'the church by law established' and the constitutional reforms of 1641 reflects relatively little interest in the actual content and derivation of the fundamental laws.[90] Defending the ancient constitution *per se* was never his priority. In constantly advising Charles to stick to 'foundations' he was articulating not a legalist position but a basic political strategy: 'for your Majesty well knows that your greatest strength is in the hearts and affections of those persons who have been the severest assertors of the publick liberties'.[91]

The government and function of the church was a major issue in the struggle between the contending counsels of force and love. One of the most effective instruments for governing the people's affections, thought Hyde, was the episcopate. As he explained:

There is no question the Clergy will always have an extraordinary influence upon the people; and therefore ... there must be a way to govern the Clergy absolutely, and keep it subject to the rules, and orders of State; which never was, nor ever can be, without Bishops; so that in truth civil prudence would make unanswerable arguments for that order, if piety did not.[92]

88   *CSP*, vol. II, p. 307.
89   Wheatley (ed.), *Evelyn Diary*, vol. IV, pp. 89–90, 96.
90   *Ibid.*, pp. 102–3.
91   *CSP*, vol. II, p. 139.
92   *Ibid.*, pp. 365–6; Brownley, *Clarendon*, p. 64; Martin Dzelzainis, ' "Undoubted Realities": Clarendon on Sacrilege', *HJ*, 33 (1990), 516.

The 'right and reverence of the Crown' were thus inseparable from episcopal government of the church.[93] The king agreed. 'Religion [i.e. episcopacy] is the only firme foundation of all power', he told Jermyn, Culpeper and Ashburnham; 'Religion will much sooner regaine the Militia, then the Militia will Religion.'[94] 'Civil prudence' as much as piety led the king and Hyde to argue that it was politically imprudent to sever conscience and policy as the Jermyn–Culpeper group advised. What separated the two camps was their differing conceptions of the church as an institution and its relationship with monarchy; devotional preferences or confessional loyalties contributed relatively little to their disagreement. Ashburnham did as much as any man in 1646 to persuade Charles to forsake the bishops, and yet was acknowledged to be 'a great lover of the church in the right protestant way'.[95] In fact most of the leading members of the foreign-alliance faction were Protestants of some description. Some of them, like Ashburnham, even had a genuine attachment to the Church of England. But what they all had in common was a willingness to subordinate public religion to political necessity.

There is no easy answer to the questions posed at the start of this section. That Tacitist concepts and language were pervasive in English political culture by the mid-seventeenth century is beyond question. The Civil War, as Richard Tuck has reminded us, 'was waged by *humanists*, and its public rhetoric ... was drawn from history and from Tacitism'.[96] The polemicist (and admirer of Strafford) James Howell was probably not the only royalist to discover that Lipsian Tacitism afforded a particularly appropriate discourse for interpreting and negotiating the traumas of civil war.[97] Unfortunately, the evidence for the emergence of this Lipsian strain of Tacitism in royalist counsels is suggestive rather than conclusive. We cannot be certain that the Jermyn–Culpeper grandees, for example, were consciously applying Tacitist precepts, or ideas drawn from Machiavelli, or simply reacting expediently to events. But certainly, on one reading of the evidence, the queen and her circle were ideologically committed to prudential politics and (in Strafford's words) 'everything that power might admit' to crush the king's enemies. Always influential, their counsels acquired more force from late 1643 as the balance of military power began to tilt decisively towards parliament.

---

[93] *CSP*, vol. II, pp. 417–18.
[94] *Ibid.*, p. 248.
[95] Carte, *Life*, vol. VI, p. 147; *CSP*, vol. II, p. 270.
[96] Tuck, *Philosophy*, p. 225 (Tuck's emphasis).
[97] James Howell, *Parables Reflecting upon the Times* (1643), p. 13; *Lustra Ludovici* (1646), epistle dedicatory and p. 183; *The Instruments of a King* (1648), pp. 1–9; D. R. Woolf, 'James Howell', *Oxford DNB*.

The dynamics of royalist counsel – Charles's preference for unsworn councillors – probably favoured those urging Straffordian remedies. In the process a factional divide emerged in the king's party between those, such as the queen's circle, who had adapted to an England where politics conformed to something like continental patterns – in other words where Tacitist and statist ideas prevailed – and those such as Hyde who regarded that development as a betrayal of their hopes for the restoration of a relatively non-coercive and fundamentally English polity. Only by keeping to 'known ways' in church and state, Hyde insisted, could Charles rekindle the love of his subjects, which was the surest means of reviving his political and military fortunes. The queen's circle, by contrast, put little faith in people power. Popular approval, or disapproval, hardly figured in their calculations, and could be set aside altogether for the sake of obtaining foreign military assistance. Like Strafford, they believed that 'Majesty without force is unassured'. Strafford's ghost may have haunted not just Viscount Lisle and the parliamentarian Independents, but also royalist counsels in the England-turned-Ireland of the 1640s.[98]

[98]   John Adamson, 'Strafford's Ghost: The British Context of Viscount Lisle's Lieutenancy of Ireland', in Jane H. Ohlmeyer (ed.), *Ireland from Independence to Occupation 1641–1660* (Cambridge, 1995), pp. 128–59.

7 'I doe desire to be rightly vnderstood': rhetorical strategies in the letters of Charles I

Sarah Poynting

In December 1642 Charles I expressed his regret to the marquess of Hamilton for being 'ill at words'; it was not the only time he made such an apology.[1] This is, however, in itself a commonplace rhetorical technique, and, like his similar confessions of laziness in writing, should not necessarily be taken at face value. If his letters are not masterpieces of English prose, they are often very carefully structured and phrased, being, as they were, a key means of establishing political and personal relationships, raising money, gaining support, putting across contentious arguments, or enforcing his will. Letters in his own hand, considered especially important both by himself and by their recipients, are particularly revealing of the ways in which the king shaped his language to achieve his ends. This chapter is concerned less with what may be seen as 'official' rhetoric (the wording found in declarations, proclamations, speeches and public correspondence) than with the linguistic and literary formation of the king's personally written correspondence.

Despite Charles's often reiterated desire to be 'rightly vnderstood',[2] like many modern politicians he appears to have believed that if his policies faced opposition, the fault lay not in the policies, but in their opponents' faulty perception of them: if properly comprehended, they could not fail to win support from all but the wilfully ill-affected. He twice repeated this sentiment (variously worded) in an irritable speech on tonnage and poundage to both Houses of Parliament at the Banqueting House on 24 January 1629, some six weeks before the dissolution. He saw no reason at that time to embellish his assertion that he claimed the duties from present necessity and not as his prerogative right: a plain statement was considered sufficient. The onus was on his listeners or

---

[1] NAS, GD 406/1/168, 29 December 1642. All letters are holograph unless otherwise stated.

[2] The title quotation is taken from Charles's speech on Strafford to both Houses of 1 May 1641 (TNA, SP 16/480, fo. 1), this version in the hand of Edward Nicholas. Similar phrasing is found in speeches and letters from 1629 to 1648.

readers to understand rather than on him to make himself understood. There is a decided irony in his next recorded utterance of the phrase, to the Assembly of Peers at York on 24 September 1640, when he declared that, desiring 'nothing more then to be rightlie vnderstood of my people', he had 'to that end' resolved to call a parliament.[3] By April 1642 he was complaining bitterly in messages to the two Houses of Parliament of their restrictions, as he saw it, on his freedom to express himself in such a way as to be understood.

It was during the 1640s that being rightly understood became most urgent. However, the developments in Charles's manner of communication occurred not in his letters to his enemies but to his followers. In the course of this decade the king's relationship with his supporters, as it is reflected in his correspondence with them, underwent a radical change as he found himself obliged to engage with their arguments and justify his policies to them. It is a change, nevertheless, that is anticipated in a number of his earlier letters. The need to argue and persuade that became ever more pressing as the royalist cause was crushed was evidently felt less strongly and less often by the king earlier in his reign, but it was not wholly absent. Letters to the marquis of Hamilton, in particular, in the late 1620s and early 1630s suggest that Charles never found it easy to issue direct orders to him, and rather than stating his royal will directly, preferred to use linguistically more oblique ways of exerting pressure; and it is in his well-known correspondence with the marquis in 1638–9 that his first more obvious rhetorical flourishes begin to appear.[4]

The start of the new decade did not, of course, mark an instant alteration in Charles's mode of communication, which was increasingly influenced by the immediate situation in which he found himself. If this seems obvious, it is nevertheless worth stating, given the tendency to view the king as incapable of genuine development in response to changing circumstances. As was the case during the 1630s, it is often Charles's curt apostiles (marginal responses) on letters from Sir Francis Windebank which provide the plainest glimpses into his state of mind in the early 1640s. In September 1640, annoyed by what he saw as foot-dragging by the Privy Council during his absence in York following the Scottish invasion, he ordered Windebank in a postscript to 'Tell the E. Martiall and all the Councell, that wee heere preache the Doctrine of seruing the king euerie one upon his chardge, for the defence of the

---

[3] Bodl., MS Clarendon 19, fo. 41.
[4] Examined in my article ' "From his Matie to me with his awin hand"': the King's Correspondence during the Period of Personal Rule', in Ian Atherton and Julie Sanders (eds.), *The 1630s: Interdisciplinary Essays on Culture and Politics in the Caroline Era* (Manchester, 2006), pp. 74–91.

Realme; wch I asseure you is taken as Canonicall heere in Yorkeshire, & I see no reason why you of my Councell should not make it bee so understood there.' A week later he added 'I see ye ar all so frighted, ye can resolue on nothing.'[5] In longer letters Charles frequently weakened the clarity of his message with qualifications, but the necessary constraint on the length of apostiles almost always gives them a decisive – indeed peremptory – quality that can be lacking in his correspondence. They present his first thoughts before doubts had a chance to be felt, sometimes revealing a sharp-tongued sarcasm otherwise veiled by a monarch who liked to present himself as endlessly patient and forbearing.

From 1642–5, once key decisions had been taken (and taken in meetings rather than in writing), the main purpose of Charles's letters was inevitably practical: issuing orders and ensuring that they were carried out. However, there are a number of letters whose aim is rather different. The king's correspondence with Hamilton after the latter's return to Scotland from York in July 1642 was resumed, but with the unsettling events in Edinburgh in 1641 ('the Incident') intervening since Charles had last written regularly to him in 1639.[6] Their once close friendship had presumably been at least superficially patched up, although it was not until March 1643 that Charles wrote to Henrietta Maria that he was 'now confident that 173: [Hamilton] is right for my seruice' and proposed that he be rewarded with a dukedom, which was indeed conferred in the following month.[7] The trust that the king evidently had in Hamilton in the 1630s could never, once shaken, be wholly restored, but its appearance needed to be convincingly performed. To Charles the ideology of monarchy and absolute loyalty to himself were indistinguishable: a close relationship suffering an ideological breach had to be recreated also – perhaps primarily – on a personal level. This is part of the intention of the letters he wrote to Hamilton in late 1642. One of the most significant ways in which he did so was to draw on their previous intimacy: 'you know mee too well to haue more words spent upon you', he wrote in a short letter of 17 October.[8] This was reinforced, as so often in Charles's letters to his followers in this period, by a promise of future reward, perhaps intended to keep Hamilton on-side until the king was more sure

---

[5]   Bodl., MSS Clarendon 18, fo. 273 and 19, fo. 3: from Windebank 1 and 7 September, apostiled by Charles 2 and 9 September, York.

[6]   In August 1641 Hamilton's alliance with the earl of Argyll led to accusations that both were traitors, and a plot was hatched to murder them, to which Charles almost certainly gave his approval. They fled Edinburgh in October, returning in November when the Scottish parliament guaranteed their safety. These events became known as 'the Incident'.

[7]   Bodl., MS Nalson 1, fo. 25, 2 March 1643 (presumably intercepted).

[8]   NAS, GD 406/1/166.

of him. While the former tactic (creation of intimacy) can be seen again in the letter of 29 December already briefly cited, the latter (promise of reward) has, for the time being, been dropped:

> ye know I am ill at words, wherfor I thinke it were best < for me > to say to you, ... you know my mynd; & indeed I know none of my subjects that knowes it better, & that hauing, for the present litle else to giue my seruants but thankes, I hould it a particular misfortune that I can doe it no better; therfor this must suffyse.[9]

The regret expressed by the king for his literary inadequacy here encompasses a more significant apology for his inability to offer a material reward. However, the balanced clauses and compact self-reflexiveness of form and content used by Charles belie any failure of verbal dexterity. The graceful deftness with which his self-reproach is offered serves to gloss over the lack of more substantial recompense.

In a letter earlier the same month, the reminders of their old familiarity were intensified. Charles referred to making 'laizie use' of the bearer to provide the marquis with both news and indications of his own wishes in a way reminiscent of two letters to Hamilton in 1631 in which he apologized for being 'lasie anufe in writing'.[10] The reason then was also that the letters were carried by a trusted bearer. The plea of laziness was even more redundant in 1642, but it served to establish a moment of private understanding between them in which this most reserved and bureaucratically conscientious of monarchs presented himself with apparent frankness as suffering from an all too ordinary human failing. The central part of the letter bears strong similarities to Charles's correspondence with the marquis in the late 1630s, particularly in his declaration that he would 'eather bee a glorius King or a patient Martir', which recalls similar assertions in 1638. The intention may again have been to evoke a sense of their former closeness in the recipient, but perhaps it had this effect on the writer himself, as he went on to confide about the one subject on which he felt true guilt:

> the failing to one frend, hes, indeed, gone very neere mee; wherefor I am resolued that no consideration whatsoeuer shall euer make mee doe the lyke; upon this ground I < am > certaine that God hes < eather > so totally forgiuen me, that he will < still > blesse this good Cause in my hands, or that all my

---

[9] NAS, GD 406/1/168. Angled brackets in all quotations indicate words interlined by Charles.

[10] NAS, GD 406/1/154 and 157: the former (in which Charles wrote that sending Henry Vane 'willbe a good excuse for my laziness in wryting shortlie') dated 21 September 1631, the latter, from which the quotation in the title of this chapter is taken, 31 December.

punishement shall bee in this World, wch without performing what I haue resol-
ued, I cannot flatter my selfe will ende here.[11]

The letter then closes, in a very characteristic turn of phrase, with: 'This
accustomed freedome will, I am confident, ad cheerefulnesse to your
honnest resolutions.' But this assertion of confidence was, as with similar
claims in letters of 1638–9, undermined by qualifications, in this case by
Charles's doubt as to whether God had fully forgiven him for the death
of Strafford (which would prey on his conscience for the rest of his life).
A sentence which begins by affirming the king's certainty that he has
been forgiven ends in a tangle of alternatives that envisage divine punishment if he does not achieve his ends. His amendments only add to the
tone of uncertainty. This is directly followed, somewhat startlingly, by
his expression of belief that the marquis will be cheered by the letter.
Charles's rhetorical control over his intended message is not always
perfect. Nevertheless, the phrasing suggests that it was less the content
of the letter than the freedom with which he claimed to share his
thoughts with Hamilton that he saw as generating 'cheerefullnesse': it
was the relationship between them that was significant.

    This freedom, and the consequent establishment of a flatteringly fa-
miliar relationship, is also reflected in letters to the earl of Newcastle,
who was distinguished by Charles at the beginning of the English Civil
War in being addressed in a relaxed, chatty style. In a letter of 29
December 1642 discussing the problem of arms supply in the North,
he used proverbial expressions and homely allusions, along with oral
speech patterns to give the effect of immediacy: the king told Newcastle
that 'Charity begins at home', and that he should 'on Gods name inquyre
what is becume' of the arms belonging to the Trained Bands, and 'make
no bones to take them' from the ill affected. He assured the earl that,
according to his own rule, he did not command, but only desired him to
make use of General King in his army – although the repetition of the
word 'desire' could leave Newcastle in no doubt as to its force: 'I earnest-
lie desyre you to see if you can comply with this my desyre'. In a postscript, though, he added 'I promis you, to be as wary of a Treatie, as *you*
can desyre' (my emphasis). There is a positive anxiety not to appear
overbearing that is found even more strongly in letters to Prince Rupert.
The suggestion given by this air of comfortable friendship and near
equality that this is Charles at his most natural could be accurate;
equally, this impression may be a calculated one. This letter was written
on the same day as the much shorter one to Hamilton in which the king

---

[11]   NAS, GD 406/1/167, 2 December 1642.

apologized for being 'ill at words'. Perhaps the difference between the two lay in Charles's desperation to hear news from the campaign in the North: every letter to Newcastle ends by pressing him to write, and in February 1643, the king wrote urgently to him that 'neuer Woeman with Chylde more longed for any thing, then we for newes from you'.[12] The nature of the relationship being stylistically established by him may have depended more on the needs of the moment than on Charles's personal feelings. Letters to Newcastle in April 1644 after he attempted to resign because of criticism aimed at him from the Court are, unsurprisingly, severer and more formal in tone: 'remember all Courage is not in fyghting; constancy in a good Cause, being the cheefe, & the dispysing of slanderus tonges & pennes being not the least ingredient'. In a second short letter the king referred him to Lord Digby for particulars after pointing out that 'wee, lyke you, cannot doe alwais what we would': there was no friendly apology for his laziness in not providing information himself.[13] Moreover, none of the letters to Hamilton or Newcastle reflect the real warmth that emerges from Charles's letters to Buckingham, almost the only person other than Henrietta Maria whom he addressed with the intimate 'thou'.

It is unexpectedly used, however, in another letter of December 1642.[14] After commiserating with Sir Arthur Aston (whom he had recently left in charge of the garrison in Reading in order to establish the Court in Oxford) on his 'untoward Soldiers, wch must needs be a great vexation to anie braue Man' and assuring him that it was impossible for 'the baceness of Roges' to injure the reputation of 'a galant Man', Charles closed with: 'Therefor I desyre you to be in good hart, for I dout not, but ... to see you enjoy a good Reward for the seruice thou now doest / Thy asseured frend'. While Aston was not addressed solely by his Christian name, as a very small number of the king's associates were, the opening 'Arthur Aston' (rather than the more usual surname alone) emphasized Charles's desire to ensure that the recipient knew that he had been singled out for royal recognition and sympathy.[15] It is impossible to know whether Aston could have been aware of the subtle differentiation in style of address employed by the king, but the connotations of 'thou'

12   BL, Harley MS 6988, fo. 133, 13 February 1643.
13   Ibid., fos. 173 and 175, 5 and 11 April 1644.
14   Belvoir Castle, MS QZ. 22, fo. 40, 12 December 1642. I am grateful to the duke of Rutland for access to the archives.
15   It is very rare to find Christian name and surname together: Sir Thomas Roe is once 'Tom Roe' in a short note of thanks for his pains in 'so difficult and unpleasant an imploiment' (27 March 1642, TNA, SP 16/489, fo. 214). The usage is clearly intended to signify a greater degree of familiarity or approval than the surname on its own.

would have been as obvious to him as they were to Shakespeare's audiences. Small lexical shifts can carry a significant semantic load.

The conversational style used with Hamilton and Newcastle contrasts strongly with that adopted by the king with his wife, although there are common elements. Charles, for example, excused his inability to express his love for her eloquently enough in much the same way as he apologized to Hamilton for his linguistic inadequacy. He similarly enlarged on his love for her by belittling his verbal efforts; though in this case he indicated that action to make up for his failure in words would not be lacking ('when I shallbee wanting, in any other way ... of expressing my Loue to thee, then, lett all honnest Men, hate & eschew me, lyke a Monster').[16] Until 1646 he showed much more concern to explain himself to her than he did to anyone else. The letters captured at Naseby show how deliberately he drafted his letters to her, both in defending his own decision to treat with parliament at Uxbridge and in questioning her judgment on Irish affairs. Concerning the former, Charles wrote:

though I judge my selfe secure in thy thoughts, from suspecting me guilty of any basenesse, yet I held this account necessary, to the end ~~that~~ thou may make others know, as well as thy selfe, this certaine trewth, that no ~~aprehention~~ <danger> of Death, or Misery (w^ch ~~is~~ I thinke much worse) shall make me doe any thing unworthy of thy Loue.[17]

The revulsion which the publication of his letters caused is unsurprising, given their evidence not only of the king's emotional dependence on his wife, but of the possible inference that can be made from them, perhaps most clearly shown here, that it was her opinion rather than the good of the kingdom that was driving his decisions. However, the dual nature of the letters should be taken into account. These are both love letters and letters concerning matters of state, and it is easy for the manifestations of the former to cloud judgment of the content of the latter. Stylistically, from the invariable opening 'Deare hart' to the closing 'Eternally thyne', they are throughout worded in the language of love, which is sometimes used by Charles more to maintain a fiction of their ideological unity than to signify his submission to her advice.

For example, his letter to her of 14 January 1645 is phrased with particular care to suggest that her 'giuing eare' to a proposal for her to go to Ireland was 'most asseuredly, only to expresse my [sic] loue to me, & not thy judgement in my Affaires'.[18] Those making the proposal, he argued, did not have her interests at heart: 'is not the proposall of

[16] Bodl., MS Nalson 1, fo. 25, 2 March 1643.
[17] HLRO, Naseby Papers (10), 19 December 1644.
[18] HLRO, Naseby Papers (13).

thy jurny to Ireland a pritty instans for seriuly [*sic*] of it selfe, I hould it on of the most extrauant [*sic*] Propositions that I haue hard'. Thus he implied that her real opinion must be the same as his, and threw the blame for her acceptance of what he evidently regarded as a wholly un-acceptable idea onto others. The language that he uses, though – a rhe-torical question, the contrast between the contemptuous 'pritty' and 'extrau[ag]ant' with the 'seriu[s]ly' applied to his own point of view – makes it quite plain to her that it is a venture not to be further contem-plated. Charles's deletions in the draft of a letter written to Henrietta Maria in April 1645 manifest the strength of his concern not to disquiet her, as he struck through repeated references to the impossibility of his feeling anger towards her, even when grieved by her silence:

~~I hope~~ though thou ~~lets~~ omittes dyuers occasions of wryting to me yet ~~it~~ < that > is no warant for me to follow thy example, it not being waranted by the law of Kyndness ~~no more then for me to be angry with thee for any thing~~, (~~for thou maist doe that, will troble, greeue me, nay what I will not name, but Anger~~ < for that > ~~is a Passion, I am not capable of, as in relation to thee~~) but ~~I am enjoyned by~~ the same law, < enjoynes me > to deale freely with thee by confessing that thy last melancoly letter, seconded by thy sylence, does troble me.[19]

The king's own distress is much more strongly manifested in the passages deleted. He has similarly altered the desolate 'one kynde word from thee, mends this' to the more light-hearted 'I expect no volumes a word or two satisfie me'. Reading Charles's fair copy of this letter, with no knowledge of the deletions, produces a very different effect from its passionate draft: his desire to protect her from unpleasantness evidently extended to the turmoil of his own emotions.[20] Any criticism of her was always made obliquely. It is undoubtedly the case that the expressions of love and of political argument in his letters to Henrietta Maria are so intertwined as to appear at times to coalesce, but closer analysis shows that the king was not so much incapable of weighing and dissenting from his wife's opin-ions as of clearly telling her so, despite his claim to 'deale freely' with her.

The use of rhetorical questions followed by a partial displacement of blame occurs even more strikingly in letters written to Rupert and Maurice after the former's surrender of Bristol to Sir Thomas Fairfax in September 1645. The king expressed his shock in terms not only of its military implications, but of his personal grief that it should be his

[19] HLRO, Naseby Papers (21), 11 April 1645. Single strike-through indicates deletion of first thoughts, double strike-through of Charles's second attempt at expressing him-self. A second passage begging her to write contains so many layers of deletions and interlineations as to make it exceptionally difficult to represent in print.

[20] Bodl., MS Clarendon 91, fo. 19. The fair copy incorporates all the changes made to the draft.

much-loved nephew who was responsible for it, in a series of epiplectic
questions preceding his announcement of his decision to send Rupert
into exile:[21]

the losse of Bristoll . . . is likewise the greatest tryall of my Constancy that hath yett
befallen mee, for what is to be done? . . . I must remember you of your letter of the
12 Aug: whereby you assured mee (that if noe mutinye happned) you would keepe
Bristoll for fower monthes, did you keepe it fower dayes? was there any thinge like
a mutinye? more questions might bee asked, but now I confesse to little purpose.[22]

However, in a letter to Maurice a few days later he wrote of Rupert
having had his 'Iudgement seduced by some Villaines', which he then
emphasized by neatly interlining 'rotten harted' before 'Villaines'.

The evidence of Charles's letters is that (not unnaturally) he strongly
disliked being at odds with those he was close to, a feeling not restricted
to members of his own family. In the late 1630s when he suspected that
his correspondents might find his actions or judgments questionable he
tended to explain himself to them; even, rather unexpectedly, to Sir
Francis Windebank. By 1646 he was faced with distinctly more robust
argument than he had ever been likely to encounter from his old Secretary of State. Henry Jermyn and John Culpeper, writing to the king from
Paris, were astonishingly blunt in their criticisms of his intended
responses to the Newcastle Propositions.[23] They agreed that he should
do all in his power to maintain the episcopacy. If, however, he meant that
under divine law no Christian church could be acknowledged as such
without bishops, they must 'craue leaue wholy to differ'. If in error on
this point, they were, they wrote, in good company: even at the Treaty of
Uxbridge, none of his divines would maintain this 'we might say uncharitable' opinion. The king was not obliged to perish along with his
bishops out of pity '(& certainly you haue nothing els left to assist them
with)'. While recognizing that manuscript survival is such a matter of
chance that it is always a risk to argue anything on its basis, for Charles
such outspokenness from his followers must have been unprecedented,
at least in writing; there is nothing like it earlier. In response he chose
not simply to assert his regal authority, but to argue back. This is not to
suggest that he made no use of his sovereignty; but he did so in subtle
ways, constructing in these letters a persona through which he could
cajole rather than command them into agreement. He was sure he was

---

[21]   Epiplexis: a form of rhetorical question intended to reproach or upbraid; used rela-
       tively often by Charles in his private letters and also found in his later public messages.
[22]   Bodl., MS Clarendon 25, fo. 147, 14 September 1645.
[23]   The Newcastle Propositions: their normal designation by modern historians. Charles
       himself always termed them the London Propositions.

right; but he seems genuinely to have wanted them to agree with him, as he wrote in August 1646: 'thus in my harshe breefe way (not hauing tyme to make large discourses) I doe ~~what I can~~ < my > endeuor to make your judgements concurr with myne'.[24] Like Charles's description of himself as being lazy and ill at words, this self-presentation is, if not exactly disingenuous, somewhat lacking in accuracy. For the first time in years, he did have time to sit down and write 'large discourses', and he proceeded to do so in these long and frequent letters. His 'harshe breefe way' manifested itself in a sermon composed of a series of rhetorical questions rounded off by a sententious chiasmus:

how can I ~~pre~~ keepe that innocency w[ch] you (with so much Reason) oft & earnestly ~~preache~~ < perswade Me > to preserue, if I should abandon the Church? beliue it, Religion is the only firme foundation of all Power; that cast loose, or depraued, no Gouernement can be stable, < for > where was < there > euer obedience where Religion did not teach it? but w[ch] is most of all, how can we expect Gods blessing if we relinquishe his Church? & I am most confident that Religion will much sooner regaine the Militia then the Militia will Religion.

However, the most dramatic method by which Charles appealed to his royalist supporters in Paris, who included John Ashburnham as well as Jermyn and Culpeper, was to present himself to them as a victim, not so much of parliament or the Scots, as of their misunderstanding, compounding the faithlessness (as he saw it) of his followers in London who urged him to accept the Newcastle Propositions. In July he wrote with a strong sense of pathos that 'It is no smale comfort to me to fynde that I haue some frends yet, that nether hath forsaken me nor is doubtfull of me.' By referring to his inconstant supporters as 'Demases', he identified himself as St Paul, imprisoned for his faith.[25] Sarcasm was next employed: 'I am faced doune, that this is all for my seruice, & if I will be ruled by them, I cannot miss to be a great & glorious King, it being upon debat the result of all my faithfull seruants in London.' On the assumption that his recipients would note the irony in the juxtaposition of 'seruice', 'faithfull seruants', and above all 'ruled' with 'great & glorious King', he appealed, with patterned repetition (anaphora), to their contrasting steadfastness:

I conjure you, by your unspotted faithfullness, by all that you loue, by all that is good, that no threatnings no aprehensions of danger to my Person, make you stire one jot from any foundation, in relation to that Authority w[ch] 364: [Prince

---

[24] Bodl., MS Clarendon 91, fo. 28, 19 August 1646.
[25] In the Epistle to Philemon 1:24 Paul refers to Demas as one of his 'fellow labourers', but in 2 Timothy 4:10 writes: 'For Demas hath forsaken me, having loved this present world.'

Charles] is borne to: I haue alreddy cast up what I am lyke to suffer, wch I shall meete (by the grace of God) with that Constancy that befits me; only I desyre that consolation, that asseurance from you, as I may justly hope that my Cause shall not end with my misfortunes by asseuring me that misplaced pittie to me doe not prejudice my Sones right.[26]

By typifying himself as a potential martyr in need of 'consolation' from the purest of his adherents, Charles made it emotionally very difficult for them to argue with him without ceasing to be the paragons he had described. His rejection of 'pittie' while deliberately evoking it is particularly elegant. This evocation of victimhood becomes even more apparent in later letters. He was replying, he wrote, to one of theirs:

with a sader hart then I euer thought that any of you could haue caused, for when those few from whom I can only expect encouradgement in my Constancy shall condem me ~~for~~ <of> willfulness <by it> & ~~of that kynde as~~ <it makes so mee> the distr~~uction~~ <oyer> of my Crowne & family, ~~what joy~~ <how> can you thinke it possible for me to joy in any thing after this? it is such a greefe, that must sinke any honest hart, & I am sure would <soone> doe myne if I did not hope (& that shortly) to make you see & confess your error, nor will it satisfie ~~my~~ <me> that you pitty my misled or too strict Conscience, <no>, I must make you acknowledge, that the giuing <such> way to P[r]esbiteriall Gouer:^{mt} ~~with the absolut abolution of Episcopacie~~ <as will content the Scots> is the absolut distruction of Monarchy, for with it ~~not only~~ Episcopasy must be totally abolished, the dependancy of Church torne from the Crowne & the Couenant firmely established: I hope you will not deny my major, (if you doe, ~~I confess~~ I shall leaue thinking of any thing but how to dye).[27]

These high-flown impassioned sentiments are the outcome of painstaking thought. They may contain an outpouring of genuine emotion, but that emotion is framed in standard rhetorical figures, the effect strengthened by alterations to the detail of the wording. As we can see, Charles first wrote that they were condemning him of wilfulness that would cause the 'distruction' of his crown and family. This he amended to wilfulness that would make him the 'distroyer' of crown and family, the personalization of the word increasing its emotional punch. The grief that would sink any honest heart '& ... would doe myne' has had 'soone' inserted ('would soone doe myne'), while 'I confess' has been deleted before 'I shall leaue thinking of any thing but how to dye', with the same result. When he engaged with their argument, that emphatic – and characteristic – 'no' has been added preceding 'I must make you acknowledge'. It is a powerful piece of writing that draws on the formal principles of classical oratory in its structure and it inspired a similarly

[26]   Bodl., MS Clarendon 97, fo. 23, draft of 22 July 1646.
[27]   *Ibid.*, fo. 41, draft of 31 August 1646.

magniloquent response without in the least having the intended effect.[28] Jermyn and Culpeper replied with equal sadness that their letters to him and his to them met with the same fate: neither having any effect 'upon the understanding to the ends they were intended for', and making no impression other 'then by adding affliction to affliction the tender sence where with should perpetually silence vs (as to this subject) if there were lesse concerned in the Question then your Crowne lyfe Posterity & Monarchy it selfe'.[29] Given the stakes involved, they presumed on his goodness to offer their own opinions; which, as we have already seen, they did with remarkable freedom.

Finding pathos unsuccessful, Charles turned to indignant sarcasm and world-weary cynicism, asking them to excuse his vanity in believing that he had as much knowledge as any of them on the implications of Presbyterian government; dismissing their argument on Ireland as 'a poore jugling answer, & such a one that the silliest understanding must easily detect'.[30] '[S]uppose they thanke me for my Concessions & demur upon the rest, what then? ... I may expect the rest when all the lower house turns Saints, or Mankynde leaues Factions.'[31] In changing his approach, Charles also changed the register of his language: the lofty terms of his earlier letters are correspondingly exchanged for a bluntly abrupt lexicon: 'for the rest < I confess > it smels much of the owld straine'. The king endorsed the letter 'To Lord: Jermyn: Lord: Culpeper: & Iohn: Ashburnham: 21: Sep: 1646 by London sensure upon theire draught for an Answer to the Pro[ns].'

Two weeks later, in a letter that combined this sarcasm with the pathos of the earlier correspondence, he half apologized for chiding them, assuring them that he had no doubts as to their loyalty, fidelity and affection. There is a significant deletion at the end, though, where he concluded with 'nether anger nor greefe shall make me forgett my frendship to you'; this originally read 'my frendship to those who will harken & submitt to Reason'.[32] There is no way of knowing, of course, which version, if either, was a truer reflection of Charles's feelings, but his letter of a week later suggests that he was becoming tired of the

---

[28] See Richard A. Lanham, *A Handlist of Rhetorical Terms*, 2nd edn (Berkeley, CA, 1991), pp. 171–4: in his letters to his Paris correspondents Charles followed the arrangement of a classical oration, though not all elements are present in every letter.

[29] Bodl., MS Clarendon 91, fos. 35–6. Jermyn and Culpeper to Charles, 18/28 September 1646. Deciphered version of letter in Charles's hand.

[30] *Ibid.*, fo. 38, draft of 21 September 1646. He emphasized his condemnation of their intelligence by inserting 'at first sight' after 'must'.

[31] In his use of the word 'Saints', Charles may be playing ironically on its employment by Calvinists to refer to God's elect.

[32] Bodl., MS Clarendon 91, fo. 47, draft of 3 October 1646.

seemingly interminable argument: 'but to vindicat my selfe from the slander of Willfullness (& of that horrid Nature as to Cause the distruction of my Crowne Family & Frends) I would haue beene sylent, my desyre of being rightly understood by my best Frends, forcing this Answer from me'.[33] Making himself rightly understood had ceased to be a simple and public assertion of monarchical will, becoming rather a protracted and tedious wrangle with his closest supporters.

The letters that Charles was writing to the queen at this time tend to follow the same pattern as the earlier ones captured at Naseby, although he argued with her rather more freely than before, particularly on the subjects of Presbyterianism and the militia. While the variety of style and tone found in his letters to Jermyn, Culpeper and Ashburnham is lacking, the objective is much the same. Reading these letters to Henrietta Maria on their own, or without sufficient regard for their rhetorical style, can, as demonstrated above, give the impression that Charles placed more weight on the assurance of her love than on his own beliefs or principles. The sentiment that 'I hope, (whatsoeuer becomes of me), to haue this Comfort that I shall not in any kynde be lessened in thy opinion, wch is the only thing that can make him truly miserable who is eternally Thyne' is typical of those expressed by him.[34] However, the assertion made by John Bruce in the introduction to his edition of the king's 1646 letters to her, that 'the fortunes of England were laid with the most abject humility at the feet of this imperious lady' is deeply misleading, not only in terms of content, but in its misunderstanding of their literary style.[35] The 'abject humility' that Bruce evidently found so contemptible was, as in Charles's earlier letters, the king's very conventional mode of expressing his undoubtedly deeply felt love for his wife. Nevertheless the letters suggest clearly that while he wanted her to agree with him and respected her opinions, he was not looking to her for decisions: 'thyne of the 23: gaue me much comfort to fynde thy judgement of Affaires so right in all foundamentalls, not without some wonder that in some particulars thou canst be so mistaken'.[36] In a letter of 21 November it is made evident that, in his view, what would make him unworthy of her love was his acting not against her advice but against God:

I made that basse unworthy concession concerning Straford; for w^{ch} ~~as~~ < & > lykewais ~~the~~ < for that > great wronge & unjustice to the Church, of ~~turning~~

---

[33]   *Ibid.*, fo. 51, draft of 10 October 1646.
[34]   *Ibid.*, fo. 64, draft of 16–17 October 1646.
[35]   John Bruce (ed.), *Charles I in 1646: Letters of King Charles the First to Queen Henrietta Maria* (Camden Society, Series I (63), 1856), p. xxvi.
[36]   Bodl., MS Clarendon 91, fo. 73, draft of 5 December 1646.

< taking a way > the Bishops Votes in Parlament, < though as > I haueing beene most justly punished, yo < yet > I hope that God will so accept, of my harty, houeuer weake, Repentance, & my constant adhering to my Conscience, that at last his Mercy will take place of his Iustice; but a new relaps (such as abjuration of Episcopacy, or my engagement, without reserue, for the perpetwall establishing of Presb^all: Gouernement) will both procure Gods further wrath upon me as also make me inconstant in all my other Grounds, such a negligent dispaire must < in such a Case > posesse my spirit; wherfor, Deare hart, albeit thou art < may be > sory for my Perswasion, yet I know that what I haue sayd, will make thee desyre me, rather to be constant to, then change my Resolution.[37]

If he frequently expressed the need for Henrietta Maria's approval, he was even more insistent that 'if I should forsake my own Conscience, I cannot be true to or worthy of thee'.[38]

The deliberately constructed nature of Charles's letters to Paris, whether in their deployment of victimhood as a form of emotional blackmail, their offended sarcasm, or passionate desire for harmony with his wife, can be seen most clearly when they are read alongside the king's other correspondence of the same period, in which he employs quite different styles. A few days before Charles sternly preached in his 'harshe breefe way' to the triumvirate in Paris, the marquis of Ormond (who probably had more reason to be driven to despair by his king than almost any other of his followers) can hardly have been cheered by receiving a jocular letter complaining of being unable to read his dispatches because of the use of an old cypher: 'aske Digby (for this I lay to his, not your, falt) if he & I, did not chyde one an other hansomly, in an other Cypher, alitle before I cam from Oxford? ... well, a smale pennance shall expiat this Cryme: Now as to my Business, I must doe lyke a Man in the darke, groape & goe slowly'.[39] It is difficult to understand how this can have appeared to Charles to be the appropriate tone to adopt. Perhaps its light-heartedness was intended to deflect attention from his sidestepping of responsibility for Ireland; if so, it seems unlikely to have succeeded.

Correspondence with Hamilton in 1646, and the following year with his brother William, earl of Lanark, is similarly couched in wholly dissimilar terms from those of the letters to Paris, though it is no less carefully structured than they are. Charles wrote to Hamilton and Lanark in a much more down-to-earth way, selling itself as open and candid, and decorated with allusions appropriate to this 'plain style': familiar Latin

---

[37] Bodl., MS Clarendon 97, fo. 55.
[38] *Ibid.*, fo. 64, draft of 16–17 October 1646.
[39] Bodl., MS Clarendon 98, fo. 119, 15 August 1646.

tags, references to a song, a fable by Gabriel Faerne (misattributed to Aesop), and a Scottish proverb.

Hamilton had expressed his desire to retire abroad, and the king, whatever his private suspicions of the duke as expressed to Henrietta Maria, wished to dissuade him. This, though the entire purpose of his letter of September 1646, is deferred until its end, presented as an afterthought, although Charles opened with a claim to be in haste:

> I haue so much to wryte & so litle tyme for it, that this letter willbe sutable to the tymes, without Method or Reason, & yet you will fynde lusty Trueths in it, wch puts me againe out of fashon, but the fitter for him to whom I wryte: now to my Business; but least I should forget it; I must first tell you, that I heare those at London thinkes to gett me into theire hands, by telling our Countrymen that they doe not intend to make me a Prisoner, o by no meanes, but only to giue me an Honnorable Guard forsuth.[40]

After amplifying his own feelings about being abandoned in England, and assuming, in parentheses, that he could leave it to the duke to make these known, he closed this passage with the business-like 'so much for that'. So, having flattered Hamilton and appealed to him as a fellow-Scot, he also called on his sense of responsibility (and, perhaps, vanity) by suggesting that he would know without further instruction how to disseminate Charles's views on his imprisonment in England for the king's 'best aduantage'. Before even touching on the question of the duke's departure, a task had been given to him that would make his leaving a little more difficult.

Charles then almost casually referred to Hamilton's decision to leave for Europe ('I esteemed you a Man no more of this part of the World'), and disclaimed any premeditated intention of raising the subject because he had believed the duke's decision to be 'lyke the Lawes of the Meds & Persians': that is, unalterable. Robert Murray (or Moray) having mentioned that this might not be the case, Charles thought that perhaps he might 'stay your Forraine Iurney by Perswasion'. He did not, however, continue by any obvious attempt at persuasion, instead referring Hamilton to 'Robin' for the arguments. However, the apparent digression in the opening paragraph ('I must first tell you') is crucial: juxtaposed with the reference to the law of the Medes and Persians, it allows Charles implicitly to identify himself with Daniel about to be cast into the lions' den for remaining steadfast to religious truth. The Scots are thereby envisaged as the honourable and well-meaning king Darius, tricked by envious princes into having Daniel thrown into the den; from which, of course, he was delivered by God for his innocence and faith.[41]

---

[40]   NAS, GD 406/1/170, 26 September 1646.
[41]   Daniel 6.

The impression of busy spontaneity given by brisk syntax, exclamatory interjections, digression (itself a formal rhetorical technique), and the shameless claim to be written without method or reason, camouflages what is in reality an expertly crafted work making the strongest possible appeal to the duke's sense of duty. Only a few days earlier the king had written of his 'unexpressable greefe & astonishment' to Jermyn, Culpeper and Ashburnham concerning their proposed answer to the Newcastle Propositions. His entirely different approach to Hamilton was clearly tailored to its recipient. Moreover, it worked: pressured by both his brother Lanark and the king, Hamilton remained in Scotland.

The complexity of this letter is unmatched in Charles's letters to Lanark, who superseded Hamilton in 1647 as the king's chief Scottish correspondent. The manner adopted is not unlike that used in 1642 to the earl of Newcastle, though with rather less of the 'man-to-man' tone in it. While a sense of urgency generated by the circumstances of his imprisonment may have been the primary cause of this blunt style, Charles must also have believed that the earl would not respond negatively to it. Nevertheless, the king clearly took pains as to how this urgency would be best conveyed. In a letter of September 1647, written from Hampton Court, Charles chose epiplectic questions and terse precepts capped by an appropriately Scottish proverb. Like many of Charles's most carefully shaped pieces of writing, it is not only very tidy, but heavily overpunctuated. The sense of immediacy is deliberately formulated:

is this a tyme for Scotland to vye punctillios of Honnor with England? & therby neglect, euen almost to loose, the oportunity, of rediming that falt wch they committed at NewCastell? ... In a word; tyme is not altogether lost; redeeme it for shame; ... remember the Prouerb: *Il Bairnes are best hard at heme.*[42]

John Scally's assessment of Lanark cites comparisons made by Gilbert Burnet and Sir Philip Warwick between the two Hamiltons. Burnet wrote of William that he was 'brisker, so he was the more frank' than his elder brother, while Warwick described James as preferring to gain his point by 'serpentine winding ... which was very contrary to the nature of his younger Brother'.[43] Perhaps Charles made the same judgment about them and adapted his style accordingly.

Until 1648 the recipients of the letters written personally by the king were members of his family, Court, political and ecclesiastical bureaucracy or military command. Imprisoned in Carisbrooke Castle from mid-November 1647, and with his own attendants dismissed, Charles

---

[42]   NAS, GD 406/1/2174, 10 September 1647.
[43]   John Scally, 'William Hamilton, Second Duke of Hamilton', *Oxford DNB*.

came to rely on a very small and rather less grand group of supporters, both inside the castle (until they too were removed following the king's failed attempt at escape) and in the Isle of Wight. Chief among these were Henry Firebrace, Silius Titus and Sir William Hopkins;[44] Jane Whorwood could be added to this trio, although only two letters to her from Charles survive.[45] The judgment that these were the most significant of Charles's local correspondents is based not only on the accident of manuscript survival, but on the frequency of cross-reference in the king's letters to each of the recipients.

Because Charles no longer dared to keep drafts and very few letters that were sent to Europe by him have survived, no comparison can be made with what he was writing to Henrietta Maria or his followers in exile at this time. Nevertheless, what is most unexpected about his letters to Firebrace, Titus and Hopkins is that if they are read with no prior knowledge of the relative status of the correspondents, it would be impossible to guess that they are from a monarch (let alone one who had shown himself so concerned with the maintenance of hierarchy) to rather minor members of the gentry. Charles addresses them in an open, easy, cordial way: 'I pray you thinke well upon it, for I am most confident that I am in the right; yet, for Gods sake, make your objections freely to what I haue said; or, if you doe not understand me, tell me in what, & I hope, that I shall satisfie you'; 'I haue receaued this Morning your yesterdays letter ... being extream glad that you understand & approue of my Answer.'[46] It could be argued that there were purely pragmatic reasons for this, constituting a further safeguard against his letters being identified in addition to the employment of cypher and Charles's use of his disguised 'slow hand' rather than his normal italic. The king's occasional references to himself in the third person would lend support to this explanation if they were not so rare,[47] and if he were not otherwise so

---

[44] Both Firebrace and Titus were appointed by parliament to serve Charles early in 1647; the latter was later marked on a list of cypher names by Firebrace as having 'Prou'd faulty', though there is no other evidence that this was so. Hopkins was traditionally identified as schoolmaster of the Newport grammar school, but seems rather to have been a member of the local gentry of whom little is known (he merits no *Oxford DNB* entry). His wife, however, was the sister of Sir David Kirke, an adventurer made first governor of Newfoundland by Charles in 1639, and it seems possible that this connection was the origin of his friendship with the king.

[45] See my article 'Deciphering the King: Charles I's Letters to Jane Whorwood', *Seventeenth Century*, 21 (2006), 128–40.

[46] BL, Egerton MS 1533, fo. 11, to Titus, [n.d., c. 12 April 1648]; Royal Library, MS RICN 1080413 (unfoliated), to Hopkins, 17 July 1648.

[47] See, for example, BL, Egerton MS 1788, fo. 41, to Firebrace, 1 August 1648: 'I haue now written clearly to E: [Lady Carlisle] concerning what the king said of the Gouernor.'

unguarded, particularly in his correspondence with Hopkins. Since it was also the latter whom he addressed with the greatest personal freedom, and with whom he used no cypher other than for names, pragmatism alone is not a sufficient motive. Charles's letters to the younger men, Titus and Firebrace, were largely concerned with various escape plans, in relation to which he asked their advice, argued and became excited about their increasingly unrealistic suggestions (usually known to the Derby House Committee almost as soon as they had been made). The social status of these correspondents seems to have been wholly irrelevant to him. This is even more true of the older Hopkins, on whom his dependence appears not merely practical but emotional: they had become friends. He apologized for his 'sower lookes', explaining that 'I had so ma[n]y things that day in my head, that I wonder not though euery one thought that I looked doggedly on them'.[48] He sent little messages to Hopkins's wife and complained, perhaps teasingly, when she visited the castle without speaking to him. It was, of course, Hopkins's house that he stayed in during the negotiations for the Treaty of Newport. One of Charles's last letters was to Sir William, written from Windsor Castle on 30 December 1648, expressing his contentment that the latter had succeeded in finding a way of continuing their correspondence.

Caution, however, must be exercised. If the king was so skilled in adjusting his writing to suit circumstance and person, is it possible to distinguish what he really felt towards his recipients at this time? There can be no certain answer to this. Indeed, in a letter to Hopkins requesting him to convey his thanks to '49', Charles advised 'for the expressions I leaue to you; only, lett them be harty, & kinde, generalls, sutable to the humor, & quality, of the Man'.[49] He clearly wrote with this final tenet, to suit expression to the recipient, in mind. A sentiment that is constructed in identifiable rhetorical figures may be none the less real for being so; conversely, one that is more simply expressed, and therefore appears less artificial, may rather be an example of plain style 'sutable to the quality of the Man'. Nevertheless, when the choices made by the king in his manner of writing are assessed on the basis of need, they provide evidence as to how to judge them. After his accession to the throne, Charles wrote to very few people with the openness seen in his letters to Sir William Hopkins in 1648, for which there was no practical necessity. Hopkins's side of the correspondence was presumably burnt by Charles, but he obviously expressed himself with a degree of freedom, which was evidently accepted by the king without demur. The self-image so skilfully

---

[48]   Royal Library, MS RICN 1080413, 2 September 1648.
[49]   *Ibid.*, 23 July 1648.

constructed by and for Charles cloaks the human being from us throughout most of his life, and especially after he became king, but there are
moments in his letters from Carisbrooke when he becomes a little more
visible. He was cut off from friends and, above all, family; evidence from
throughout his life suggests that he was someone with a strong need for
emotional intimacy and support. Sir William Hopkins appears to have
been one of those from whom he gained it in his increasingly despairing
last days in the Isle of Wight. Charles wrote to him in October 1648 that:

> to deale freely with you, the great Concession I made this day, was meerely in
> order to my escape of w^{ch}, if I had not hope, I would not haue done; for then I
> could haue returned, to my straight Prison, without reluctancy, but now I con-
> fess it would breake my hart; hauing done that, wch only an escape can justefy.[50]

The wording of the letter bears signs of characteristic attempts at rhetorical control aimed at strengthening the urgency of its message, but
also manifests uncharacteristically unconcealed fear and desperation to
escape, tinged with shame at the terms he had accepted. Perhaps Charles
did not mind revealing himself in this way to Hopkins; or perhaps, for
a time, the burden of maintaining the kingly image had become too great.
That this might be the case is suggested in a letter to his twelve-year-old
daughter Elizabeth written a few days later, in which his dejection is
obvious:

> it is not want of Affection that makes me write so seldome to you, but want of
> matter such as I could wishe; & indeed I am loathe to write to those I loue, when
> I am out of humore, (as I haue beene these Dayes by past,) least my letters should
> troble those I desyre to please; but hauing this oportunety I would not loose it;
> though, at this tyme, I haue nothing to say, but God bless you.[51]

Of all of the king's surviving correspondence, this offers the most transparent and unvarnished testimony to his state of mind. There is no effort
here to convey an emotion appropriate to the occasion, as happened so
obviously in the letters to Paris, or even in those to Hopkins. Perhaps for
that reason it is a letter that still has power to move its readers. It is
unfortunate for Charles that his other letters rarely achieved the same
effect.

---

[50]   Royal Library, MS RICN 1080413, 9 October 1648. The 'great Concession' almost
certainly refers to the king's second 'Paper concerning ye Church' (Bodl., MS
Clarendon 33, fos. 54–7), although he also submitted an answer on the militia the same
day.
[51]   BL, Sloane MS 3299, fo. 145, 14 October 1648.

8   Royalists and the New Model Army in 1647: circumstance, principle and compromise

Rachel Foxley

In the summer of 1647 the parliamentarian New Model Army decisively asserted its right to act according to its own political conscience, defying parliament's attempt to disband it. Some royalists were prepared to go a long way towards rapprochement with the army, defending its actions as a return to true obedience – to the king – and urging army and king to make a deal which would restore Charles I but protect the interests of the soldiers. Among the army and their political allies the Independents there were men who were also interested in just such a settlement, and some of them, as well as some of the royalists, began to advocate such a solution publicly almost as soon as the army gained custody of the king.

This potential rapprochement invites two extremes of interpretation. One is to see these moves as simple switches of allegiance: these particular army men had simply become royalists, or at least flirted with something that was recognizably 'royalism'. Those historians who deploy the terms 'royalism' of New Model Army men, or 'crypto-royalism' of some Presbyterian and City ringleaders, may be boxing themselves into an overly rigid framework in which 'parliamentarian' and 'royalist' identities are fossilized and all the historical actors can do is change one for the other. Given how much we know about the complexities of politics *within* each side, this seems a peculiarly reductive model of the relationship *between* the sides. Alternatively, we might think that civil war politics was a constant game of political recalculation and reorientation based on the 'interests' of various factions and micro-factions, and that the events of 1647 are a perfectly normal example of this. This would be a significant misrepresentation in the other direction: during the Civil War period many people developed a keen sense of their own, and their enemies', political identities: indeed the seventeenth-century labels have become part of the historiography. For a 'Cavalier' and an 'Independent' to start talking publicly about uniting their interests behind a particular kind of settlement was likely to be distinctly uncomfortable for both of them. David Scott, as part of a brilliant analysis of the factional politics of these years, has suggested that 'there are grounds for arguing that the fundamental division in British politics by late 1646 was no longer that of royalist versus parliamentarian and Covenanter, but between Hyde's royalist 'patriots' and leading Independents on the one hand, and the covenanting interest and pro-Scots royalists on the other.'[1] Maybe; but would any contemporary have been capable of viewing the situation in those terms?

This chapter approaches the thinking of royalists and of army men and Independents through published works which illuminate the genuine strains of this rapprochement as well as the grounds on which it could occur. Adopting Jason McElligott's helpful stricture that 'royalists' are those who are intent on achieving the best possible settlement for the king (and not just restoring him on their own terms),[2] this chapter examines some published writings which are clearly royalist in this sense, and which in some cases make clear that their authors are coming from a position of committed royalism, rather than being new advocates of the king's rights. When I refer to 'royalist' tracts and authors, these are the criteria on which I have labelled them. The royalist group of tracts includes works by David Jenkins, but also other (mostly anonymous) pamphlets. From the other side of this potential rapprochement, this chapter looks at published writings by army men and Independents. Here I pick out in particular a series of works (which I will call the 'army-radical' pamphlets) which were printed on the press obtained by Sexby and operated by Henry Hills and John Harris on behalf of the agitators, and which have been identified and discussed by Michael Mendle.[3] In addition I will look at other tracts, again often anonymous, which identify themselves as being from the viewpoint of 'Independents' or the army, but which show no particular sign of originating from radical circles.

It is of course well known that the army leadership in the summer of 1647 negotiated with the king on the basis of the *Heads of the Proposals*;[4] in the rank-and-file of the army, too, historians have seen signs of a surprising willingness to contemplate a speedy settlement with the king (at

---

[1]   David Scott, *Politics and War in the Three Stuart Kingdoms, 1637–49* (Basingstoke, 2004), p. 122.

[2]   Jason McElligott, *Royalism, Print and Censorship in Revolutionary England* (Woodbridge, 2007).

[3]   Michael Mendle, 'Putney's Pronouns: Identity and Indemnity in the Great Debate', in Mendle (ed.), *The Putney Debates of 1647: the Army, the Levellers, and the English State* (Cambridge, 2001). The four 'army-radical' pamphlets which I discuss here are: 'Amon Wilbee', *Plaine Truth without Feare or Flattery* (Oxford, [2 July] 1647), attributed in its second edition to 'I. L.', intended to be understood as John Lilburne; *The Grand Informer. Or the Prerogative of Princes, Priviledge of Parliaments, Propriety of the Subject* (Oxford, [15 July] 1647); I[ohn] H[arris], *The Antipodes, or Reformation with the Heeles Upward* ([22 July] 1647); *The Grand Account* (Oxford, [29 July] 1647).

[4]   David L. Smith, *Constitutional Royalism and the Search for Settlement, c. 1640–1649* (Cambridge, 1994), pp. 132–4, on the genuine army origins of the *Heads*.

the expense of the Presbyterians in parliament).[5] Mark Kishlansky sees a willingness to offer an honourable settlement to the king as part of an 'army' ideology which was relatively solid and untroubled through the ranks. Morrill and Baker, keen to undermine any idea that the grandees were royalist and the rank-and-file anti-monarchist radicals, have argued – with an element of truth – that divisions over the issue of the king at Putney in the autumn were vertical rather than horizontal.[6] As suggested above, these feelings within the army should not be labelled simply as 'royalist', and this chapter will look at the precise nature of the views expressed about the king and the political situation by army men and Independents. Michael Mendle, although he does label the army-radical tracts 'royalist', opens up more provocatively the question of the *nature* of this 'royalism', and proposes a different kind of split between the radicals and the grandees: essentially one between conservative royalist grandees and radical royalist activists. For Mendle the 'royalism' of the agitators in the spring and summer becomes comprehensible when it is seen as a different type of royalism from that which their leaders were expressing. Radicals found appealing the notion of a king who was indeed naturally in authority over them – but equally over their leaders and social superiors; not at the pinnacle of a hierarchy, but 'outside and beyond it altogether', like the popular monarchs who might seem to be more on the side of a humble apprentice than of their own courtiers in a Deloney romance. Mendle amplifies the usual explanation that it was simply spiralling distrust which drove a wedge between radicals and grandees in the autumn, suggesting that it was due to the realization of the radicals that they would not be able to achieve the restoration of the type of non-hierarchical kingship which could have secured them; on the contrary, they began to see a conspiracy of their social superiors with the king which would entrench tyranny over them even more firmly.[7]

My conclusion about the types of royalism which were attractive to the army, and particularly to the radicals, differs from Mendle's. The issue which was likely to be the greatest sticking point for the radicals

---

[5] Austin Woolrych, *Soldiers and Statesmen* (Oxford, 1987), pp. 69–71, 142–3; Ian Gentles, *The New Model Army in England, Ireland and Scotland, 1645–1653* (Oxford, 1992), pp. 153–4, 171 (suggesting that there was a basic unity of purpose in the army in favour of an honourable restoration of the king); p. 215 on the change of mood by the time of Putney, when the king's flirtations with the Scots were becoming known.

[6] Mark Kishlansky, 'Ideology and Politics in the Parliamentary Armies, 1645–9', in John Morrill (ed.), *Reactions to the English Civil War* (1982); John Morrill and Philip Baker, 'The Case of the Armie Truly Re-stated', in Michael Mendle (ed.), *Putney Debates of 1647*, p. 123. The element of truth is that William Allen professed himself willing to see the king restored, while Cromwell himself seemed rather more troubled at the prospect.

[7] Michael Mendle, 'Putney's Pronouns', in Mendle, *Putney Debates*, pp. 134–6.

was one of political principle: the uniqueness of the king's power. Certainly for the Levellers, and probably for many in the army, the extension of 'kingly' (or even 'tyrannical') powers throughout society,[8] meant that it was reasonable to 'balance' the dangers of these powers as exercised by different persons or bodies: at some points the king might be the least dangerous. For grandees as well as radicals this was because government, whether of the king or of parliament, rested ultimately on consent and trust, and the king *was* in some sense accountable to his people. As Cromwell pointed out at Putney, even the grandees had not entirely flattered the king, insisting that 'the King is king by contract'.[9] For royalists, in contrast, the king's unique power was precisely what gave him the ability to offer a secure settlement to the soldiers, and while they might accept consent theory to explain the role of parliament, royalists – however 'constitutional' – would certainly not accept it to explain the role of the king.[10] Thus this chapter argues that throughout all of these army and Independent tracts, even the army-radical tracts, one sees not Mendle's non-hierarchical royalism, but a contractual approach to the monarchy, whose evils can be balanced against the tyranny of an also supposedly contractual parliament. This view of the king's potential role meant that collaboration with long-term royalists had to gloss over certain fundamental differences of view – and this is apparent in the sometimes strained rhetoric of both sides of the alliance.

We will see that there were some substantial grounds on which authors on both sides could base their arguments for a novel alliance between the king and the army that had been fighting against him. However what is initially striking is the enormous rhetorical difficulty, for authors on both sides, of making this case. The pamphleteers were well aware that the views both they and their opponents were associated with might need to be reassessed or explained away before the alliance could become a realistic option. One royalist author cleared the way for an alliance with the Independents by admitting that some of their writings suggested that they were 'worse principled for Magistracy' than the Presbyterians, but drew on his personal dealings with Independents to demonstrate their fairness, civility and piety.[11] Both sets of authors were

---

[8]   David Loewenstein, 'The King among the Radicals', in Thomas Corns (ed.), *The Royal Image: Representations of Charles I* (Cambridge, 1999), on the widespread radical perception that the king was not the only exerciser of 'kingly' power.

[9]   A. S. P. Woodhouse, *Puritanism and Liberty: being the Army Debates (1647–9), from the Clarke Manuscripts* (London, 1938), p. 96.

[10]   Smith, *Constitutional Royalism*, ch. 7.

[11]   *An Answer to a Letter concerning the Kings going from Holdenby to the Army* ([17 June] 1647), pp. 2–3.

aware of the labels attaching to themselves, and their presumed allegiances, and might go out of their way to explain why they were now changing their alignments. One author pleaded with his correspondent 'Mistake me not yet, Sir, I am ... no Pleader for Episcopacy; I am an Independent ... still I am, as I was then, a perfect Bishop-hater' – even though he was now contemplating concessions to episcopacy. In politics he was still a parliamentarian, but now only 'politickly' rather than 'sincerely', as he had realized the need to repent and offer his support to Charles I – through the agency of the New Model Army.[12] Labels of allegiance were very consciously at issue in these pamphlet debates, and could be qualified to make the new alignments less of a stretch – hence such titles as *A Letter Really Written by a Moderate Cavalier to an Intelligent and Moderate Independent*.[13] One of the army-radical tracts, having made its case, also felt the need to protest that 'I speak not in favour of his Majestie further then conscience and equity', perhaps implying that someone who could fairly be called a royalist would not be so critical.[14]

So what caused these people to reassess their alignments in such potentially uncomfortable ways? One overriding issue was freedom of conscience, widely seen to be seriously imperilled by any forthcoming Presbyterian settlement. Clearly for the Independents, and their more radical allies in the army, religious freedom was a crucial precondition for any treaty with the king. The king, too, was presented by both royalists and army men and Independents as desiring freedom of conscience in his own right; it was pointedly reported by many proponents of a deal in the wake of the seizing of the king at Holmby that under the army's custody he was allowed access to his chaplains. Authors on both sides – at least if they were unaware of the less demanding private terms being offered to the king by English and Scottish Presbyterians – might well feel that a guarantee of liberty of conscience might be welcome to a king who was otherwise faced with a requirement to sign the Solemn League and Covenant.[15] The material which followed the seizure of the king, emanating both from army/Independent and from royalist sources, emphasizes freedom of conscience as a common desire binding the king and his new gaolers: the king had been denied his choice of chaplains,

---

[12] *A Letter of an Independent, to his Honoured Friend in London* ([21 June] 1647), pp. 3, 7–8.
[13] Dated '26 June' 1647 by George Thomason.
[14] 'Amon Wilbee', *Plaine Truth without Feare or Flattery* ([2 July] 1647), p. 18. Attributed in its second edition to 'I. L.', intended to be understood as John Lilburne.
[15] Scott, *Politics and War*, pp. 133, 143–4; Gardiner (ed.), *CDPR*, pp. 291–2; Smith, *Constitutional Royalism*, pp. 129–131, on the king's absolute refusal to compromise on religion, even when urged to by his counsellors.

and the army promised him his freedom of conscience if they might have theirs. The royalist *Answer to a Letter* both made clear the need to fulfil the Independent desire for freedom of conscience, and suggested the reciprocal nature of it: 'as they [the Independents] desire to exercise no severe jurisdiction over other men's consciences, so they seeme to desire in like manner that none may over theirs'.[16] All of the royalists who wanted the New Model Army to act to restore the king made a point of conceding freedom of conscience for the Independents. David Jenkins included the demand in his standard litany of requests at the end of each of his pamphlets, but even the wilier but less tactful royalist pamphlet *The Riddles Unridled* was careful to applaud sectaries as better and more loyal protestants than the 'king-selling' presbyters.[17] Marchamont Nedham was one of those apparently tempted over (for the time being) to the royalist side for reasons which included the need to secure freedom of conscience; crossing over in the other direction was John Hall, at this point a royalist, but to become a republican early in 1648: it is interesting that Hall was the kind of royalist who did support a degree of freedom of conscience and a limited episcopacy, and felt that at an earlier stage in the summer Fairfax had missed a reasonable chance of restoring Charles I on this basis.[18]

On the Independent and army side of the alliance, there was scope for an acknowledgement that freedom of conscience cut both ways, and that they might have to accept the re-establishment of a (non-compulsive) national church structure which they had worked hard to dismantle and found it difficult in conscience to accept. The 'Bishop-hater' we met above had come to the conclusion that 'Episcopacy may stand, and we enjoy our Consciences; Presbytery will not allow it.'[19] Such a limited episcopacy was of course the solution proposed by the army and Independent grandees later in the summer.[20] Some royalists, too, were happy with that proposal. Jenkins is typical of David Smith's

[16] *An Answer to a Letter* ([17 June] 1647), pp. 3–4.
[17] *The Riddles Unridled* ([14 July] 1647), p. 10.
[18] Marchamont Nedham, *The Case of the Kingdom Stated, According to the Proper Interests of the Severall Parties Ingaged* ([12 June] 1647); Nedham, *The Lavvyer of Lincolnes-Inne Reformed: Or, An Apology for the Army* ([1 July] 1647); John Hall, *A True Account and Character of the Times, Historically and Politically Drawn by a Gentleman to give Satisfaction to his Friend in the Countrey* ([9 August] 1647), p. 7. Joad Raymond, 'Nedham, Marchamont (*bap.* 1620, *d.* 1678)', *Oxford DNB*; Joad Raymond, 'Hall, John (*bap.* 1627, *d.* 1656)', *Oxford DNB*. On Nedham's career see Jason McElligott, *Royalism, Print and Censorship*, ch. 4 which emphasizes that Nedham's royalism from 1647–9 was more committed than sheer anti-presbyterianism can explain.
[19] *A letter of an Independent*, p. 5.
[20] Articles XI–XII of the *Heads of the Proposals*: Gardiner (ed.), *CDPR*, p. 321.

'constitutional royalist' sympathizers in this and in making much of the fact that he had opposed the excesses of the Laudian bishops.[21] There was potential for a genuine middle ground to be found which could serve the interests of both royalists and Independents in avoiding the feared Presbyterian tyranny over consciences.

Common enemies could be a powerful uniter. There is no avoiding the fact that the Presbyterians, considered both religiously and politically, were powerfully resented by both royalists and radicals; linked to this was the anti-Scottish feeling which had become crucial to the cohesion of the 'Independents' as a political force in England. The fact that royalists might have equally strong reasons for distrusting the Scots ('the first Nation that ever I read of who *sold their King*'[22]) lent significant rhetorical possibilities to the advocates of an army-royalist solution. Nedham, coming around to a royalist view and defending the actions of the army, saw only the 'Scottish-mist' of the Presbyterians and their allies to the north as obscuring the advantages of an alliance between the king and the army.[23]

But the rhetoric of parliamentary tyranny was perhaps an even more powerful uniter of erstwhile enemies. This is key to the alliances explored in this chapter, and while it was far more than just a rhetorical trope for both sides, it did offer a satisfying rhetorical means of playing up the potential unity between them. The fear of parliamentary tyranny was immediate and overwhelming for the threatened New Model in the spring and summer of 1647; royalists had been making mileage out of parliamentary illegality since the start of the conflict. Shared horror at the actions of parliament could be exploited particularly well when parliament's propagandists justified its actions by necessity rather than law, explicitly arguing that law could be overridden. The widely appealing language of the common law could then be used in retaliation, and this is clearly one of the points on which Leveller authors could find themselves thinking in parallel with royalists.[24] An alliance partly grounded in such arguments could appeal deeply to the principles of both sides – but the coincidence of principled belief between the two sides might still be partial and unsatisfactory as a basis for a viable deal. Army feelings about parliamentary tyranny ran high during 1647, and the Leveller account of the political principles which could be invoked in understanding and

[21] David Jenkins, *To the Honorable Societies of Gray's-Inne* (28 April 1647), sig. A.
[22] *An Answer to a Letter*, p. 5.
[23] Nedham, *The Lavvyer of Lincolnes-Inne Reformed*, p. 4.
[24] Martin Dzelzainis, 'History and Ideology: Milton, the Levellers, and the Council of State in 1649', *HLQ*, 68 (2005), for a helpful discussion of the dynamic of the argument between Leveller legalism and parliamentary extra-legalism.

resisting it was certainly useful to army men. But while these feelings enabled army men to build bridges with royalists, it was unlikely to create in them anything that could reasonably be called 'royalism'.

What we do see, rather, are statements comparing parliament unfavourably with the king – under present circumstances; not suggestions that the king's cause was to be preferred. The Leveller John Lilburne may have set the tone for the army radicals, remarking in *Rash Oaths Unwarrantable* that parliamentary tyranny had become worse than that of the king, but not declaring himself for the king.[25] In *The Grand Account*, one of Mendle's 'determinedly royalist' army-radical publications, references to the king were used purely to point up the current tyranny of parliament. The author pointed out with evident approval that the Civil War had been fought to bring about freedom 'after so hard a servitude under an unlimmited Monarchicall power', and was fought so that 'Regall power might be limmited by Law, not proportioned by will'. Clearly this author felt, as royalists would, that there could be a regal power which was not tyrannical; but he did not think that Charles I's rule had exemplified it. The rhetorical point recurring throughout the pamphlet was simply that all that the parliament had said about necessary limits on the king's power must also apply to parliament's power. There was only one suggestion that the king's power was preferable to parliamentary power: talking about the shielding of alleged offenders from justice by Charles, and now in the case of the Eleven Members by parliament, the author wrote that for such an obstruction of justice 'the Kings Prerogative is a much better Plea, then your priviledge'.[26] Clearly he was not endorsing either plea.

Some of the other pamphlets from the army radicals and other Independents did, however, take a further important step: they started to treat the king himself as one of the *victims* of parliamentary tyranny. The author of *A Letter of an Independent* viewed Presbyterian tyranny as a dethroning of the king.[27] 'Amon Wilbee', the author of one of the army-radical tracts, took a similar line about royal rights, both in religion and government. In his *Plaine Truth without Fear or Flattery*, what bridged the gap between army and royalist perspectives was the behaviour of the House of Commons, particularly considered as the work of a Presbyterian faction within it. The whole pamphlet was directed against Presbyterianism, seen as a religious and political force – not

---

[25]   John Lilburne, *Rash Oaths Unwarrantable*, preface dated May 1647 but bought by Thomason on or after 25 June 1647.

[26]   *The Grand Account* (Oxford, [29 July] 1647), pp. 6–7.

[27]   *A Letter of an Independent*, pp. 5–6.

a new theme for Independents and radicals. Yet here, the *radicals'* dislike of Presbyterianism was combined with the notion that such a form of church government was *anti-monarchical* in its refusal to allow the 'Supreme Magistrate' to have a role in religious affairs. The writer argued that Presbyterianism conduces to tyranny, 'even to abolish all rules of Law and civil liberty, it is an antipathy to Monarchy, and the legall power of civill Magistracy and brings under a yoake (where it is predominant) both King and People'.[28] This was a theme also developed in the other works of 'Amon Wilbee': in the first of a tripartite work he argued explicitly that because parliament was controlled by a corrupt faction, the king was preferable.[29]

The Antipodes again stressed the parliament's derelictions of duty, but here the tone and argument may come close to justifying Mendle's label of 'royalism'; the arguments are very close to those found in some of the pamphlets by royalists appealing to the army. MPs, according to this writer, are 'by the free Commons chosen servants, yet by their usurpations become Masters, ney Kings; commanding both King and People without controule'.[30] Their status as chosen trusted representatives ought to limit the Commons; but the status they assumed in overstepping the mark was more like the status of the king – and it does not sound like a very limited kingship. Often in these writings, excessive use of parliamentary 'priviledge' was compared to the exorbitant kingly 'prerogative' which the war had been fought to limit; but in this pamphlet the comparison to prerogative was completely omitted. The writer simply demanded that 'the iust priviledges of the Parliament may be by Declaration made manifest to the Kingdome, and the Kingdome not inslaved by an unknown and unlimitted priviledge'.[31] The pamphleteer used consent theory to taunt England with being 'a servant to thy servant' (the House of Commons), and said that in future it would be said 'that thou brokest the bonds of thy Soveraigne, and became a slave to thy equals'.[32] As in the royalist material, one theory of government seems to apply to parliament, and another to the king. The usefulness of consent theory for this author was simply as a means to deflate the claims of

---

28   *Plaine Truth*, pp. 6–7.
29   'Amon Wilbee', *Prima Pars. De Comparatis Comparandis: seu Iustificationis Regis Caroli, Comparatè, Contra Parliamentum. Or The First Part of Things Compared: or Of the Iustification of King Charles Comparitively Against the Parliament* ([3 July] 1647).
30   I[ohn] H[arris], *The Antipodes, or Reformation with the Heeles Upward* ([22 July] 1647), p. '12'.
31   *The Antipodes*, p. '9'.
32   *The Antipodes*, p. '6'.

parliament: it disposed of the parliament's claims to obedience and left the king intact.

Issues of real political principle could be very hard to negotiate. To establish common ground, both sides resorted to the declared aims of king and parliament in fighting the war. These slogans had been strenuously uncontroversial – indeed, it was hard to tell apart the rallying cries of the two sides – and at this moment of rapprochement they came in extremely useful. In some cases the return to these slogans may reflect a genuine reassessment of commitments – an attempt to establish how deeply held beliefs applied to changed circumstances. Thus the still nominally parliamentarian author of *A Letter of an Independent* argued that although he was a committed parliamentarian, he had never been an opponent of the king, having (foolishly) believed the line that the parliament was fighting to recover the king from the clutches of his evil counsellors. He invoked the stated parliamentarian aims to explain why his political allegiance had now changed:

To preserve our Antient and Fundamentall Lawes, to purchase our just Liberties, To preserve the Kings known Rights, were our solemne Protestations. All these being now like *Sampsons* cords, broken, I believe myself disengaged.[33]

Royalists, too, made use of the similarity of parliamentarian and royalist slogans to demonstrate the potential closeness of honest men on each side. Jenkins made the point most explicitly in a pamphlet of 1648: 'The King and the two Houses of Parliament declaring mutually, that they took up Arms for the same reasons, intents, and purposes, 'tis a wonder how at first they fell out, and a greater wonder that hitherto they are not reconciled.'[34] Jenkins made the charitable assumption that parliamentarian soldiers had fought precisely for the things the parliament declared for – and that they had now realized they had been duped:

the Army doth now evidently perceive, that they were mis-led by the specious pretences of *Salus Populi*, the maintenance of the Kings Honour, and of the maintenance of the Lawes of the Land, and liberties of the Subject, to take up Armes against their naturall Liege Lord and Soveraigne, the King.[35]

The anonymous author of *The Riddles Unridled*, a royalist pamphlet directed at the parliamentarian army, and framed as a defence of them, in mid-July 1647, went even further. He reminded the parliament's army that the Houses declared that they were to fight for 'the Kings Authority

---

[33] *A Letter of an Independent*, pp. 7, 1.
[34] David Jenkins, *A Short, Sure, and Conscientious Expedient for Agreement & Peace* ([31 July] 1648), p. 1.
[35] Jenkins, *An Apology for the Army, Touching the Eight Quaere's upon the Late Declarations* (1647), p. 1.

and his person in his Royall dignity ... the Laws of the Land ... and the just priviledges of Parliament'. He then replied to concern that soldiers who had been in arms against parliament had come into the New Model's ranks by arguing that

> we know not of any English or Irish Souldiers now listed in the Army, that hath heretofore borne Armes against the Parliament, for such as were listed under the Lord *Goring*, or any others by the Kings Commissions were listed, ingaged, and taken on for the defence of his Majesties Royall person, the maintenance and preservation of the known and established Lawes, the just ... Privileges of Parliament, and Properties of the Subject. And if any such are now listed under Sir *Tho. Fairefax*, who heretofore served the K, we know not that they can be imployed for better ends then what they formerly were ingaged to maintain.

Continuing in his utter denial of the categories of the Civil War, he argued that 'those that did formerly serve the King, did not serve against the Parliament; for we hold that the King is a part of the Parliament'.[36] Presumably the converse applied, and parliamentarian soldiers did not need to castigate themselves for any disloyalty to the king, or to fear reprisals from him or his party.

The army-radical pamphlet *The Antipodes* is strikingly similar to the royalist works appealing to the army at this time, particularly in its appeals to the official war aims of parliament, which it saw as utterly hypocritical. Soldiers should 'remember the end of your taking up armes was to defend the Kings maiesty'; the parliament was covenanted 'To preserve and defend the King in his Person and authority, and not to usurpe his power, and imprison his Person'.[37] Obviously this attitude to the hypocrisy of the parliamentarian slogans was the other side of the coin from the more thorough-goingly radical attitude which might require the parliament to admit that it had really been fighting against the king himself, and even (eventually) to put him on trial.

Fleshing out their commitment to the original slogans of both sides, writings from both royalists and army men/Independents tried to emphasize potential middle ground in some form of limited monarchy. We here return to Mendle's question of what *kind* of 'royalism' is discernible in the writings of both sides – or, to put it in more neutral terms, whether the army men and Independents had a view of the king which could ever enable them to make an effective deal with the royalists. It is unclear whether any common ground between them was firm enough, or extensive enough, to build on.

---

[36]   *The Riddles Unridled* ([14 July] 1647), p. 7.
[37]   *The Antipodes*, pp. 9, 7.

David Jenkins, the royalist judge, placed himself firmly in this middle ground; David Smith classifies him as one of the royalist writers whose theories were closely aligned with the views of the 'constitutional royalists' advising Charles.[38] We know from Jenkins's own assertions in his publications at this time that he was one of the many royalists who had opposed some of the royal practices of the 1630s. He asserted that he '*ever detested the Shippe-mony, and Monopolies*', and while his works make clear that he was solidly Anglican, he had opposed '*the excesses of one of the Bishoppes*'.[39] These grievances had been remedied, with Charles's assent, before the outbreak of war.[40] Given the nature of the grievances, Jenkins's emphasis on the fundamental nature of the law is to be taken very seriously. As he himself wrote:

We of the Kings party did and do detest Monopolies, and ship money, and all the grievances of the people as much as any men living, we do well know that our estates lives and fourtunes are preserved by the lawes, and that the King is bound by the lawes.[41]

The remedy for all these grievances was the rule of law, and the king was within, rather than above, this system of law. While he frequently referred to the notion of the king as the fountain and life of the law, he also referred to the king's prerogative as part of the law.[42] He argued that the king was bound by law, although he also cited the conventional claim that the king was punishable by none but God. His interpretation of *Magna Carta* was a typically common-law one: that it was a confirmation of the subjects' 'Rights and Liberties, which were no other then their ancient Customes'; as he pointedly added, 'the fundamentall Rights of the King as *Soveraigne* are no other'.[43] The king's sovereignty belonged within the same system of common law as the subjects' liberties – and presumably the implication was that there should be little conflict between them. The king's possession of the various marks of sovereignty was shown by their existence time out of mind.[44] Again, while Jenkins was careful to say that the monarchy antedated parliament and insisted that the king was the head of parliament and summoned it,[45] he also

[38]   Smith, *Constitutional Royalism*, ch. 7.
[39]   Jenkins, *To the Honorable Societies*, sig. A.
[40]   *Ibid.*, p. 14.
[41]   *Ibid.*, p. 22.
[42]   Jenkins, *The Vindication of Judge Jenkins Prisoner in the Tower* (29 April 1647), p. 2 (the King as 'the Fountaine of justice, and the life of the Law'); *To the Honorable Societies*, p. 1, marginal note using Littleton places the king's prerogative within the system of law.
[43]   *Ibid.*, p. 1.
[44]   *Ibid.*, p. 2.
[45]   *Ibid.*, p. 12; Jenkins, *The Armies Indemnity*, p. 4.

more than once placed the origins of parliament before the Norman Conquest,[46] and was prepared to cite the statute which suggested that parliament should be annual, as well as apparently supporting the Long Parliament's Triennial Act.[47] In short, Jenkins was very much a constitutional royalist. Similarly, a 'moderate cavalier' objected to the actions rather than the intentions of the parliamentarians: they had brought about 'an Eradication of the Kings Prerogative, while they pretended onely a circumscription, or modest limitation'; presumably limiting the king's prerogative would have been acceptable.[48]

From the parliamentarian side, we see again attempts to set out what the common ground of political principle might be. Among the army-radical tracts, *Plaine Truth* objected to 'a new Hidra-headed prerogative' being exercised by the Presbyterians in parliament; readers were left to conclude that the king had now renounced similar uses of *his* prerogative, as the author had made clear that true 'Regall power' was 'just and mercifull, regulated by Law, preservative and corrective'.[49] Here we can perhaps see how the legalist royalism of someone like Jenkins could begin to appeal to army men. Indeed, in some cases we can see the Independents expressing genuinely nostalgic and conservative views: it was not just law which had been broken by the war and the Presbyterians, but any recognizable structure and hierarchy in government: the self-declared 'Independent' mourned that there were now many kings and no subjects, and urged a return to the king who was set over the nation by God.[50]

But the fundamental principles of both sides also placed serious barriers in the way of cooperation. Some potential limits to the royalists' appeal to the soldiers are made clear in Jenkins's account of the difference between his and a parliamentarian view of kingship: '*We* maintayne that the King is King by an inhaerent birth-right, by nature, by gods law, and by the law of the land, *They* say his Kingly right is an office upon trust.'[51] This of course goes to the heart of the issue: the constitutional royalists insisted just as strongly as the more absolutist royalist thinkers that taking up arms against the king was never justified; the king was bound by law but not accountable to his people for breaches of it.[52]

---

[46] Jenkins, *An Apology for the Army*, p. 3; Jenkins, *The Armies Indemnity*, p. 4.
[47] Jenkins, *A Discourse Touching the Inconveniencies of a Long continued Parliament* (1647), pp. 1–2; evidently the idea of a triennial or an annual parliament was useful against the now 'perpetual' parliament.
[48] *A Letter Really Written by a Moderate Cavalier*, p. 5.
[49] *Plaine Truth, without Feare or Flattery*, pp. 15, 4.
[50] *A Letter of an Independent*, p. 6.
[51] David Jenkins, *To the Honorable Societies*, p. 21; my emphasis.
[52] See Smith, *Constitutional Royalism*, ch. 7.

Linked to consent theory and important in parliamentarian and radical argument was the distinction between person and office; royalist writers courting the army were merciless with the 'fiction', as Jenkins calls it, that the king's natural body and body politic might be separated.[53] Again, the royalist *Riddles Unridled*, having employed a rather half-hearted consent theory (to argue that the army need not obey the parliament, who are, after all, their own trustees), moved to an entirely royalist line of argument to conclude that the real 'higher powers' referred to in the Bible were the king and those deputed by the king.[54]

On the side of the army radicals, too, we see arguments being developed which were totally incompatible with the assumptions of royalist writers, even within Mendle's series of 'determinedly royalist' pamphlets. This is unsurprising in what, by Mendle's own criteria, is the least 'royalist' of these pamphlets, *The Grand Informer*. Where royalist writers defended the army's action on the grounds that it was not disobedient to the parliament because it was in fact displaying a higher obedience to the king, this writer took his cue from the parliamentarian and radical writers, arguing that in acting for the safety of the people, the army were playing out the logic of magistracy in the absence of an adequate government. He mobilized a set of resistance arguments – complete with their sources in Peter Martyr and Calvin – on behalf of the inferior magistrates' also having their power from God, and claimed that 'our Land' was one of the countries where the people had the right to elect magistrates. He was entirely committed to the distinction between the office and person of a magistrate, though he did not apply it specifically to the king, but used it in his analysis of the corruption of the present parliament. The consent theory of government pervades the pamphlet: the powers of a magistrate were those, and only those, originally possessed by and transferred by the people. No ruler, of any kind, was infallible and hence none should be entrusted with 'unlimmited power'. The only role left for the king would be as a limited and entrusted chief magistrate.[55] Again, the foundation of the pamphlet *The Grand Account* is a consent theory of government, where one of the most emotive pleas made to the parliament is to 'looke unto the

---

53   Jenkins, *The Vindication of Judge Jenkins Prisoner in the Tower*, p. 5: 'this vertuall power is a meer fiction'; [Anon.], *Riddles Unridled*, p. 1 on the idea that the king needed to be reunited with 'his imaginary Office'.

54   *Riddles Unridled*, p. 8.

55   *The Grand Informer. Or the Prerogative of Princes, Priviledge of Parliaments, Propriety of the Subject* (Oxford, [15 July] 1647), *passim*. Mendle suggests that the lack of royalism and the style of this pamphlet may point to Edward Sexby as the author: Mendle, 'Putney's Pronouns', p. 131.

Rocke from whence you were hewen; were you not fellow Commonners with us? . . . Did not you receive your power from us, for our good; to be accountable to us, by whom you were impowred and intrusted?'[56]

The army-radical pamphlet *Plaine Truth* did make clear that under the circumstances the king was to be preferred to parliament, but there were still clear sticking-points. Unlike the royalist pamphlet *The Riddles Unridled*, this author was not prepared to embrace former royalist soldiers who had come into the parliamentarian armies; rather, it was because the Presbyterian faction were traitors that they had put militia in the north into the hands of 'Malignants', some of whom were said to have been in arms with the king against parliament.[57] Most strikingly, towards the end of the pamphlet the author addressed head-on the question of his attitude to the king:

I speak not in favour of his Majestie further then conscience and equity, the Lord my Maker knows I am sincerely for truth and justice, without partiality, and against the contrary, wheresoever, or in whomsoever I find it: but a traytor or felon by the Law looseth not any of his franchizes, possessions and estate, before he be convict: let Cesar have his due, and us the free Commons ours . . . If the King be King let him raigne: if he have otherwise deserved, why proceed ye not legally against him, that the World may see and judge, and ye be cleared of all calumny and aspersion?[58]

This is instructive because, however clearly the author implied the need for a swift royal settlement in the rest of the pamphlet, he felt obliged to put his views into a framework of neutrality and openness which could actually envisage putting the king on trial. Whether the author himself was here giving voice to the weighing-up process which had led him to conclude that the king at this point was the best option, or whether he simply felt that his army and civilian parliamentarian audience would require qualifications put on his advocacy of restoration, it clearly suggests that he was working with ideological constraints that might be very difficult to negotiate.

Ultimately the proponents of an army-royalist deal could find themselves resorting to arguments which were not just unlikely to be compatible with each others' assumptions, but which seem simply

---

[56] *The Grand Account. Or a Remonstrance* (Oxford, [29 July] 1647), p. 7.

[57] Three cavalry regiments of the Northern Association army under Sydenham Poyntz had been chosen to remain in England by the Presbyterians, while the bulk of the New Model Army was to be either disbanded or sent to Ireland. Poyntz was both seen as an ally of the Presbyterians (and potentially of a further Scottish invasion), and suspected of Catholicism, which might naturally cause suspicions of malignancy (*Oxford DNB*).

[58] *Plaine Truth without Feare or Flattery*, pp. 12, 18.

disingenuous and twisted. Jenkins and other royalist writers made a play for the trust of the army by defending the soldiers against their attackers, at least earlier in the summer, but the logic through which they did so was distinctively royalist. Sharing with the army and the army radicals an account of the current House of Commons as arbitrary, tyrannical, or oppressive, they sought to show that in rebelling against it, the army was – at least potentially – acknowledging that the Houses of Parliament had, all along, been illegitimate as a commander of armed forces, and that the army was now reverting to the true source of its authority, the king. The soldiers were not rebels against the Houses, precisely because the Houses *were* rebels against the king, and to obey such rebels was unlawful. *The Riddles Unridled* used a similar ploy in defence of the army, again arguing that the House of Commons was not owed obedience as a higher power, because MPs were merely the 'trustees' of those who had sent them. Such a use of consent theory seems somewhat insincere, and it certainly did not extend to the royalist authors' interpretations of the power of the king. Rather, the parliament's consent theory could be used against it, but the king, whose power rested on quite different foundations, was not (however limited) answerable to the people. Having said this, *The Antipodes* confirmed its position as the most 'royalist' of the army pamphlets by employing rather similar arguments.

The last argumentative resort was fear. It is well known that indemnity was one of the 'bread and butter' issues spurring the army's resistance to disbandment throughout 1647, and Mendle has drawn attention to the importance of this for the army's thought, seeing the *Agreement* as – among other things – a crucial device to guarantee indemnity.[59] Indemnity for the soldiers of the New Model was one of the key demands which Jenkins included at the end of each pamphlet at this time. *The Riddles Unridled* tackled the issue less benignly and more shamelessly, pointing out that after the army's actions against its masters in Parliament in 1647, it had even more to fear than before. The pamphlet's last few pages are devoted to extravagant warnings that the army should not think their safety would be guaranteed if they lived in a 'free state', a claim backed up by invocations of classical examples of such states turning against their military commanders.[60]

Fundamental differences of view contributed to the souring of the potential alliance on both sides, no doubt helped by propaganda spread by Presbyterians and other enemies of the alliance. Such authors took

---

[59]   Mendle, 'Putney's Pronouns', p. 141; for the practical issues see also Barbara Donagan, 'The Army, the State and the Soldier in the English Civil War', in the same collection.
[60]   *Riddles Unridled*, pp. 17–21.

care to remind their readers of the 'contrary ends' of the two sides,[61] and spread lurid and hyperbolic ideas about the real intentions of the army. Many authors, including William Prynne, turned to the Leveller statements of anti-monarchical principles to be found in *Regall Tyranny Discovered*, which had been published as recently as January 1647, to argue that the army's real intentions towards the king were extremely sinister, and that they were only being gracious towards him 'to take off the envy and opposition of his party'.[62] As fast as army and Independents tried to build up the grounds for an alliance of interests, other propagandists undermined them – and some potentially optimistic royalists did begin to waver: one author detected attitudes in the army's treatment of the king which were not acceptable to his royalist sensibilities.[63]

It is hard to avoid the question of where the Levellers belong in this story. They were undoubtedly involved in the radicalization of the army, and the turning of some elements in the army against the leadership over the question of the nature of any settlement with the king. They were relatively theoretical political thinkers, and they had already in January of 1647 very explicitly committed themselves to a negative view both of the monarchy and of Charles I. How did they react to the possibility of an army deal with the king? Were they, like some of the authors of the army-radical pamphlets, interested in the option?

There were certainly accusations that they, or at least Lilburne, belonged squarely with those who were prepared to strike a deal with the king, if it was done through the army; but as we have seen, there were also vocal reminders that as recently as January 1647 Lilburne and his allies had denounced both the institution of monarchy and the person of Charles I in *Regall Tyranny Discovered*. We should notice that the army-radical pamphlets, as well as the *Letter of an Independent, to his Honoured Friend in London*, named Leveller prisoners among the victims of the current regime. Supporting Levellers, in this respect at least, was not incompatible for them with supporting an army-royalist deal. Contemporary (if rather excitable) evidence for meaningful Leveller–royalist

---

[61]   *A True Alarum to England, but more Especially to the City of London: and a Relation of the Treacherous Combination Between Errorists and Malignants* ([29 July] 1647), p. 4.
[62]   William Prynne, *The Totall and Finall Demands already Made by, and to be Expected from, the Agitators and Army* ([21 July] 1647), pp. 5–8. Similar views are to be found in *A Coppie of a Letter, sent from one of the Agitators in the Army, to an Agitator in the City* [a hostile satire, not an army or agitator document] ([22 July] 1647); *Match Me These Two: or The Conviciton* [sic] *and Arraignment of Britannicus and Lilburne* ([29 July] 1647); *Some Queries Propounded to the Common-Councell, and Citizens of London* ([30 July] 1647); G. R., *The Intentions of the Army Plainely Discovered* ([3 Aug.] 1647).
[63]   *Certaine Observations on that Letter Written to the Two Houses from the Army* (1647).

links is provided by Sir Lewis Dyve, one of Lilburne's royalist fellow-prisoners. Dyve reports Lilburne's claim that he told Cromwell in September 1647 that the crimes of Charles I's government were 'glorious and righteous' when seen in comparison with those of the parliament; and that the peace of the kingdom should be settled according to the army's declarations – 'both in reference to your Majestie [Dyve was writing to Charles I] and the subjects' libertys'. Lilburne's reported words focus on the perennial issue of tyranny, and opposing it wherever it was found – which, as we have seen, could well play in favour of the king at a time when parliamentary tyranny was seen as overwhelming. In Dyve's account, written to Charles I himself, Lilburne draws the conclusion in favour of the king by going on to try to agitate for Charles in the army. But as Dyve notes, Lilburne's words 'were enough to undoe him with his owne party, if it were knowne'.[64] It is perhaps unsurprising that when Lilburne argued in *Rash Oaths Unwarrantable* that parliamentary tyranny was worse than that of the king, he did not draw the conclusion there that a deal with the king was indicated.[65]

As well as Dyve, Lilburne got to know Jenkins in prison, and plenty of rumours circulated at the time about the effects of this acquaintance on the ideas of both men, although it was only systematically used against Lilburne once political circumstances had changed, from 1648 onwards.[66] In the light of Lilburne's willingness to consider tactical use of the king or his son to balance other dangerous powers in 1648–9,[67] and the royalist friends he later made in exile in the 1650s, we may take the stories as plausible – particularly when we know that Jenkins was appealing to the army just as Lilburne himself was. However it is very striking that whatever kind of friendship this was, and whatever ideas were exchanged, Jenkins did not come within the circle of those whom Lilburne and other Levellers were prepared openly to defend. The strong emphasis in Jenkins's writing on his royalist beliefs was evidently not offset by his willingness to attack the regime in ways helpful to the army and the Levellers. Enough has been said about Jenkins's legalist royalism to suggest why he and Lilburne – an inveterate user of the common law, albeit in combination with consent theory and for radical

---

[64]   H. G. Tibbutt (ed.), 'The Tower of London Letter-book of Sir Lewis Dyve, 1646–7', *Bedfordshire Historical Record Society*, 38 (1958), pp. 86, 88, 90–96.

[65]   Lilburne, *Rash Oaths Unwarrantable*.

[66]   [Sydenham], *An Anatomy of Lievt. Col. John Lilburne's Spirit and Pamphlets* ([16 Oct.] 1649); Henry Parker, *Letter of Due Censure and Redargution* ([21 June] 1650), p. 12; Walter Frost, *A Declaration of some Proceedings*, in William Haller and Godfrey Davies (eds.), *The Leveller Tracts 1647–1653* (Gloucester, MA, 1964), p. 105.

[67]   Andrew Sharp, 'The Levellers and the End of Charles I', in Jason Peacey (ed.), *The Regicides and the Execution of Charles I* (Basingstoke, 2001).

purposes – apparently got on so well, but while Lilburne may have learnt some specific legal arguments and references from Jenkins, Jenkins's general views would have been anathema to the Levellers. Some of the authorities used by Jenkins were also used by Lilburne, and in similar ways: demands for jury trial as 'the birthright of the Subject' and references to Pym's speech against Strafford, and to chapter 29 of Magna Carta, setting out the rights of a 'free man' to his freehold and to duly administered justice. But Jenkins also insisted that 'The King can doe no wrong' (here he used Pym's speech for purposes Lilburne would have avoided) and that parliament had no legitimacy if it was not composed of king, Lords and Commons.[68] As we have seen, he also insisted that the office of king was not elective.

It seems that however the balance of power was shifting in 1647, Leveller denunciations of Charles I were too recent, and too vehement, to be publicly revoked; and that even if Lilburne had wanted to put such views, he had good cause to suspect that they would alienate his allies. The sources we have do not enable us to consider what kind of royal restoration Lilburne might have been contemplating, if he was contemplating one at all – Dyve was hardly likely to discuss a minor firebrand's plans for limiting the monarchy in his letters to the king, and the friendship with Jenkins produced no direct evidence on Lilburne's views either. What is clear, in both cases, is that the driving logic behind Lilburne's comments was his calculation of the balance of tyranny; however much he felt that the balance might be redressed by turning back to the king, he would not have wanted the balance to tip too far in the direction of the 'regall tyranny' he had only recently denounced. Given that Lilburne had been a passionate parliamentarian, and that his interlocutors were imprisoned royalists, their views of where that tipping point was were not likely to be compatible.

We have seen that there were clear circumstantial prompts for the royalist attempt to woo the army in 1647. But the royalists, while they could be wily in their arguments, did not compromise the core of their views in their writings for the army; and we can see that someone like Jenkins had a particular brand of royalism that might be relatively appealing to some in parliamentarian and radical circles. There were stubborn points of royalist specificity in the argumentation which were picked up in one, at least, of the army pamphlets (where consent theory was not extended to the kingly office) but firmly rejected in others.

---

[68] Jenkins, *Iudge Ienkins Remonstrance* (dated 21 Feb. 1647), pp. 5–7; Jenkins, *A Declaration of Mr. David Ienkins* (dated 17 May 1647), unpag.; Jenkins, *The Armies Indempnity* ([31 May] 1647), p. 3.

The most fundamental common ground was simply the existence of a common enemy, the parliamentarian Presbyterians, and writers on both sides made their stand on the issue of parliamentary illegality, tyranny and oppression. Clearly, soldiers of the New Model Army, feeling this parliamentary persecution directly, would have responded to this picture: but would they have responded as royalists wished? Some might have felt that parliament's behaviour indicated the need for a return to arguments from law, rather than arguments from necessity – but would they accept the king's role as central to that system of law, as Jenkins wished? The rejection of consent theory as applied to the king must surely have limited the appeal of this royalist thinking to many Independents, army men, and Levellers, even when lip-service was paid to consent theory as applied to the parliament. Many of those who might have welcomed a royal settlement at this point would still have viewed this as a pragmatic return of the king to his betrusted office, rather than a restoration of England's innate governmental order.

1647 was a year of reorientation and realignment.[69] People's decisions in and after the war were not once-and-for-all expressions of allegiance to a fixed ideology, but personal calculations about the best way to serve principles, country – and of course themselves – at any given time. Yet both principles and prior commitments put limits on how flexible people could be, and while we certainly need to recognize the contingent nature of allegiance, we should not forget that people did come to identify, and to be identified, as 'Cavalier', 'Independent' and so on, and that such identifications affected what they could then say; in the case of the Levellers, it seems to have prevented any open support for the king's restoration by the army being expressed at all. We can see shared feeling, shared belief, and perhaps most importantly, opportunities for powerful shared rhetoric, as well as a simple coincidence of circumstances, as bringing royalists and their former opponents together at this point. Yet the alliance was self-conscious and uncomfortable, and even in the public documents which tried hardest to smooth over the differences, the sharp corners of stubbornly divergent beliefs poked through.

---

[69]   Jason McElligott, *Royalism, Print and Censorship*, ch. 4 points out that four of the key royalist propagandists only became active as royalists in 1647.

9   The royalist origins of the separation of powers

Michael Mendle

I

Of all political notions floating about the seventeenth century, perhaps the most seductive was the sovereignty of parliament. By that idea is meant precisely this: that parliament is the final arbiter of whatever is undertaken by the monarch and nation, and the actions of the executive and the judges are subject to parliament's rule and, if need be, reversal. Such a view had its sixteenth-century origins, before Jean Bodin elevated the concept of 'sovereignty' itself to a political commonplace. Famously, Henry VIII himself said his 'estate royal' was greatest 'in the time of Parliament'; Sir Thomas Smith held the parliament was the 'most high and absolute power of the realme'.[1] Whether, though, the notion of parliamentary sovereignty was mere political boilerplate or a contentious and, indeed, a revolutionary doctrine depended entirely upon what one held to be the composition of a parliament. Both Henry and Smith – and, following them, the overwhelming preponderance of informed pre-Civil War opinion – thought a parliament included the king as a fundamental part. Without the king, the two houses were no parliament. Yet common if unthinking usage held that the Lords and Commons alone constituted the parliament. King versus parliament, royalists versus Roundheads – sophistications or sophistries aside, that was what the conflict seemed to be about.

Of course, those self-serving and conscience-assuaging equivocations had their uses. Members of the army of the earl of Essex swore they were fighting *for* the king as they were fighting against his army; Charles's forces fought for the king *and* the parliament. It was confusing, but so were the issues and the times. But when the bicameral parliament operating independently of the king claimed the sovereign powers that

---

[1]   Henry VIII, quoted from Holinshed in G. R. Elton, *The Tudor Constitution* (Cambridge, 1968), p. 270; Sir Thomas Smith, *De Republica Anglorum* (1583, repr. 1970), p. 34 (Book 2, Ch. 1).

common opinion had acknowledged to be in the king-in-parliament, the sovereignty of parliament took on an entirely different aspect. When, further, these powers were used to override the prerogatives of the king alone, the bicameral parliament seemed to be arrogating to itself all possible power. As Charles, acting alone, had earlier been accused of usurping the powers of parliaments, and thus of acting absolutely, so now the sovereign and perpetual bicameral parliament could be accused not only of usurping the powers of the king, but also of being as absolute.[2]

Similarly, while both a monarch and a parliament *might* be said to be subject to law, a single ruler and a corporate one such as a parliament ended up as a *lex loquens*, to use an expression of James VI and I: they were equally the final judges of their own legality, their own righteousness. In the seventeenth century, this difficulty was also acutely, indeed painfully felt. For all those excluded from the direct exercise of power, parliamentary sovereignty was little different in form from the pretensions to supremacy of prerogative power. For those who had resisted what they thought was the tyranny of Charles I – that is, for those for whom the crime of Charles was his supposed abuse of power – it was cold comfort to find that one oppression had been replaced by another.

Out of such a predicament, an important constitutional sensibility was born. The problem, so it was argued, was not monarchy *per se* but unrestrained, unlimited power. The remedy was to divide power, to separate it into kinds and functions and to place these in different hands, so as to prevent power's monopolization by any single individual or entity. This notion, which in the eighteenth century became most commonly identified with Montesquieu (although earlier it was at least intimated by the largely forgotten George Lawson (d. 1678)),[3] was in turn linked to notions not of parliamentary but popular sovereignty, and so became a core principle of the American constitution.[4] But what is not well appreciated is that the origins of the separation of powers lie in a famous royalist critique of parliamentary aggrandizement, *The Answer to the XIX Propositions*. What is more, that royalist critique provided a recurrent *leitmotif* of much political–constitutional thought of the Civil Wars and Interregnum – a feature not only of royalist but also radical, republican and Protectoral analysis of the continuing difficulty in

---

[2] Because Charles had agreed (in May 1641) to waive his prerogative to dissolve the present parliament without its own consent, the current parliament lacked the check provided by the king, and was now all but perpetual.

[3] On Lawson, Conal Condren, *George Lawson's 'Politica' and the English Revolution* (1989).

[4] The most useful survey is M. C. J. Vile, *Constitutionalism and the Separation of Powers*, 2nd edn (Indianapolis, 1998).

establishing effective but not overbearing power. By 1659 and early 1660, the separation of powers had its own role to play in creating the Restoration scenario, the script of coming events.

Even so, in England, the heyday of the separation of powers was relatively brief. Like other elements of England's seventeenth-century experience, the separation of powers became a fork in a road that eighteenth- and nineteenth-century Britain bypassed, and the United States followed, as each community selectively drew upon a once-common past. Precisely because later British sensibility turned from the separation of powers, its place in seventeenth-century conceptualization has been largely overlooked.

II

Though written by Lucius Cary, Viscount Falkland and Sir John Culpepper, *The Answer to the XIX Propositions* will forever be identified with Charles I.[5] It was written in June 1642 in response to the Nineteen Propositions offered by the two houses to Charles as a basis for a war-averting settlement. The houses demanded a large measure of control over the independent executive power wielded by Charles I, what (in a famous and enduring formulation of the fifteenth-century lawyer Sir John Fortescue) was dubbed the *dominium regale*, as opposed to the unquestionably limited, joint authority the king had with the Houses of Parliament and the courts of law, the *dominium politicum*. Charles and his advisers had no interest in making further concessions of this sort – he had agreed to important qualifications of his power to call and dissolve parliaments but had rejected surrender of his sole control over the military might of the kingdom – and so *The Answer to the XIX Propositions* was an emphatic rejection of the executive-grabbing pretensions of the Nineteen Propositions.

But *The Answer* did so in an odd, conflicted way, one that all but guaranteed that differing (and self-serving) interpretations would be made then and later of what the king had actually said. For *The Answer* was rich in the idiom of mixed government, of the shared and conjoined power of the king, Lords and Commons, which in turn were identified (albeit inconsistently) with the classical forms of monarchy, aristocracy, and democracy. For those who wanted to see things that way, Charles had conceded that England was a 'mixed' monarchy, in which the modal activity was the undeniably shared or 'coordinate' legislative authority of

---

[5]   On the *Answer*, Michael Mendle, *Dangerous Positions: Mixed Government, the Estates of the Realm, and the Making of the* Answer to the XIX Propositions (Alabama, 1985), pp. 5–20.

king, Lords and Commons. Further, if legislation was taken to be the controlling activity of governance (as Bodin seemed to suggest that it was), then the case was largely closed. Power was, in a sense, divided amongst the three 'estates' (as the *Answer* called them) of king, Lords and Commons, but it was essentially shared, 'coordinate'.

However, *The Answer to the XIX Propositions* stubbornly and perhaps perversely held to a vastly different construction, one that made its 'mixarchic' parts seem a mis-step. It crucially defined the separate, incommensurable, and unfungible activities of king, Lords and Commons in a way that combined a functional distinction with conventional notions of social aptness. Each part did what it was 'naturally' suited for, according to the common (if badly skewed) identification of king, Lords and Commons with monarchy, aristocracy and democracy. The only business for which the three constituents were equally and jointly suited was legislation. All the rest was separate. To the king was entrusted 'the government' (the medieval *gubernaculum*), or the packet of powers often called his prerogatives. These powers were also understood as the 'royal' or 'regal' component of the *dominium politicum et regale*. The Lords was entrusted a judicatory power, and, implicitly, an advisory role that conflated the institutional House of Lords with the council. The House of Commons was given a special subset of legislative power, the sole power to initiate taxation, as well as the power, by virtue of impeachment, to identify (but not unilaterally to punish) those they thought their enemies.

In the language of *The Answer*, each 'estate' was likened to a river. Kept within its 'proper channel', each river of power begat 'verdure and fertility' all around. Unrestrained, each river threatened the general welfare with its particular 'deluge or inundation' of evil, its natural vice. For 'absolute [i.e. pure] monarchy', the corresponding ill was 'tyranny'; for aristocracy, 'faction and division'; for democracy, 'tumults, violence, and licentiousness'. This was conventional – it conformed to the operative stereotypes – and apparently even-handed or moderate, both in acknowledging the evil of an unbridled monarchy, and speaking to the necessity of a distinctive role for the Commons. But the whole structure was turned to a special purpose: to argue the king's case. In the current juncture, he had not encroached upon the others. Rather, the Commons had indulged in an orgy of power-grabbing, arrogating to itself what belonged to the king. *The Answer*'s listing of his prerogative powers, the Fortescuean *dominium regale*, was in itself a shorthand formula of rejection of the executive-grabbing Nineteen Propositions. If the king was stripped of these particular, functionally distinct powers, he would be unable to prevent the ill of aristocracy ('faction') and of democracy. The Commons would in time devour the Lords, and England would descend by stages into the nightmare of early-modern order theory, the 'dark, equal chaos of confusion'.[6]

This separation was precisely the non-negotiable element in *The Answer*. It was used to explain the king's position on the constitutional crux that *as theory* was the grounds of war and *as practice* was its precondition – who controlled the military might of the kingdom? Charles had been offered legislation to remove his sole control over the armed forces – the militia bill – and had refused to agree to it. That is, he used his 'negative voice' or veto, because the bill, if he accepted it and it became law, divested him of the key power that marked his 'government' and 'regal authority' and thus broke with the 'known law', the ancient constitution. The Houses had responded with an emergency, a supposedly nonce-enactment taken by virtue of their own supposed executive authority (as the king's great Council), which the king vigorously denied existed. This was the militia *ordinance*, which compounded the injury because it claimed the Houses possessed an executive authority to deprive the king of his. Similarly, the Houses, particularly the Commons, took upon themselves judicial authority that had previously been accorded the courts at Westminster.[7] For *The Answer*, this was tantamount to constitutional revolution.

In the immediate context of spring and summer 1642, as England descended into civil war, *The Answer* was, like most other pieces in the war of words, a preachment to its own choir. John Selden, whose temperament joined his intellect in being able to understand both sides, caught well the limitations of the king's argument: it depended upon the belief that the king's missteps were *in fact* of the same kind and no worse for the kingdom at large, indeed less so, than those of his opponents. Whatever their reasons, the parliament's partisans would not see it that way, and for them, the king's logic (as Selden put it of Charles's attempt to arrest the Five Members) was that of a child who explained to his father that he had a right to have sexual relations with his paternal grandmother: 'You lay with my Mother & why should I not lye with yo^{rs} [?]'[8]

---

[6] Here and elsewhere, the *Answer* had to step lightly around one of its own inconsistencies, as it by turns equated the Commons with the democracy and at others separated the Commons from the real *canaille*, 'the common people' and their presumed natural leaders, the likes of 'Jack Cade or ... Wat Tyler'.

[7] *The Answer* did not assert the independence of the judiciary from either the legislature or the executive. If anything it tacitly assumed the judicial function to be in some sense under the king; this is the point of assertion that the king was obliged to obey the law, 'if he knows it'. Yet *The Answer* also assumed that 'the Law' functioned as a constant, independent element in the constitutional equation – the king could not create it, indeed could not know it independently of his judges.

[8] *Table Talk of John Selden*, ed. Sir Frederick Pollock (1927), p. 65. This remark and the next in the section headed 'The King' speak to the noncommensurability of his position with that of the Houses; others address his plight more sympathetically.

Nevertheless, as the major political drift of the 1640s and beyond until Cromwell's death in 1658 was the progressive falling away of the more conservative, or socially and religiously frightened of parliament's original supporters, even as successive regimes at Westminster and the army consolidated their practical control over England, the warnings of *The Answer* were remembered. As he lost on the battlefield, Charles belatedly (and for him personally, pointlessly) won the war of words. The problem was the abuse of power when it was concentrated; the solution was its separation.

III

The broad coalition that had brought Charles to his knees at the summoning of the Long Parliament in November 1640 had fragmented sufficiently by the summer of 1642 to give Charles a party prepared to fight for him. The parliamentary remnant continued to fragment thereafter. Some – the more cautious or frightened – moved quietly toward a new appreciation of the royalist argument, and a desire to find a basis for settlement with the king. But this also occurred among the more radical. Nothing, of course, brings out latent tensions and animosities like victory; in 1647, when the First Civil War seemed won, the combination of parliament and army that paid for and won the war faced a crisis of dissolution. Many, in short, were prepared to acknowledge the existence of 'roundhead [particularly, parliamentary] tyranny'.[9] Clearly present-tense transgressions were those in mind; it is notable, however, that the war of words of 1641–2 was used to understand the current predicament. The royalist judge David Jenkins quoted John Pym's law-loving speech against the earl of Strafford in 1641 as an arch-example of the parliament's decline from its own professions; Jenkins's friend and pupil, John Lilburne, would do the like.[10] The sense was general. As an army declaration of June 1647 put it,

Parliament Priviledges, as well as Royall-Prerogative, may be perverted and abused to the destruction of those greater ends for whose protection and preservation they were admitted or intended (*viz.* the rights and Liberties of the people and safety of the whole).

[9]   Robert Ashton, 'From Cavalier to Roundhead Tyranny, 1642–9', in John Morrill (ed.), *Reactions to the English Civil War* (1982), pp. 185–207.

[10]   David Jenkins, *The Works of that Grave and Learned Lawyer Iudge Jenkins* (1648), p. 98, from Jenkins's *The Armies Indemnity*, which Jenkins self-dated 17 May 1647. On Lilburne and Husbands's *An Exact Collection*, see Andrew Sharp, 'John Lilburne and the Long Parliament's *Book of Declarations*: a Radical's Exploitation of the Words of Authorities', *History of Political Thought*, 9 (1988), 19–44. On Lilburne and Jenkins, see Pauline Gregg, *Free-Born John* (1961), pp. 169, 197.

The danger being no less great, the remedy was 'no lesse to be endeavoured'.[11] But just what was the remedy? Here there was no shortage of answers, most of which could be combined. For some, the cause of the decline was the infrequency of election; the remedy was self-evident. Somewhat later, for others, notably Harrington and his friends in The Rota, rotation of office supplied what even elections could not. For still others, the best or only remedy was virtue, as it was theoretically attempted in the Nominated Assembly and as Milton proposed in *The Ready and Easy Way*. And, to the point of the present chapter, for some, the cause of the problem being the fusion of powers that ought to have been kept in separate hands, the solution was their re-separation.

For Charles and his royalist advisers in 1642, the key violation was the assumption of executive authority by the two Houses. They presumed to *govern* without him, which was no more clearly to be seen than in their appropriation of power over military might. In 1647 and beyond, that could hardly be the issue. The New Model had emerged as an independent political presence and the prime antagonist of the conservative forces at Westminster. But the doctrine of the separation of powers spoke to another consequence of improperly conjoined powers: the judicial 'tyranny' exercised in various ways by the Houses of Parliament. The House of Lords attacked its enemies through judicial proceedings conducted by itself; the Commons did the like, and, much more significantly in terms of general effect, its committees (of Compounding, of Sequestration) functioned as administrative–judicial tribunals of original jurisdiction. Those who smarted under the judicial power of the Houses had no doubt that it was an illegitimate usurpation of power. But there was no consensus how to characterize it. One writer, Charles Dallison, devised a terminology remarkably close to the modern notion of executive, legislative and judicial power. Others seem more to have viewed the aggrandizement as against the king's 'government', here obviously conceived more expansively than the prerogative alone to include the general supervision of the courts. This, in fact, may have conformed closely to the largely tacit assumptions underlying *The Answer*. In either case, though, the message was the same: the Houses had stepped out of their proper channel, to use the idiom of *The Answer*. And it is unmistakable as well, that whatever the real and perhaps ultimately unbridgeable differences, royalists and radicals synergistically developed their notions of the separation of powers.

---

[11] *An Humble Remonstrance from his Excel. Sir Thomas Fairfax and the Army under his Command ... Presented to the Commissioners at St. Albanes, Iune 23* (1647), p. 6.

Not surprisingly, this olla of ideas first developed in that cauldron of possibilities, the summer and autumn of 1647, when royalists, army interests, radicals in the army and in London, and 'Presbyterian' and parliamentary interests jostled for place in what was believed to be an imminent settlement. We have already noted David Jenkins's and John Lilburne's shared view of parliamentary aggrandizement. Importantly, Jenkins went further, trying to convince John Lilburne (and, through him, the army) that no settlement without the king's active participation would secure the army's interests, above all, the key issue of indemnity from prosecution for actions committed while under arms. The short-lived army press at Oxford in the summer of 1647 shows at least traces of guarded royalism, or at least sympathy for the king's position; one of its principals, the actor-printer-radical journalist John Harris, was in fact married to a royalist, Susannah Harris, and came from an Oxford roy-alist family.[12] Arguably, its sympathy for the king was fragile and situ-ational, but its analysis of the parliament's misdeeds was drawn from the royalists' stock arguments. Thus *The Grand Account*, an analysis of parliamentary financial shenanigans, closed with a coda ('Vox Populi') that cleverly pitted the pre-war abuses of 'Prerogative' (viz. the king's misdeeds) with those of parliamentary 'Privilege' in the present. 'Did you so vehemently declare against Prerogative, with intent to destroy us by Privilege? Did you exclaime against injustice in others, that your selves might be singular, yea superlatively uniust?' In that comparison, *The Grand Account* found the king's prerogative 'much the better Plea', though it would have been better still if parliament had adhered to its pretensions: 'that they that give Law to others, ought not to be above Lawe themselves'.[13] John Harris, who certainly authored another of the tracts he printed, *The Antipodes*, similarly used 'an unknowne and un-limited Priviledge' as a marker of parliament's illegitimate violation of the separation of powers: to all who opposed its exorbitances, parliament claimed that 'we that are the makers of a Law, are best able to iudge of the sense and meaning of the Law'.[14] In the name of the common good, the Houses had arrogated to themselves, and naturally abused, powers that ought to have been separate.

---

[12] On Harris's family and Oxford background, see Stephanie Jenkins's web page on Francis Harris, Mayor of Oxford at http://www.headington.org.uk/oxon/mayors/1603_1714/harris_francis_1633.htm.

[13] *The Grand Account* (Oxford, 1647), pp. 7–8. There was another printing, not of the Oxford press (possibly issued in London), which unfortunately bears the same Wing number, G1486.

[14] I. H., *The Antipodes* (Oxford, 1647), pp. 6 and 9 mispaged (viz., sigs. A3 verso and A4 verso).

When the army press closed in August 1647, John Harris went back to London. There he continued his Leveller-royalist activities, as printer/publisher and writer, usually under an anagrammatic shuffle of his name (Sirraniho or Sirrahnio, Ja. Hornish, Jah. or J. Norris). The separation of powers followed him back as well. As Levellers curiously and importantly took up the case of one of the secluded members, Sir John Maynard (1592–1658), they and he spoke to his difficulties in the idiom of the separation of powers. Maynard thought he taught the lesson to Lilburne, whose great error was '*idolizing this House* [the Commons]' as

the Supream Authority, and the chiefe Judicatory, in representing the People, from whom All POWER *is derived* ... But I have shewed him the contrary ... I conceive it not honourable, not just, *that We, that are Legislators, should be Administrators or Executioners of justice.*[15]

John Wildman, writing in Maynard's defence, concurred. It was 'a grosse mistake, confounding the legislative power, with the power judiciall and executive'. But he also tried to integrate the separation of powers with the principle of popular sovereignty, hinting that the courts were as much the repositories of the people's executive and judicial power as parliament was of the legislative.[16] In spite of Maynard's efforts, Lilburne remained foggy. He thought it 'most irrationall and unjust' for legislators to meddle in affairs cognizable in ordinary courts of justice.[17] But Lilburne also could not abandon his vision of a world created anew in an agreement of the people or his naive excitement in the promise of 1641 even in the disillusion of 1647–9. A settled, 'known' law and a world of one's own making remained painfully in tension.

Maynard's partially successful efforts at tuition reflected the ongoing importance of the doctrines of *The Answer to the XIX Propositions*. It was to be seen especially clearly in a tract written by Charles Dallison, at one time the Recorder of Lincoln. *The Royalists Defense* was a rousing vindication of the need for a separation of powers, even as Dallison veered away from *The Answer*'s denomination of the king, Lords and Commons as 'estates' and also as Dallison went much further than *The Answer* in asserting an independent role of the judiciary. Dallison summarized his own views unmistakeably. As any royalist would, he denied

---

[15]   *A Speech Spoken in the Honourable House of Commons*, pp. 6–7.
[16]   *The Lawes Subversion: or, Sir John Maynards Case Truly Stated* (1648), pp. 13, 14–15, 24.
[17]   John Lilburne, *A Defiance to Tyrants. Or The Araignment of Two Illegall Committees* (1648), sigs A2v, A4r.

that the Houses alone had any power of legislation. He went further, arguing

[t]hat the King, the Lords House and the Commons House concurring, have not an unlimited power to make Laws, it being in the brest of the Judges of the Realme, to determine which Acts of Parliament are binding, and which void, and to expound the meaning of every Act.

Instead, the judges to whom the 'people are bound lastly and finally' are the judges of the Westminster courts. At a stroke, therefore, the claims of the Houses to act as courts of original jurisdiction and of appeal were shattered. Likewise, execution and the '*Soveraigne* power of Government' belonged in '*one* hand' and 'the absolute determination of that Law, by which (under the Supreame Magistrate) the people are governed, in an *other* hand'. In making this move, Dallison was following a particularly law-inflected species of royalism seen in Hyde's description of the law and the church as 'Hippocrates' twins', and in Sir John Spelman's quasi-mystical endowment of 'the law' with agency.

IV

These issues, of course, remained unresolved. The execution of the king and the eventual collapse of Leveller-inspired constitutional schemes in no way altered the theoretical role of the single-chamber parliament, the power of which was justified, to the extent that it was at all, by recourse to the amalgam of notional popular sovereignty and practical parliamentary omnicompetence that underlay the parliamentary case during the war years and beyond. But when Cromwell dissolved the Rump, a new round of constitutional theorizing was inevitable. And once again, strikingly, the idiom and logic of *The Answer to the XIX Propositions* re-emerged. In his puff piece on behalf of the Instrument of Government – the constitutional scheme making Oliver Cromwell the Lord Protector – Marchamont Nedham defined the cardinal sin of the Rump to have been the 'placing the *Legislative* and *executive Powers* in the same persons'. This was, he argued, 'a marvellous In-let of Corruption and Tyranny', which was so whether the two powers were held by 'any single person' or 'by many'. In deliberative and extensive echoes of *The Answer*, Nedham found 'the keeping of these two apart, flowing in distinct Channels, so that they never meet in one (save upon some transitory extraordinary occasion) ... a grand Secret of Liberty and good Government'. He continued in like vein: 'And therefore it was the wisdom and care of our Ancestors, so to temper the Government of our Nation in time past that they left the Supreme *Law-making Power* among the people in Parliament' and '*Execution of Law*, with the mysteries of Government, in the hands of a single person and his Council'.[18] While the Instrument of Government, unlike the Humble Petition and Advice to follow, made no provision for a surrogate House of Lords (the 'Other House'), Nedham nevertheless found it important, in his rephrasing of *The Answer*, to find the aristocratic element in the Council of State: the Instrument provided for

the good of all the three sorts of Government ... bound ... all in one. If War be, here is the Unitive vertue (but nothing else) of *Monarchy* to encounter it; and here is the admirable Counsel of *Aristocracie* to manage it: If Peace be, here is the industry and courage of *Democracie* to improve it.

Again, and above all, 'the *Legislative* and *Executive* Powers' were separated, avoiding the ills of parliaments ('Division, Faction, and Confusion') as well as the 'Inconveniences of absolute Lordly power'.[19]

Cromwell himself was later reported to have said the same thing. In the discussions he had in April 1657 with the promoters of the Humble Petition and Advice, Cromwell allegedly drifted into what he called 'a little short Chronology' and gave his view of what caused him to dissolve the Rump. Neither 'recruiter' elections to supply the places of dead members nor wholesale replacements of perpetually sitting parliaments would do what was required, he said. Rather, parliament had arrogated authority beyond the due limits. It had 'assume[d] to it self the authority of the three Estates that were before ... if any man would have come and said what are the rules you judge by? Why, we have none but we are supream in legislature, and in judicature'. A parliament was 'pitiful remedy ... when soever a legislature is perpetually exercised, when the legislative and the executive powers are always the same'.[20]

The Answer, or Nedham's rephrasing of it, is to be heard repeatedly in the debates of the Protectoral parliaments established by the Instrument of Government and the Humble Petition and Advice. Indeed the terminology probably assumed its greatest currency in those years, as members sought to cope with the Protectorate's constitutional conundrums. The first problem was the result of the Instrument itself, which

---

[18] Marchamont Nedham, *A True State of the Commonwealth of England, Scotland, and Ireland* (1654), pp. 10–11. *The Answer*, however, made no exception for an emergency. Without such an exception, of course, the case for war, as it was actually presented, would have collapsed. Moreover, Nedham's classical republicanism would have made him at least theoretically sympathetic to the occasional necessity of a Roman-style dictatorship.
[19] *Ibid.*, pp. 51–2.
[20] *Monarchy Asserted, to be the Best, Most Ancient and Legall Form of Government, in a Conference had at Whitehall with Oliver Late Lord Protector & a Committee of Parliament* (1660), pp. 89, 94. Cromwell also described (p. 96) such a parliament as 'absolute'.

immediately became the subject of debate in the first Protectoral parliament in September 1654. The prime issue was the relation of the Protector (or single person) to the parliament, which, it was agreed, was to be accomplished by 'distinguish[ing] the word "Government" into the legislative power and the executive power'. Without much ado, it was decided that 'the executive part of it ... [was] ... not exercisable by the Parliament'. More complicated was whether the Protector was to have a share in the legislative power. Republicans stood determinedly against it, but with the Protector's camp both arguing the case and hinting that the Protector would brook no opposition, the parliament agreed he was to have a share. '[I]f the supreme legislative power should rest only in the Parliament, they might have opportunities to perpetuate themselves as the old Parliament did' – or so proponents argued, adding such a 'check' (a word repeatedly used in the discussions) was part of 'the natural constitution, and most suitable to the governing of the nation'. Evidently *The Answer* and perhaps Nedham had done their work well.[21]

The case of the Quaker James Nayler provided another occasion for sustained discussion of the separation of powers. Nayler's exhibitionistic display at Bristol brought out the worst in most members of the Parliament. While death had been taken off the menu of punishments, one snatch of debate had members offering up punishments like so many bidders at an auction: 'his tongue might be bored through ... his hair might be cut off ... his tongue might be slit or bored through, and that he might be stigmatized with the letter B ... [s]lit his tongue, or bore it, and brand him with the letter B'.[22] Nayler's case raised several constitutional issues, which characteristically were handled in terms of the separation of powers. Was Nayler to be proceeded against by legislative action or judicially? If the former, the Protector's assent (at least the seeking of his assent) would have been required under the Instrument of Government. Since Cromwell, along with other senior officers, was known to have his doubts about the Quaker's extreme punishment, this put the parliament's ability to act in the matter in jeopardy; for the squeamish, it also raised the issue of the legitimacy of *ex post facto* legislative attainder as well as of the extent to which the parliament had absorbed the constitutional rights of the now abolished House of Lords. Legislative action (even if it was also routinely described in the debate as setting Nayler's 'punishment') did at least avoid raising the now-widespread dislike of the parliament's exercise of judicial authority.

---

[21]   J. T. Rutt (ed.), *The Diary of Thomas Burton, Esq.*, 4 vols. (1828), vol. I, pp. xvii–xliv (9 and 11 September 1654).

[22]   Burton, *Diary*, vol. I, p. 153.

Not surprisingly, the debates on the constitutional issues raised by Nayler's case showed opinions of every stripe whether to proceed 'upon the legislative way or the judicatory way'.[23] Eventually the latter route was the one chosen. Sir Walter Strickland went so far as to argue that if Strafford's case had come up anew, the parliament would proceed judicially, no longer having to worry about the complication of a House of Lords. 'We are another Jurisdiction now, a judicial Court. If we lose this privilege, if we own it not now, we shall have much ado to resume, to regain it. I desire you would trouble yourselves no further in this business. If you talk of a Bill, it will all come to nothing.'[24] Cromwell's response to Nayler's judicial condemnation and punishment was to question its legitimacy, implying that a legislative approach (and hence his right to assent) was required. This provoked a new crux: as quickly as the House's judicial power was asserted ('our jurisdiction ... is the essence and being of a Parliament' and a 'Parliament cannot subsist without a judicatory power, as well as a legislative') it was denied (such jurisdiction could not be unlimited, 'for then all other powers are swallowed up in the legislative').[25] If anything, continuing debate emboldened some members to be more resistant than ever to forgoing the judicatory power, while others continued to insist that it was dangerous to 'confound' them.[26] Nevertheless, both sides seem to have realized they were entering a dangerous zone of uncertainty, which, while it seemed to call for a 'tertium Arbiter', revealed there was none.[27]

V

The Humble Petition and Advice further restored the ancient constitution, albeit in different terms. The 'Other House' of Cromwellian life-nobles and supportive peers may not have been called a House of Lords, but debates within the Protectoral parliament of Oliver's son and successor Richard rotated around whether the difference in name was indeed a difference in substance. Equally, although Oliver Cromwell had again passed by the title of king, the power of the Protector was routinely evaluated as if monarchy was the only standard of comparison. Most strikingly but routinely, the Protector and Houses were the three estates, as if 1642 had returned.

---

[23] Burton, *Diary*, vol. I, p. 32.
[24] Burton, *Diary*, vol. I, p. 157.
[25] Burton, *Diary*, vol. I, pp. 253, 255.
[26] See the debates for 27 and 30 December 1656. For confounding, vol. I, pp. 271, 278.
[27] Burton, *Diary*, vol. I, pp. 249, 251.

From the beginning, the Other House was treated as a House of Lords by another name, and so the language and logic of *The Answer* was once again heard. Burton reported the discussions between Oliver and his officers on the topic as rooting the logic of the new body in the need to 'lay aside arbitrary proceedings, so unacceptable to the nation' by means of the 'check, or balancing power' that amounted to a 'House of Lords, or a House so constituted'.[28] In Richard's parliament, the Other House was repeatedly spoken of (as in *The Answer*) as a screen, as when Francis Drake, thanking God for having restored the ancient constitution of 'a single Person' and two Houses, called the Other House 'a screen between us and the people, as well as between us and the single person'.[29]

Oddly – and pertinently – the last debate of a Protectoral parliament (21 April 1659) reprised the very issues that had provoked the Nineteen Propositions and the king's answer to them, and did so in *The Answer*'s idiom. 'Major Beale had moved that the militia be declared to be in three estates', the report of the debate began. Henry Vane replied that this was 'the quarrel you had with the late king'. He added that the dispute should focus not on the 'legislative' but the 'executive power'. Others agreed and disagreed. Some suggested that the militia belonged with all three estates; but a member replied that to 'have this militia every where, is to have it nowhere. Two suns cannot shine in one firmament.' Another insisted that '[w]herever the legislative is, the militia is'. The debate carried on into the afternoon. The young Viscount Falkland, whose father had helped to pen *The Answer*, worried that the question of the locus of the militia's power was to 'our ancestors ... a secret of state; and they would never define where it was'. Argyle remembered that it was 'the executive power of the King, singly ... that brought on the war'. Another member, with an eye on the present, replied that if the 'legislature of the militia be in one single estate, then all is there'.[30] The debate was to be resumed the next day, but on that day the parliament was dissolved.

VI

Conceptualization of the restoration of monarchy and the Stuarts drew upon many strands of royalist thought, but amongst them once again was the logic of the separation of powers. Even in the semi-chaos of the winter of 1659, the old distinctions were found useful. *The Agreement of the*

---

[28] Burton, *Diary*, vol. I, p. 384 (7 March 1656/7). The arbitrary power referred to was that used in Nayler's case.

[29] Burton, *Diary*, vol. III, p. 349 (19 Feb. 1658/9). See also vol. III, p. 412 (22 Feb. 1658/9), vol. IV, pp. 55, 65, 67 (7 March 1658/59).

[30] Burton, *Diary*, vol. IV, pp. 472, 476–80.

General Council of Officers naturally upheld a commonwealth without
a king and House of Lords, but also insisted '[t]he Legislative and Executive power be destinct [sic], and not in the same hands'.[31] As the return
of the monarchy grew more likely in February and March 1660, the
newly re-energized presses of London churned out speculations on both
sides on the nature of the Restoration scenario. And in these, the separation of powers and other elements of *The Answer to the XIX Propositions* were often to be found. Of all the tracts and single sheets, the most
important and earliest in this vein was Roger L'Estrange's *A Plea for
Limited Monarchy*, which Thomason acquired on or shortly before 20
February 1660.[32] L'Estrange wrote this to counter what seemed to be
General Monck's flashy repudiation of monarchy in response to an appeal
of his Devonshire countrymen to admit the secluded Members. Most
likely, Monck's response was part of his negotiating strategy with the
royalists; some royalists, however, clearly were rattled.[33] L'Estrange's
general tack – in phrasing that recurred in other pieces – was to argue
that the old monarchy before the war was 'the Kernel, as it were, of a
Common-wealth, in the shell of Monarchy',[34] and also to cloak the monarchy in the full raiment of the ancient constitution ('more ancient then
story or record, more Venerable than Tradition it self') and 'our English
nature'.[35] The circumstances of early 1660 dictated that L'Estrange min-
imize the danger of the king's 'executive' power and 'that Bug-Bear' of the
king's and the Lords' negative voice. Nevertheless, he was surprisingly
insistent upon the necessity of the separation of powers. The veto was
only a 'Target' (i.e., a shield) to 'shelter and preserve the Government
from being altered', fixed so as to prevent 'Power [from] being engrossed
by one of the Estates' and made to serve 'the Interests of a Faction'. That
was no better than 'a Ballance consisting of but one scale'.[36] While prerogative had the role assigned it by *The Answer*,[37] L'Estrange could only
'wish' that the current commonwealth would 'so perfectly ... distinguish
the Legislative from the Ministerial Authority, as we once did; when the

---

[31] *The Agreement of the General Council of Officers* ([23 Dec.] 1659).

[32] The title page of L'Estrange's *An Eccho [sic] to the Plea for Limited Monarchy* (1660),
which (p. 8) is self-dated July 1660, says that *The Plea* first appeared in January. I take
this simply to be a faulty recollection.

[33] Michael Mendle, 'News and the Pamphlet Culture of Mid Seventeenth-century
England', in B. Dooley and S. Baron (eds.), *The Politics of Information in Early-modern
Europe* (2001), pp. 57–79.

[34] R. L'Estrange, *A Plea for Limited Monarchy, as it was Established in this Nation, Before
the Late War. In an Humble Addresse to his Excellency General Monck* (1660), p. 5.

[35] *Ibid.*, p. 4.

[36] *Ibid.*, pp. 5–6.

[37] *Ibid.*, p. 8: 'Tumult was curbed, Faction moderated, Usurpations forestalled, Inter-
vales prevented, Perpetuities obviated, Equity administered, Clemency exalted.'

House of Commons had not the power of a *Court Leet* to give an Oath, nor of a Justice of the Peace, to make a *Mittimus*'. That distinction, he argued, was 'the most vitall part of Freedome, and far more considerable to poore Subjects, than [Harrington's] pretended Rotation'.[38]

The message was reiterated often, almost unceasingly, in late February and March 1660. Some of it, to be sure, was L'Estrange quoting himself; other pieces he may well have inspired. To the casual consumer, however, the message was unavoidable. One 'Tho. Le White, Esq.' wondered the same day that *A Plea* appeared whether the 'absolute and Arbitrary Power' of those few who assumed 'the sole power of Government to themselves' could be 'regulated and balanced' by a House of Lords.[39] Days later, another piece mourned the loss to liberty by the removal of 'Negative Voices, and balancing Interests of King and Lords'.[40] Early in March, another item in the campaign to pressurize Monck spoke of monarchy as 'our antient (and best fabricated Government in the world)'.[41] Several days later, two pieces addressed how Monck's terms for a restoration (indemnity and security of lands being high on the list) were best to be met through the 'ancient constitution of King, Lords, & Commons'.[42] So it continued, most strikingly when later in March the arguments of *A Plea* were reprised in a broadside.[43]

VII

By summer 1660, the argument had been won. L'Estrange celebrated in *An Eccho to the Plea for Limited Monarchy*, congratulating Monck and England for their good work. The king had been restored to his 'regall

---

[38]   *Ibid.*, pp. 7–8.

[39]   Tho. Le White, *Considerations by Way of Sober Queries* ([20 Feb.] 1660). Very possibly this is a L'Estrange pseudonym; cf. the other piece supposedly by Le White, *A Brief Character of Englands Distraction being the Copy of a Letter Sent into the Country by a Gentleman of the Middle-Temple* (1660).

[40]   *The Copy of a Letter from a Lincolne Shire Gentleman; Sent to his Friend in the City of London* ([23 Feb.] 1660), p. 4.

[41]   *The Coppy of a Letter to Genereall Monck* ([4 March] 1660), p. 6.

[42]   *A Short Discourse upon the Desires of a Friend* ([8 March] 1660), pp. 11–12. Similarly themes were pursued in *Englands Monarchy Asserted, and Proved to be the Freest State, and Best Commonwealth ... With a Word to the Present Authority, and Excellency General Monck* ([8 March] 1660). As the title intimates, this tract closely mirrors the argument and idiom of *A Plea*.

[43]   *No King but the Old Kings Son* ([23 March] 1660). Other similar pieces in the second half of March include *The Qualifications of the Succeeding Parliament* (1660), *A Pertinent Speech made by an Honourable Member of the House of Commons, Tending to the Establishment of Kingly Government* (1660), and *The Case Stated Touching the Soveraign's Prerogative and the Peoples Liberty, According to Scripture, Reason, and the Consent of our Ancestors* (1660).

Power', the Lords to their role as 'just and wise Mediatours' and a 'skreene' to keep the king from 'popular encroachments'. As in *The Answer*, all this was claimed as the 'wisdome of many ages', not least in separation of the 'Legislative and Ministerial' power.[44] In a way, though, *A Plea* would prove a valedictory. Charles II's addiction to his promise of religious toleration made at Breda would lead him to assert his separate power of dispensing, and so the argument would begin anew, though pitting the Anglican victors against their Cavalier king. Nevertheless, the notion would not die. Locke would try to settle an old ambiguity by distinguishing judicial from 'federative' power, placing in the latter category the complex of prerogatives belonging to foreign policy. Nevertheless, he remembered enough of the Civil War years to think the placing of executive and legislative authority in the same hands was a bad idea, whether those hands were those of an absolute monarch or a perpetual parliament. Even in crucially assisting an argument against his son, Charles I's *Answer to the XIX Propositions* and the experience of decades had done their work: an old argument about kings had become a new one about power. So, indeed, the pedigree of a foundation text of liberal thought was to be found in part in the constitutional position of royalists on the eve of the Civil War.

[44]   *An Eccho*, pp. 4–6.

10 'A No-King, or a New'. Royalists and the succession, 1648–1649

Sean Kelsey

In the autumn and winter of 1648–9 Charles I came as close as he would ever come to negotiating a peace with the rebellious Westminster Parliament. As usual, his willingness to talk peace was just one element in a strategy of war. Militarily, the king's best-laid plans once again lay in ruins, strewn across the northern counties of England with the remnants of the Scots army of the Engagement. But with a fleet of warships still at his son's disposal, and an alliance with the Irish confederates still a possibility, the king's hopes were little diminished. Politically, his prospects remained good, and in order to take advantage of the differences within the parliamentarian coalition he agreed to sit down with his adversaries. Believing that he could negotiate without in fact committing himself to anything, the king apparently abandoned power, authority and even his principles. His objective was to dupe his opponents, either into allowing him to return to his capital to conclude the deal, or else to permit him sufficient personal freedom to engineer an escape. But unaware of his calculations, or else unconvinced of their wisdom, some of the king's closest supporters found the seemingly imminent prospect of a peace without honour or security hard to reconcile with the best interests of either the crown, the church, the House of Stuart, or indeed themselves. Pride's Purge and the collapse of the treaty of Newport offered little solace as it soon became apparent that a similar deal to that tabled at Newport might still be struck by the king and the leaders of the new military regime. This was by no means the first time the king's scheming had put his supporters' loyalty to the test. Royalist reaction to his flight to the Scottish army in 1646, and to the terms of the king's Engagement with the Scots in 1648 had demonstrated the limits of what many of the king's supporters would put up with.[1] Their

---

[1] David Scott, *Politics and War in the Three Stuart Kingdoms, 1637–49* (Basingstoke, 2004), pp. 121–2, 166. I am indebted to Dr Scott for reading and commenting on this chapter prior to publication.

prospects would have seemed worse than ever by the winter of 1648–9 were it not for the fact that by then there was available a credible alternative to awaiting the outcome of the king's questionable gamble.

This chapter argues that partisans of the House of Stuart began seriously to think about life after Charles I some considerable time before the king himself submitted to exchange his mortal crown for an immortal one. Although Charles had long believed that a martyr's death surely awaited him, it was for him axiomatic that whilst he drew breath he might hope, and the hope of fresh armies in Ireland and a fleet at sea must have been positively exhilarating.[2] The treaty of Newport from September to November, and much of what followed at Westminster and Whitehall in December and January, gave substance to the king's assessment that, one way or another, his various English enemies all still needed him.[3] But whilst Charles strove manfully to give destiny the slip; and even as fate seemed to afford him fresh opportunities to outmanoeuvre his bitterly divided opponents; some of those most loyal to the Stuart cause began deliberately to disregard the possibility that the king's day still might not yet be done. Some of the king's supporters may even be said to have anticipated the possibility of regicide with rather more equanimity than most of those who would eventually take responsibility for that dreadful act. To some, even king-killing had begun to seem acceptable by comparison with the possibility of an accommodation, however disingenuous, with the common enemy. The king's restoration at the hands of either a Presbyterian majority in parliament, or else an army of sectaries and their Independent supporters, would constitute an enormous gamble on his resumption of the authority and power necessary to restore the fortunes of the crown, the church, his family and their supporters. The king's murder, on the other hand, would present the House of Stuart with at least the glimmer of an opportunity to outwit its enemies; to reinstate, even enhance the ideological power and moral authority of the crown and the church; and to establish redoubtable new strongholds from which to mount fresh military offensives by land and sea against the Westminster rebels and their cohorts. Quite some time before England's reluctant king-killers finally resigned themselves to the execution of Charles I, not a few royalists were already pinning their hopes on the prospective succession of Charles II.

<hr/>

[2] John Adamson, "'The Frighted Junto'': Perceptions of Ireland, and the Last Attempts at Settlement with Charles I', in Jason Peacey (ed.), *The Regicides and the Execution of Charles I* (Basingstoke, 2001), pp. 36–70.

[3] *Eikon Basilike* (1876), p. 184; *Memoirs of the Two last Years of the Reign of ... Charles I*, by Thomas Herbert (1702), p. 174.

The treaty of Newport had its genesis in the Newcastle Propositions of 1646.[4] These were subsequently recycled in the autumn of 1647 when the English parliament and its army put to the king at Hampton Court their respective proposals for settlement.[5] The king chose the army Heads over the parliamentary propositions, but within a short space of time all dialogue had halted with the king's flight to the Isle of Wight in November. In December, parliament demanded that, prior to the resumption of talks, the king sign into law four Bills, which included provisions placing the power of the sword in parliament for twenty years and withdrawing all royal proclamations and declarations condemning the Westminster rebels. The king refused to cooperate, and further dialogue was proscribed entirely by the Vote of No Further Addresses in January 1648. When it came to talking with the king self-denial came easier to some than to others, and the vote was honoured more in the breach than the observance. The prohibition collapsed altogether in the face of Lord Inchiquin's abandonment of the parliamentary cause in Ireland, renewed preparations for war in Scotland and the outbreak of revolt in the provinces of England and Wales. On 28 April 1648 parliament voted to revive the substance of previous propositions made to the king as the basis for a settlement.[6] Opponents of negotiations, hoping to scupper them before they began, tacked on three preconditions, two of which replicated two of the four Bills. Before talks proper could begin, the king had to cede the militia and cancel his proclamations, as well as granting a Presbyterian church settlement to last for three years. But with a Scots army once more on English soil, London itself on the verge of combustion, and the Prince of Wales at the mouth of the Thames with the largest single body of English naval shipping under sail at his command, the preconditions were dropped by both Houses on 28 July.[7] Shortly thereafter a deputation set out from Westminster for the Isle of Wight where they formally offered the king talks. On 10 August the king made his acceptance conditional on the withdrawal of the Vote of No Further Addresses and the admission to his presence of those he chose – without which he could not regard himself as treated with 'honour, freedom and safety' – as well as the participation of the Scots nation

---

4   For the Newcastle Propositions, see David Scott, 'The "Northern Gentlemen", the Parliamentary Independents, and Anglo-Scottish Relations in the Long Parliament', *HJ*, 42 (1999), 365–70.

5   Gardiner, *HGCW*, vol. III, p. 355; Richard Cust, *Charles I. A Political Life* (Harlow, 2005), p. 434.

6   David Underdown, *Pride's Purge. Politics and the Puritan Revolution* (Oxford, 1971), p. 97; Scott, *Politics and War*, p. 171.

7   *Ibid.*, p.178.

in the negotiations.[8] On 25 August, parliament informed the king it had repealed the Vote of No Addresses, and invited him to submit the names of those whom he desired to attend him if he now wished to enter talks. On 28 August, the king formally accepted the treaty.[9]

Talks began on 18 September and continued, on and off, until 28 November.[10] On 25 September the king agreed to assent to a Bill withdrawing his proclamations in denunciation of the Westminster rebels, the preamble to which openly stated that parliament had lawfully waged war against the king and his supporters. On 9 October he granted command of the militia to parliament for twenty years. On 11 October he granted parliamentary control of affairs in Ireland for twenty years. On 21 October he assented to the abolition of the entire English church hierarchy, from archbishops to sacrists, vicars choral and choristers, save only for bishops. On 4 November he accepted the absolute proscription of the Book of Common Prayer, even in his own household. On 8 November he granted parliamentary control over the appointment of ministers of state in England for twenty years. There were only two genuine sticking points in the course of the negotiation. The first issue was episcopacy. By the time the treaty ended, the king had come as close as he would ever come to conceding episcopal supremacy. Since 1646 he had managed to reconcile his conscience to the temporary abandonment of bishops.[11] At Newport he held to the same line, offering to suspend episcopal jurisdiction, the monopoly power of ordination included, for three years. On the penultimate day of the treaty the king declared that he could not, yet, accept the abolition of episcopacy, but he offered that the suspension of episcopal authority should last until he and his two Houses agreed on a form of ecclesiastical settlement. Moreover, although he still refused to alienate church lands in perpetuity, nevertheless he consented to an Act which would reinvest church lands in the crown in order that they then be granted on long leases to those who had acquired them on the authority of parliamentarian Ordinances for their sale. A few days later, a majority of MPs accepted the king's answers as a basis on which to settle the kingdom. Had these terms ever been translated into a political settlement, then all else being equal (which of course the king calculated it would not be) it would have taken the best part of a generation at least

---

[8] *His Maiesties Most Gratious Answer to the Votes of the Two Houses of Parliament* (14 August 1648).

[9] *A Letter Sent from the Speakers of Both Houses of Parliament to His Majestie* (31 August 1648), pp. 4–6.

[10] Sir Edward Walker, *Perfect Copies of all the Votes, Letters, Proposals and Answers . . . in the Treaty held at Newport* (1705); Underdown, *Pride's Purge*, chapter five.

[11] Cust, *Charles I*, pp. 18–19, 424–6.

for episcopal authority to reassert itself. The second issue on which the king took a stand had not even arisen until six weeks into the treaty. In late October it was confirmed that the marquis of Ormond was once again in Ireland, seeking an alliance with the confederate Catholic government at Kilkenny. The king came under pressure at Newport to disown the marquis and to order him publicly to cease negotiating with the Irish Catholic rebels. Charles steadfastly declined to issue a proclamation to that effect, but at the very close of the treaty he handed the parliamentarian commissioners a letter to the marquis giving the required order.

During the talks at Newport, the king had seemed – and had certainly been seen – to grant practically everything. Amidst all his sham concessions it is easy to overlook the fact that this was in some respects a genuine negotiation. Charles had twice been invited, at Newcastle and at Hampton Court, simply to set his seal to the propositions tabled at Newport, with very little time permitted in which to debate the details of the proposed settlement. That they might now be the subject of discussion at all was a step in his direction – as were the two extensions permitted to the forty-day term which parliament had originally set. In the course of talks the king persuaded the parliamentarian commissioners to put before parliament answers to their propositions which fell manifestly short of what he was required to grant. Ultimately he even succeeded in moderating some of the parliamentarian demands, particularly with regard to the government of Ireland, as well as the treatment of his friends and supporters at the hands of their conquerors. But the most important concession extracted by the king was the acceptance by the Westminster regime of his condition that nothing agreed during negotiations would actually bind either party until everything on the table had been agreed.[12] Doubtless this was of some reassurance to the king as he then set about making many of his seeming 'concessions', which were in reality nothing of the sort, and which did not by any stretch of the imagination constitute his willing capitulation to his parliamentarian captors. He himself can have had no intention of honouring the terms agreed at Newport; his advisers had reportedly counselled that he make them solely with a view to securing an invitation to go to Westminster to conclude the treaty.[13] The insincerity of the king's concessions is amply evidenced by his instruction that the marquis of Ormond ignore them and his assurance that they would come to nothing.[14]

[12] *Ibid.*, p. 443.
[13] *His Majesties Propositions Sent Yesterday to Both Houses of Parliament* ([3 October] 1648), p. 3; *The Perfect Weekly Account*, 28 September–4 October 1648, [sig. Ee3].
[14] Carte, *Life*, vol. V, pp. 24–5.

Yet there is no disguising the king's own evident distress at the nature and the scale of the terms he was forced to accept at Newport. It was one thing to stipulate that nothing bind until all was agreed, and to enter any and every additional mental reservation necessary to render his concessions meaningless. It was something else actually to be seen not only to cooperate with the parliamentarians, but even explicitly to justify and condone their rebellion. There was an awful irony of which the king could not have been aware in the fact that he assented to treat on the very day that Sir George Lisle and Sir Charles Lucas were executed at Colchester for their loyal defence of the Stuart cause, the first English combatants to suffer summary capital judgment for their armed resistance to the parliamentarian regime.[15] Whatever the niceties of the deal which the king believed he had struck at the commencement of the treaty, the moment he allowed the preamble to the first proposition his enemies began to exploit to the full what they regarded as the king's unequivocal acceptance of guilt for the wars.[16] From the siege of the last English royalist outpost at Pontefract it was reported that the king's withdrawal of his proclamations against parliament had been used by the besiegers, who sent it into the castle, scorning the loyalty of those within. 'What will he not do', they jeered, 'having yeelded thus far? where is his regard to his Party? You shall see him sacrifice all to save his owne stake.'[17] News that the king had accepted the first proposition in full prompted one supporter of the Westminster regime to crow that

the blood thirsty Cavaliers ... may now goe shooe the goose, there is no imployment for them, unlesse they will beate hempe and make halters to hang themselves in, and indeed it is but equity, that such run away Rascalls ... should never be partakers of this peace, but as they have sowed unto sorrow, so let them reape unto shame.[18]

Charles himself plainly came to fear that he might have exposed not only himself but also his closest friends and supporters to the vengeance of their enemies. He had been briefed extensively to the contrary during the treaty itself, but it is not clear whether he had consulted the lawyers who certainly attended him at Newport before or after he agreed to

---

[15] The news from Colchester, when finally it reached the king, was said to have driven him to tears. *The Kingdomes Weekly Intelligencer*, 5–12 September 1648, p. 1078.

[16] *Mercurius Pragmaticus*, 26 September – 3 October 1648, [sig. Nnv]; *The Moderate*, 26 September – 3 October 1648, pp. [90–1]; *The Declaration of the Armie* (5 October 1648), p. 2; *The Moderate*, 14–21 November 1648, pp. 153–4; *Severall Petitions* ([30 November] 1648), p. 8.

[17] *Mercurius Pragmaticus*, 17–24 October 1648, sigs. Tt1, Vv2.

[18] *Mercurius Anti-Mercurius*, 26 September – 2 October 1648, p. 3.

withdraw his declarations and proclamations.[19] In reaction to Henry Ireton's revolutionary manifesto *The Remonstrance of the Army*, which in November 1648 called for the trial of the king and the punishment of royalists, Charles posed the question 'Whether his acknowledgment of the bloud that hath been spilt in the late Warres (nothing being as yet absolutely concluded or binding) could be urged so far as to be made use of by way of Evidence against Him, or any of His Party?'[20] Lengthy legal opinion was again offered to refute the assertion that the king had indeed contracted upon himself and his party the guilt of shedding innocent blood.[21] Sir Edward Hyde followed this line in his own later account, but also remarked that the king 'said that he well foresaw the aspersions it would expose him to; yet he hoped his good subjects would confess that it was but a part of the price that he had paid for the benefit and the peace of his dominions'.[22] The insincerity of the king's concessions does not appear to have spared him the guilt of making them. Shortly after granting away the control of the militia, Charles confided that 'my too great Concessions' were such 'that ... only an Escape can justify'.[23] This is an odd-sounding plaint coming from someone who supposedly did not believe that he could be held to anything until the treaty was agreed, and not even then to anything exacted under duress. What is more, it came even before Charles made his most substantial concessions on the religious and ecclesiastical settlement. Nicholas Oudart attested to the tears of frustration which the king shed before concluding the paper touching regulation of the episcopal function presented on 9 October.[24] The king's servant Philip Warwick also described how he witnessed the king weeping in a private moment of regret for having heeded others even though their advice hurt his own conscience.[25]

If the king took little enough comfort from the insincerity of his treating, it is hardly surprising that his supporters seemingly took no heart from it whatever. In public, royalist attitudes towards the treaty varied significantly. The overwhelming reaction to news of fresh talks was to condemn the prospective negotiation as a parliamentarian deception. Once preconditions were dropped, opinion improved slightly. A few

---

[19] *CSP*, vol. II, p. 431.

[20] *His Majesties Queries upon the Remonstrance of the General Councell of the Armie* ([27 November] 1648), pp. 2–4.

[21] *Reasons and Grounds of his Majesties Answere to the first Proposition* ([11 December] 1648).

[22] *CHR*, vol. IV, p. 436.

[23] C. W. Firebrace, *Honest Harry. Being the Biography of Sir Henry Firebrace, Knight (1619–1691)* (1932), Appendix E, 'The Hopkins Letters', pp. 344–6.

[24] Francis Peck (ed.), *Desiderata Curiosa* (3 vols., 1735), vol. II, Lib. x, p. 7.

[25] Sir Philip Warwick, *Memoires of the Reigne of King Charles I* (1702), p. 326.

newswriters and commentators even professed to see the proposed treaty as a hopeful beginning for the restoration of peace and prosperity. More realistically, others saw in it at least an opportunity to build a coalition with moderate parliamentarians in order to isolate those incendiaries who sought to prolong the conflict from which they had derived so much power and profit. But there was a clear realization even in these more optimistic quarters that no real good could come of the treaty unless it was worthy the name and there was a genuine dialogue. When this was not forthcoming some consoled themselves with the thought that the king could be held to nothing which was extorted from him by force. A few remarked the fact that the king had stipulated that he not be held to his concessions until the treaty was successfully concluded. Others urged that the king grant all and did not stint to say that thereby he might trick his way back to Westminster and regain the power with which to scourge his enemies. But the only thing most royalists could find to commend the treaty once it got under way was the fact that it gave the king an opportunity to make manifest his own desire for peace, to expose the implacability of his adversaries, and to exhibit the princely virtue of putting his people's interests before his own. Commenting on what exactly it was the king was sacrificing, those most sympathetic to him did not pull their punches.

There was nothing particularly new about many of the king's concessions. He had been offering to relinquish the prerogative of the sword for almost two years by the time the treaty of Newport began.[26] Perhaps this was why so many of his supporters seem to have been braced for the worst. Before talks began the king's friends realized that the acceptance of key terms, such as surrender of the power of the militia, would render him 'a fine King of clouts', divested of sovereign power, and thereby denuded of authority.[27] After just two weeks of talks, Marchamont Nedham remarked that the king was so earnest after peace that 'he hath in a manner resigned up his Sword, Scepter and Crowne'.[28] Another writer described the king as 'bereft / Of regall power, no jot of honour left... / ...forc'd, if he his libertie will have, / To bury all his vertues in the grave'.[29] In November, the same writer wrote hopefully of 'an happy issue' of the treaty, yet nevertheless recognized that peace would be 'purchased at so deare a rate' that 'Charles must (a while) be Slave unto

---

[26] Cust, *Charles I*, pp. 427, 430, 436.
[27] *Mercurius Pragmaticus*, 5–12 September 1648, [sig. F4]. This was plainly not an edition published by Nedham. I am grateful to Jason Peacey for guidance in this attribution.
[28] *Mercurius Pragmaticus*, 3–10 October 1648, sig. Pp-[v].
[29] *Mercurius Melancholicus*, 2–9 October 1648, p. 1.

the State'.[30] All this frank ingenuity notwithstanding, there is reason to believe that many royalist commentators were biting their tongues. The fact was that in the months before the talks began, they had given up to fortune a number of hostages none of which survived the first few weeks of the treaty. Nedham had assumed that the requirement that the king revoke his declarations must surely indicate a desire to see the treaty fail, for it amounted to an impossible demand that the king 'cut the Throats of the Royall Party'.[31] Once talks began, the king's first concession was to concede the withdrawal of his declarations. In mid-September James Howell wrote that

For a King to part with the Sword politic is to render himself such a ridiculous King, as that logg of wood was which Jupiter let down among the froggs for the King at the importunity of their croaking; tis to make him a King of clouts, or as the Spaniard hath it, Rey de Havas, a Bean-King, such as we use to choose in sport at Twelf-night.

Within a few weeks of treating, albeit privately his resolution to crush his enemies remained undimmed, the king had indicated for all the world his willingness to look ridiculous to that end by offering to act the king of clouts.[32]

Charles undoubtedly negotiated insincerely. He and his advisers believed he could not possibly be held to terms dictated to him. According to a hostile source, some of his supporters openly stated that the treaty would be honoured in the same way that the Emperor honoured his undertakings to the Bohemians in 1618, or the king of Spain his, more recently, to the Neapolitans.[33] In any case, having secured his demand that nothing bind until all be agreed, he ensured that he effectively granted precisely nothing of substance at Newport. It remained open to question whether the king would ever actually sign the Bills which would transform the treaty propositions into law. It is hardly surprising that royalist polemicists chose not to labour these points in public, for fear of undermining the king's attempt to outwit his enemies. But it is therefore all the more remarkable to find that, even in private, many loyal servants of the House of Stuart were evidently hard pushed to keep faith with Charles I during the treaty of Newport. The calculations behind the king's tactical gamble cannot have been lost on these men.

---

[30]   *Mercurius Melancholicus*, 14–21 November 1648, pp. 1 and [6].
[31]   *Mercurius Pragmaticus*, 4–11 July 1648, unpaginated.
[32]   *The Instruments of a King: or, a Short Discourse of The Sword, The Scepter, The Crowne* (dated 16 September, p. 11; published [18 September] 1648), p. 9. Nedham's earnest commendation of this work is noteworthy: *Mercurius Pragmaticus*, 19–26 September 1648, [sig. Mm2v].
[33]   *The Moderate Intelligencer*, 12–19 October 1648, pp. 1692–3.

But there is no mistaking the depth of their doubts about the wisdom of holding out concessions.

Soon after talks began at Newport, anonymous newsletter writers were muttering darkly that the king 'hath a hard choice, whether he will give away his Crown, or let them take it: and which he will resolve upon, is not yet easy to inform you'. Another claimed that if the treaty came to a successful conclusion 'monarchy and religion must then conclude with it. The King (they say) is in a fair way to grant all.'[34] When, on 11 October, the news came out that the king had agreed to the abolition of the entire ecclesiastical hierarchy, save for bishops, it provoked a riot amongst the royalists who had taken to congregating at the George tavern at Newport. The assembled 'resolved against it, and made great protestations to avenge their quarrel upon some of the opposite party'. Five died in the resulting affray.[35] On 19 October 1648, Sir Roger Burgoyne told Sir Ralph Verney that the king was being very pliant (so much so that some began to fear lest he grant all), 'and I beleeve will stick at nothing, and I know no reason why he should having already taken upon himself and his party the guilt of all the blood which hath been shedd'.[36]

At some remove from events, several senior figures shared these misgivings. With the memory of the king's betrayal of the earl of Glamorgan in 1646 no doubt weighing heavily, the marquis of Ormond himself remarked that the king's concessions at Newport 'weare as large if not larger then he could give', and even expressed the opinion that 'to my sence he hath parted with more then his owne'.[37] Ormond could be forgiven for believing that his king had given away that which was not his to give. He was not alone. Sir Edward Nicholas worried that his royal master would 'not stick at any thing he can possibly grant' in order to satisfy parliament and army, and expressed his concern to see at 'how deare a rate the king is content to purchase a peace for his subjects in England'. Although he clung to the belief that the treaty would ultimately come to nothing, nevertheless he perceived grave danger in 'his majestie's strange offers', which he feared would be used 'only to defame him and his loyall party'.[38] Even before the king had granted the

---

[34] Carte (ed.), *Letters*, vol. I, pp. 171, 178.

[35] *Bloudy Newes From the Isle of Wight Since the Return of the Parliaments Commissioners from the King* ([13 November] 1648), pp. 1–2.

[36] Papers of Sir Ralph Verney, 1648–53, BL, microfilm M636(9).

[37] Ormond to Lord Inchiquin, 10 November 1648: Bodl., MS Carte 22, fos. 645-v. For the king's disavowal of the terms agreed with the confederates by Glamorgan, see Gardiner, *HGCW*, vol. III, pp. 45–7.

[38] Carte, *Life*, vol. VI, pp. 567, 569–71.

indefinite suspension of episcopal supremacy, Nicholas told Ormond that the king 'hath not totally quitted the Church, though he hath reserved very little of it', and had 'yielded to pay the greatest ransom that ever was paid'. Though he was prepared to accept that this was done merely as a means to secure the king on his throne, 'I confess, I want faith as well to believe it as to comprehend how such concessions can be the way to good either for King or people.'[39]

Sir Edward Hyde also pondered the prospect of a deal at Newport with bitter indignation. The Chancellor had left himself precious little room for manoeuvre by then. In the summer there was published at London his stinging rebuke to the four Bills and the Vote of No Further Addresses in which he had effectively stated that there were no circumstances in which a captive king might honourably and with dignity negotiate with his own gaolers. He had also declared that it was not in the king's power to divest himself of his prerogative of the sword for 'no King hath power not to be a King, because by devesting himselfe he gives away the right which belongs to others, their title to, and interest in his protection' – precisely the spirit which informed Ormond's belief that the king had made concessions which were not in his power to make.[40] Shortly before talks began, Hyde told Lord Culpeper that it would be unworthy 'to flatter ourselves that Monarchy is preserved, whilst the Monarch is stripped and robbed of his Regal power and rights'. Not surprisingly then, against the backdrop of the Newport talks, and the granting by the king of much of the substance of the Bills and preconditions, Hyde told Lord Digby that

I will censure nor rebel against no conclusion the King shall make; but by the grace of God I will not contribute towards, nor have any hand in any, which in my judgment promises nothing but vexation and misery to himself, and all honest men. And therefore you may easily conclude how fit a Counsellor I am like to be, when the best that is proposed, is that which I would not consent unto, to preserve the Kingdom from ashes.

When he came to compose his account of the Civil Wars, Hyde recorded that by the autumn of 1648 'there seemed to be no hope left, but that by treaty the King might yet be restored to such a condition that there might be those roots left in the Crown, from whence its former power and prerogative might sprout out hereafter and flourish'. But he also rather pointedly claimed that many MPs voted that the king's final answers at Newport were a satisfactory basis for settlement on the grounds that there was no longer anything to fear from him because 'if

---

[39]   Carte (ed.), *Letters*, vol. I, pp. 166–7, 168–70, 189–90, 190–1.
[40]   *A Full Answer to an Infamous Trayterous Pamphlet* ([28 July] 1648), p. 134.

he should have a mind to continue the distractions to-morrow, he would find nobody ready ever to join with him, having at this time sacrificed all his friends to the mercy of their mortal enemies'.[41]

Some of those around the king at this time did not forbear to advise him that his duty to his subjects and his posterity could not be discharged by concluding a dishonorable peace. At Newport on 29 November, the day after the treaty of Newport ended, even as the king sat back and contemplated the harvest that he hoped to reap from the 'seeds of peace' he told his son he had implanted with the parliamentarian commissioners, Henry Ferne preached a sermon before the king in which he assured Charles that whilst peace would surely return to England in the end, yet it might come the sooner to the just man who came to an acceptance of his own death and the 'Crown of Glory' which awaited him.[42] By that time the king and his advisers had in their hands the manuscript of *Eikon Basilike*, by now very close to completion, if not finished, in which the king resigned himself to Christian martyrdom. But according to one account, the king did not want the book published in his name. The time was perhaps not yet ripe.[43]

In the event, the treaty of Newport did not survive the vote of MPs to accept the king's answers as a basis for settlement, a vote which precipitated the army's purge of the Commons. But the forcible exclusion of MPs who supported the treaty of Newport did not end the search for a peaceful accommodation with the king. Delegations from each side passed back and forth between Westminster, Windsor and Whitehall at the end of December and into January, with the earl of Denbigh for the parliamentarians and the duke of Richmond for the royalists leading the efforts to broker a settlement. Back-stair dealing was still in evidence even during the king's trial, Charles and his judges keeping open channels for more constructive communication than the angry public exchanges witnessed in the Great Hall at Westminster. Many royalists plainly came to appreciate that which the king himself had long since grasped: that the ruling parliamentary junto needed him too much to kill him. Having reacted so violently to the talks at Newport, some senior royalists appeared far more sanguine about the prospect of concluding terms with the Independents, Sir Edward Nicholas openly professing that he expected they would be better than those tabled by the

---

[41]　*CSP*, vol. II, pp. 412, 459; *CHR*, vol. IV, pp. 426–n8, 453, 464–5.

[42]　Henry Ferne, *A Sermon Preached before His Majesty at Newport in the Isle of Wight, November the 29. 1648. Being the Fast-day* (1648[/9]), p. 20.

[43]　Sean Kelsey, 'The Kings' Book. *Eikon Basilike* and the English Revolution of 1649', in N. Tyacke (ed.), *The English Revolution c. 1590–1720. Politics, religion and communities* (Manchester, forthcoming).

Presbyterian leadership.[44] Nicholas was pursuing a number of schemes through agents at Westminster for the recovery of property in England at the time that he offered the opinion – his 'single fancy' – that any terms the army might offer would be 'much more moderate and honourable both for the King and his party'.[45] More disinterested royalist commentators such as Marchamont Nedham realized the price of an accommodation was the king's assent to the destruction of the crown, church and parliamentarian trinity.[46] Even when it had involved capitulation to the two Houses this had not been a handsome prospect, much less so now that it would involve surrender to a military junto. Royalists who played down the threat to the king's life in the winter of 1648–9 are often accused of indulging in 'wishful thinking'. But there was nothing necessarily 'wishful' about it.

During the treaty at Newport, royalist commentators had at least tried to maintain in public a stoic acceptance of the king's sacrifices in the face of parliamentary demands as the price he must pay for the sake of his people. When a similar offer was tabled by the army and its supporters just before Christmas at Windsor, the response was rather less philosophical. One royalist newswriter commented that the earl of Denbigh had offered the king his crown in a deal which would deny him the kingly power of both his negative voice and his right to summon parliament, 'so that you see a Jack a Lent, or a King of Clowts would be full out as usefull to us, as King Charles, if they might but have their wills'. All they would have him do would be to revoke honours he had conferred, and reconfer them instead as directed.[47] In a similar vein, one royalist lamented that, in captivity, the king was as good as dead. His enemies having subjected him to their own will there was little point in executing him. If their intention was simply to reduce the monarchy to a vehicle for their own designs, the anonymous poet advised,

> Then yet let Charles be King; he's now become
> Just such a one, by his unhappy Doome,
> As ye could wish to have him, linck't as fast
> In iron, as you'd wish in Law.

Indeed, so humiliating was his new condition that it would be better for the king to be executed, a fate which would at least grant him the

---

[44] Carte (ed.), *Letters*, vol. I, p. 191.
[45] John Lawrans to Sir Edward Nicholas, 26 January 1649: Bodl., MS Clarendon 34, fo. 87; *Nicholas*, vol. I, pp. 109–10.
[46] *Mercurius Pragmaticus,* 26 December 1648 – 9 January 1649, unpaginated.
[47] *Mercurius Elencticus,* 19–26 December 1648, p. [547].

'favour' to be 'crown'd above... / Wrap't in a Starry Chariot of his owne'.[48]

Many shuddered to discover that the king was still willing to gamble everything that remained of the constitution and his own cause. When news broke of the efforts made by the duke of Richmond and several other privy councillors to broker a settlement, one commentator remarked dismissively that

> I cannot tell how any should assume to deliver any thing as the Kings offer, what ever Lords or others pretend; But this I can assure you, that when the King was told on Monday last, that Commissioners were chosen, and a Court authorized to try him: He made Answer, That he would be tryed by none, but his God and his Conscience.[49]

Many clung to this conviction, and attempted to paint the king into a corner to which evidently he had no intention of confining himself. There is an instructive comparison here between Nedham's jeremiads about a puppet king on the one hand and the counterfeit *Pragmaticus* by whom he was supplanted after going into hiding in mid-January 1649, who insisted that the king 'will not stoop to a Subjects Triall, but rather suffer a violent Murder, then in the least seem accessary to his own death or deposition, by such a subjection'.[50] But doubt persisted amongst even the most loyal. On 11 January the future archbishop William Sancroft wrote to his father that 'there is [now] nothing left for the king and his party in this world, but the glory of suffering well, and in a good cause; which I hope nor devils nor men shall be able to deprive them of'.[51] The same day leaders of the Independent interest sat down at Whitehall with the duke of Richmond and other privy councillors in the renewed search for a negotiated settlement; whilst around the same time at Windsor the king was entertaining leading Independent divines.[52] Charles I was far from ready for 'the glory of suffering well', and with good reason. Preparations for the king's trial amply demonstrated, for their part, the near-total lack of lethal intent amongst his judges, most of

---

[48] *A Sigh for an Afflicted Soveraigne. Or, Englands Sorrowes for the Sufferings of the King* ([18 December] 1648), pp. 3–4, 5.

[49] *Perfect Occurrences*, 5–12 January 1649, p. [796].

[50] *Mercurius Pragmaticus*, 9–16 January 1649, unpaginated. For the claims to authenticity of the different versions of *Pragmaticus*, see Jason Peacey, ' "The counterfeit silly curr": Money, Politics, and the Forging of Royalist Newspapers during the English Civil War', *HLQ*, 67 (2004), 27–57.

[51] H. Cary (ed.), *Memorials of the Great Civil War in England from 1646 to 1652* (2 vols., 1842), vol. II, p. 103.

[52] F. F. Madan, *A New Bibliography of the Eikon Basilike of King Charles the First* (Oxford, 1950), pp. 164–5 and n.

whom recognized that there was too much at stake for them to sacrifice potentially their strongest card.[53]

Reasons for royalist hostility to the prospect of settlement at the end of a sword are not hard to find. But their reaction was made all the sharper by one factor in particular – the emergence of a credible alternative to a reign suborned to the will of an armed sectarian faction. On 25 January 1649, the ministers and lecturers of Banbury and Brackley presented a petition to the Lord General of the parliamentary army and his Council of Officers at Whitehall. As revolutionary events careered seemingly out of control, the ministers pleaded with the soldiers to avert regicide. They warned that such a course must inevitably result in

a perpetual engagement of the three Kingdoms of England, Scotland, and Ireland in blood ... because the Prince of Wales (the Heir apparent to the Crowns of all the three Kingdoms) is now at liberty, and may probably be proclaimed and crowned in Scotland and Ireland, and so not likely to want power to seat him on his Fathers Throne here in England.[54]

Those attempting to steer a course through the violent storms threatening to inundate the Stuart kingdoms at the time needed little reminding of the danger posed by the Prince of Wales. Five days before the lecturers' petition, the trial of Charles I had begun in the Great Hall at Westminster with the reading of a lengthy charge against the king. Echoing the angry complaints made by some of the parliamentary soldiers who had petitioned their commander-in-chief for justice in the preceding weeks and months, the charge indicted the king not only for attempting to extinguish English freedoms by raising, then renewing war against parliament and people, but also for continuing his commission to the Prince of Wales, and others, 'from whom further invasions upon this land are threatened'. During the trial, the High Court of Justice heard evidence indicating that the prince remained pivotal to schemes for the renewal of armed struggle on his father's behalf.[55]

At the time, Prince Charles was living as the guest of his brother-in-law, William, Prince of Orange.[56] The Stadtholder's support had helped to preserve substantially intact the small naval force which comprised

---

[53]   Sean Kelsey, 'Staging the Trial of Charles I', in Peacey (ed.), *The Regicides*, pp. 71–93; Sean Kelsey, 'Politics and Procedure in the Trial of Charles I', *Law and History Review*, 22 (2004), 1–25.

[54]   *The Humble Advice and Earnest Desires of Certain Well-affected Ministers* (1649), p. 6.

[55]   *Two Petitions Presented to His Excellency Lord Fairfax* (1648), pp. 4, 7; *Heads of the Charge against the King, drawn up by the Generall Councell of the Armie* ([24 December] 1648), p. 5; Gardiner (ed.), *CDPR*, p. 373; J. G. Muddiman (ed.), *The Trial of Charles the First* (Edinburgh and London, 1928), p. 221.

[56]   Pieter Geyl, trans. Arnold Pomerans, *Orange and Stuart, 1641–1672* (2001), ch. 2, *passim*.

one of the Stuarts' chief strategic assets by the winter of 1648–9. The royalist fleet of seven warships and five smaller vessels was big enough to pose a significant threat to English shipping, whose plunder paid for the royalists' passage to the Irish port of Kinsale in the last week of January 1649, an expedition which the under-strength and over-stretched parliamentarian force proved unable to prevent.[57] By the time it slipped its moorings at Helvoetsluys, the royalist fleet under the command of Prince Rupert was no longer the Stuarts' only, or even its chief, strength. On the authority of the Prince of Wales and his mother, talks had begun in October 1648 between James Butler, the marquis of Ormond and the confederate Catholics of Ireland, with the aim of creating a united royalist front in that kingdom. Mired in factional conflict and political uncertainty at Cork and Kilkenny from their commencement, negotiations finally began to accelerate towards a successful conclusion at the end of December. The protagonists were persuaded to sink their outstanding differences when news of the parliamentarian army's renewed irruption onto the English political stage reached Ireland in late December.[58] The marquis of Ormond's second Irish peace was signed and sealed on 17 January 1649. The confederates promised Ormond an army of 15,000 foot and 2,500 horse to add to the substantial Munster Protestant force already placed at his disposal by Lord Inchiquin. The arrival of the royalist fleet later that month added spurs to renewed English fears of an impending Irish invasion.[59]

The situation in Scotland, too, was ripe with potential. In the winter of 1648–9 representatives of the whiggamore Covenanters and former Engagers vied with one another at The Hague for the attentions of the young prince.[60] There were rumours that fresh armies had been promised, on condition that the prince take the Covenant.[61] A clear indicator of the prince's hopes of military assistance from Scotland was his attitude towards James Graham, the marquis of Montrose. In the winter of 1648–9, the prince and his advisers declined any public concourse with

57 Gardiner, *HGCW*, vol. IV, pp. 136, 170, 174; Bernard S. Capp, *Cromwell's Navy. The Fleet and the English Revolution, 1648–1660* (Oxford, 1989), p. 20.

58 Carte, *Life*, vol. III, p. 407; P. J. Corish, 'Bishop Nicholas French and the Second Ormond Peace, 1648–9', *IHS*, 6 (1948–9), 83–100, at p. 98; Micheál Ó Siochrú, *Confederate Ireland 1642–1649. A Constitutional and Political Analysis* (Dublin, 1999), p. 196.

59 Adamson, '"The Frighted Junto"'.

60 Sir Edward Hyde to Prince Rupert, Sunday 24 [January] 1648 [n.s.]: Bodl., MS Firth c.8, fo. 125; *Perfect Occurrences*, 5–12 January 1649, p. 791; *Perfect Diurnall … Parliament*, 8–15 January 1649, p. 2263; *Perfect Occurrences*, 12–19 January 1649, p. 803; S. R. Gardiner, *History of the Commonwealth and Protectorate* (4 vols., 1987), vol. I, p. 16.

61 *The Moderate Intelligencer*, 1–8 February 1649, pp. [1883–4]. But cf. *The Moderate Intelligencer*, 18–25 January 1649, p. [1857].

Montrose, for fear of the damage it might do to the prince in the eyes of the Covenanters who wished to cooperate with the Stuarts, yet who fought shy of any taint of malignancy.[62] In the meantime Montrose, exploiting the title of Field Marshal recently bestowed upon him by the Holy Roman Emperor, would become closely involved in the efforts made to raise fresh German and Scandinavian forces in the hope of establishing a new bridgehead for the Stuarts in the North of their dominions.[63]

The prince's strength could clearly be exaggerated. The royalist fleet was ragged and impoverished, and the arrival in Ireland of Prince Rupert and his retinue further complicated the delicate balancing act required to content all parties to the fragile peace.[64] Ormond continued to face formidable military challenges and even if his paper armies were to materialize in the field, prospects for the unity of a joint Catholic and Protestant force were uncertain at best. In Scotland the whiggamore regime would only raise arms on the prince's behalf on terms which would negate Ormond's achievements in Ireland. Any alternative strategy in the North depended almost entirely on the improbable diplomacy of the marquis of Montrose, and, as ever, hopes of foreign support would prove wildly optimistic. Many royalists may have regarded the prince as dangerously over-exposed to the likes of Lords Jermyn and Culpeper and the kind of counsels which might yet lead to the betrayal of the Church of England. This danger had become all too apparent in the summer when the prince had exceeded even his mother's willingness to accommodate the Scots by declaring a readiness to observe the Presbyterian liturgy on joining Hamilton's army. Edward Hyde, for one, looked on all this with grave suspicion, and many others must have harboured doubts.[65] But the one true strength of which there was never any doubt was the prince's greatest strategic asset – his titular right as the undisputed heir to the three Stuart kingdoms. With his father in captivity, the prince had become the natural leader and figurehead for continued royalist resistance, and in doing so he and his advisers and supporters had found it expedient to help themselves to a hefty advance on the prince's prodigious inheritance – the prerogative rights and title which he would one day come to enjoy in full capacity as king of the Stuart dominions.

---

[62]   *CSP*, vol. II, pp. 466–7, 469–70; Mark Napier (ed.), *Memorials of Montrose and his Times*, 2 vols. (Edinburgh, 1850), vol. II, p. 364.

[63]   *Perfect Occurrences*, 5–12 January 1649, p. [796]; *Mercurius Melancholicus*, 25 December 1648 – 1 January 1649, p. 8; James N. M. Maclean, 'Montrose's Preparations for the Invasion of Scotland, 1649–1651', in R. Hatton and M. S. Anderson (eds.), *Studies in Diplomatic History. Essays in Memory of David Bayne Horn* (1970), pp. 7–31.

[64]   Ormond to the Prince of Wales, n.d.: Bodl., MS Carte 23, fo. 301.

[65]   *CSP*, vol. II, pp. 411–12.

In a declaration announcing his intention of rescuing his father in the summer of 1648, the prince had invoked an authority 'inherent in our Person, during His Majesties restraint', as well as the king's commission, as the basis on which to 'require and command' the English people 'to joyn and associate themselves with us in this our undertaking'.[66] One supporter cited legal authority for his claim that the Prince of Wales was 'esteemed one person with the King and ... ought to enjoy all the antient Prerogatives of the Crowne'.[67] Key confederates at Kilkenny reportedly believed that the Prince of Wales could be persuaded to grant a toleration to Catholics within their own quarters at Kilkenny, offering that in return 'P. Charles in his Father's right shall enjoy all honours and support, due and fitting for the Crown' in Ireland.[68] Ormond, practically dependent on the prince for his authority to negotiate so controversially with the Kilkenny Catholics, seems to have come to regard him as a kind of regent in Ireland, requesting from him not only authority to appoint councillors and ambassadors, but also that he send to Ireland a sword of state, a mace and a seal to replace those Ormond had surrendered to the parliament at his rendition of Dublin back in 1647.[69] In the event, the prince was the king by the time he received Ormond's request. But whilst prince he had certainly not been shy of bestowing the badges of his father's authority, allowing his cousin Prince Rupert to set to sea in January 1649 beneath the royal standard of a regally appointed Lord Admiral, which Rupert most certainly was not.[70]

The prince's liberty, his naval potency and his military prospects – exaggerated or not – exerted a palpable influence over the course of events at Westminster and Whitehall during the king's trial. One possible explanation for the supreme circumspection with which the king's judges approached their solemn responsibility is that it reflects in large part their appreciation of the grave tactical danger to which they would expose themselves by killing one king only to set another at liberty to wreak fresh havoc.[71] By striking fear into the hearts of the beleaguered minority struggling to subdue England, let alone the rest of the British Isles, the warlike preparations made by the heir to the throne and his commanders by sea and by land strengthened the king's hand as he tried talking his way

---

[66] *The Declaration of his Highnesse Prince Charles* ([8 August] 1648), p. 3.

[67] R. M. 'of the Middle Temple, Esq.', *The Just Measure of a Personall Treatie Between the Kings Majesty and Both Houses of Parliament* ([11 July] 1648), pp. 14–16.

[68] Carte (ed.), *Letters*, vol. I, p. 186.

[69] Ormond's instructions to Lord Byron on his despatch to the prince, 26 January 1649: BL, Egerton MS 2541 (Nicholas Papers), fos. 395–9v.

[70] *CSP*, vol. II, pp. 468–9.

[71] Sean Kelsey, 'The Trial of Charles I', *EHR*, 118 (2003), 583–616.

back on to his English throne. Some contemporaries maintained that the king believed Ormond would lead an invasion force which would rein-throne him.[72] But it is unlikely that even Charles had much hope invested in the prospect of a Catholic army hacking its way to Westminster, wad-ing to his rescue knee-deep in Protestant English blood. The vigorous efforts to rekindle the flames of Stuart resistance in Ireland were useful to the king only in so far as he might offer to snuff them out again in return for limiting the scope of the concessions which parliament and the army were determined to extract from him.[73] As they went about risking their own lives and fortunes for his, recent experience cannot have inspired the king's supporters with overmuch confidence. The king's public disavowal of the earl of Glamorgan and his order to Montrose to lay down arms in 1646 amply demonstrate the utility of the king's capture by his enemies.[74] Not surprisingly, when the king once again began talking with his ene-mies in 1648, the reaction amongst royalists had been ambivalent to say the least. Charles I was really only useful to his captors as a puppet, and even then only because the heir to his three crowns was at large, free to resume at will the war of the three kingdoms.

It is easy to see how the prospective succession of Charles II might have come to look more attractive than the prospect of the restoration of Charles I on terms dictated by an army of sectaries. Peace would emas-culate the king, tear up the constitution, bury the episcopal Church of England, and seal the fate of the Stuarts' most loyal friends. Regicide would renew the war and revive the prospects of the House of Stuart, dealing a hammer blow to its godless antagonists by effectively setting at liberty the triple-crowned Stuart monarch. There were risks in such a transition. Succession would inevitably be attended by a factional struggle for supremacy between churchmen and those dubbed 'statists' by David Scott, a struggle whose outcome was uncertain.[75] But this was a struggle that would not have been worth winning if its object was a king who was formally subjected to the sovereignty of the people, the only terms on which Charles I might survive the constitutional revolution which gripped England in the winter of 1648–9. On his father's death Charles II would accede to the full panoply of prerogative power, what-ever he might choose to do with it subsequently, power which his father had little prospect of ever exercising again. Hence Ferne's stern

---

[72] Scott, *Politics and War*, p. 192.

[73] Adamson, ' "The Frighted Junto" ', p. 51.

[74] Gardiner, *HGCW*, vol. III, pp. 153–4; Napier (ed.), *Memorials*, vol. II, pp. 277, 278, 280, 282.

[75] Scott, 'Rethinking Royalist Politics'. For the struggle for influence over the prospec-tive new king, see Kelsey, 'The Kings' Book'.

admonition to a king still unwilling to accept the awful truth; hence also Sancroft's sincere hope that his royal master would defy temptation and embrace 'the glory of suffering well'. Weeks before the king's trial began one royalist newswriter published a lengthy disquisition on the legal formalities for the accession of the king's heir to the throne of England and the manner of his coronation 'after his Royall Fathers decease (whose life God continue)' – a telling afterthought.[76] From The Hague, where the Prince of Wales and his retinue were based, it was reported by a hostile source in mid-January 1649 that 'the Royal English party here are biding in their hopes, that they shal possible thrive better under a new king ... and say they shall next fight for a Master that was never sold'.[77] Even before the king's trial began, there were royalists toying with plans for life after his death.

Unsurprisingly, few were willing openly to voice such sentiments. But they were implicit in much of the trenchant private criticism which had greeted the last ditch efforts to secure a settlement made by Charles I and his advisers. Of the treaty of Newport Sir Edward Hyde had acidly remarked that

Whilst we keep ourselves upon the old foundation of the established Government, and the good known laws, how weak soever we are in power, we shall be strong in reputation; whereas, when we are devising alterations, other's judgments will be submitted to before our's, and we shall only have the infamy of being unfortunate projectors.[78]

As we have seen, Hyde pledged himself loyally to obey all his master's commands, however repugnant. Others were less circumspect. Constitutionally incapable of mincing his words, when news broke of the earl of Denbigh's mission to the king at Windsor, Marchamont Nedham presented his readers with the stark choice between 'a No-King, or a New'.[79] Having realized how desperate many parliamentarians were to avoid ceding the initiative to a king over the water, royalists began to place their hopes in the reversionary interest of the king's heir. Already, as the leader by default of the royalist resistance in 1648, the more the prince had deported, and even proclaimed himself as a sort of regent, the more some amongst his followers had begun to look to him as something rather more than merely his father's heir. Equally, the tighter the king himself was clasped to the bosom of his enemies in the autumn and winter of 1648–9, the more it behoved the Prince of Wales to adopt

[76] *Mercurius Melancholicus*, 1–8 January 1649, p. 10.
[77] *The Moderate Intelligencer*, 11–18 January 1649, p. [1847].
[78] *CSP*, vol. II, p. 459.
[79] *Mercurius Pragmaticus*, 26 December 1648 – 9 January 1649, sig. Fff.

the mantle of the Stuarts' champion and the leader of their partisans; and the more the prince deputized for his father in the exercise of his power and authority, the more pointed the contrast between him and the 'No-King' which Charles I himself recognized he was fast becoming.[80]

In an incisive aside Lois Potter once suggested that, reading royalist literature, 'it sometimes seems as if his own party was consciously *willing* the king to die' by the time he made his first appearance before his judges in Westminster Great Hall. 'Writers had created a fictitious saintly Charles I, and then fallen in love with their own creation.'[81] Knowing what the king was capable of, royalists had every reason to prefer the fantasy to the reality. Many must have pondered anxiously what Charles might do once backed into a corner, and, having seen what had happened at Newport, frankly wondered what he would *not* do in order to save his crown. And yet equally, royalists were in a sense safe, morally at least, in resorting to the dark inward contemplation of the prospects for the premature death of their king. Certainly they could console themselves, as they seem to have done, with the thought of royal martyrdom in a cause which would become deathless, safe in the knowledge that there would come afterwards one who might yet redeem all their own sacrifice and suffering.

By late 1648 the House of Stuart faced a crisis in which some of its supporters saw at least the glimmer of an opportunity – the prospective succession of King Charles II. Safely overseas, with a navy at his command, the immediate prospect of Irish armies in the field, and promises of support in Scotland, the Prince of Wales remained easily the greatest threat which faced the English parliament by the autumn of 1648. To some extent, the prince's reversionary interest gave Charles I some faint leverage in a desperate situation, first at the treaty of Newport, and then during his trial in the Great Hall at Westminster, most of his judges hoping to reach an accommodation with him rather than cede the political initiative to his successor. However, it was self-evident that any putative accommodation would inevitably give ultimate victory to the parliamentarians by placing the king in checkmate and neutralizing the prince. At least some royalists began to realize that it would be better – for the church, the monarchy, the House of Stuart, and for they themselves – if Charles I quit the field in favour of his son. By the close of the treaty of Newport royalists had begun to confront the choice between a No-King and a New. Subsequent developments did nothing to obviate

---

[80]   Firebrace, *Honest Harry*, Appendix E, p. 344.
[81]   Lois Potter, *Secret Rites and Secret Writing: Royalist Literature, 1641–1660* (Cambridge, 1989), p. 175.

the necessity of choosing, but they may have made the choice easier. Indeed, by the time of his trial, at least some of his own supporters appear to have looked forward to the king's death more enthusiastically than did most of his enemies. Some, such as Ferne and Sancroft, may have feared the prospect of settlement more than they welcomed the prospect of a succession – albeit the accession of a new king was the corollary of what they had come to hope for. Others, however, such as Nedham and the royalists at The Hague, positively welcomed the prospect of a new reign – albeit the inevitable corollary of their hopes was regicide. Paradoxical as it may seem, king-killing had actually become the last best hope for many royalists. Having mentally rehearsed his own martyrdom for a number of years, and fully appreciating how much his enemies still needed him, Charles himself almost certainly realized this. For his own part, his eldest son had enjoyed too much latitude in the second half of 1648 not to be aware, at the very least, that his father's and his family's best interests might one day diverge. But as 'the now king of England' faced his accusers, the future king of England limbered up for succession, and their friends and supporters began staking their claims on a new order, it remained to be seen whether Charles I would finally find the courage to embrace a glorious death.

11   The royalism of Andrew Marvell

Blair Worden

I

In the England of the 1640s, civil war was fought on two fronts: by the sword, and by the pen. The polemicist Marchamont Nedham, a figure with a large part in Andrew Marvell's literary career, remarked in 1652 that 'in our late wars ... the pen militant hath had as sharp encounters as the sword, and borne away as many trophies'. For while the sword may subdue men 'by force', 'the pen it is which manifests the right of things; and when it is once cleared, it gives spurs to resolution, because men are never raised to so high a pitch of action, as when they are persuaded, that they engage in a righteous cause'.[1] In the late 1640s, when the story to be told in this chapter begins, the pen was the principal instrument of defeated royalism, the cause which Nedham, the serial turncoat of the Puritan Revolution, served at that time. During the Second Civil War of 1648, it is true, it was briefly the ally and servant of the sword, but otherwise it was a substitute for it. Never was royalism more buoyant on the page than in the two years that preceded the execution of the king. The royalist cause, like the parliamentarian one, had always been a coalition of principles and temperaments. Royalist writing ranged from piety to hedonism, from Calvinism to paganism, from belligerence to Stoic resignation, from divine-right absolutism to moderate constitutionalism, from unquestioning commitment to the king to doubts about his conduct and policies. It is easier to say what the royalists of the late 1640s were against than what they were for. They were against Roundheads and puritans and against the destruction they had wrought. Whether we describe everyone who shared those antipathies as royalist is a matter of words, but if we do so we must include many people who had not supported the king in the First Civil War, or would not fight for him now, or who did not think that the damage done

---

[1]   John Selden, *Of the Dominion of the Sea* (1652), [transl. Marchamont Nedham], ep. ded. I explore the literary relations of Marvell and Nedham more fully in my *Literature and Politics in Cromwellian England* (Oxford, 2007).

to England in the First Civil War should be blamed on one side alone. Verse and prose that were unmistakably royalist strove to synthesize the various elements of anti-parliamentarian sentiment and make a common cause of them. They projected royalism not, or not only, as a commitment to a particular political or religious programme, but as a creed – an anti-puritan creed – of sociability and civility and conviviality; as a commitment to ideals of honour and loyalty; and as a longing for the civility and tranquillity of the 'halcyon days' of the pre-war Caroline world.[2]

By the late 1640s political poetry had become something like the preserve of royalism. When, at the Restoration, Dryden, in *Absalom and Achitophel*, proclaimed that 'Never rebel was to arts a friend', he drew on an established practice of deriding the philistine illiteracy of the Roundheads and of claiming 'wit' and 'learning', the two essential ingredients of poetic inspiration, for the king's side. Recent writing has protested at that equation, and has shown just how much verse was written by Roundheads.[3] Even so, there were Roundhead writers ready to concede, even to take polemical advantage of, the royalist claim to literary superiority. Marchamont Nedham was one of them. For Nedham wrote for parliament in the first war before writing for the king in the second; thereafter he would write for the successive Roundhead regimes of 1649–60, and then for the restored monarchy. He was himself a poet, whose satire has earned, at its best, legitimate comparison with Dryden's.[4] He made extensive use of verse when writing for the royalists, but mostly eschewed it in writing against them.

In the first war he did, on the Roundheads' behalf, essay literary virtuosity in prose, and so earned the derision of royalists for 'prostituting' 'wit' – anyway an allegedly clumsy wit – to 'a herd of readers'.[5] But he did not come to poetry's defence. He did not claim, as modern critics friendly to Roundhead verse might hope, that poetry, as the ally of truth and virtue, could speak for parliament but not for the king. Instead he contrasted his own 'plain' and 'naked' prose, which 'speaks truth', with the literary

---

[2] Much more attention has been given by literary critics to royalist poetry than by historians to royalist politics. Among a number of illuminating recent studies, the most comprehensive is Robert Wilcher, *The Writing of Royalism 1628–1660* (Cambridge, 2001). An older work, Peter W. Thomas, *Sir John Berkenhead 1617–1679. A Royalist Career in Politics and Polemics* (Oxford, 1969), remains a fine introduction to the royalist literary milieu.

[3] See especially Nigel Smith, *Literature and Revolution in England 1640–1660* (London and New Haven, 1994); David Norbrook, *Writing the English Republic. Poetry, Rhetoric and Politics 1627–1660* (Cambridge, 1999).

[4] Joseph Frank, *Cromwell's Press Agent. A Critical Biography of Marchamont Nedham, 1620–1678* (Lanham, MD, 1980), pp. 60–3, 171.

[5] *Mercurius Anti-Britanicus, or, The Second Part of the King's Cabinet Vindicated* (1645), p. 25.

affectation of royalist writing, which hides it. He represented the Court's taste for masques as a symptom of its dishonesty, which he would 'unmasque' or 'undisguise', and whose 'daubings', and 'paintings' he would expose.[6] Nedham, through whose writing there runs an alertness to the folly of 'fancy' or 'fantasy', saw that proclivity reflected in the royalist taste for chivalric fables.[7] He had higher literary targets too. Behind royalist propaganda, he maintained, there stood the influence of Shakespeare and Jonson, of Beaumont and Fletcher, of Shirley and Davenant. Adopting a puritan face, Nedham connected the Court's literary tastes with its idolatrous worship of God, and contrived to attack 'Shakespeare's works, and such prelatical trash'.[8] The Court, he predicted,

will go near to put down all preaching and praying, and have some religious masque or play instead of Morning and Evening Prayer; it hath been an old fashion at court ... to shut up the Sabbath with some wholesome piece of Ben Jonson or Davenant, a kind of comical divinity.[9]

In the Second Civil War, now wearing a royalist hat, Nedham became a friend to literature. But his earlier approach was adopted by a young journalist whose career and writings frequently interweaved with his, John Hall. In a newsbook with the title, *Mercurius Britanicus*, that in the first war had been Nedham's, Hall portrayed the royalist appetite for chivalry and romance as a symptom of irresponsible escapism.[10]

Where Nedham and Hall pointed, Nedham's 'great crony' and 'particular friend'[11] John Milton would follow. When, in the early 1640s, Milton turned from poetry to the prose he wrote 'of my left hand', the difference was a change of genre but not of literary spirit. To prose he brought the devices of eloquence and oratory that in his mind shared the ethical and persuasive character of verse. But by the late 1640s he was writing a different kind of prose, the austere prose of his *History of Britain*. Earlier he had seen history, no less than oratory, as the handmaid of poetry. More interested in the instructive power of history than in its factual truth, he had been drawn to the literary possibilities of Arthurian myth. Now, in the late 1640s, he strove to write a history

---

6   *Mercurius Britanicus*, 16 November 1643, p. 89; 19 August 1644, p. 10; 30 September 1644, pp. 399–400; 14 October 1644, p. 415; 28 October 1644, p. 431; 3 March 1645, p. 576; 22 December 1645, p. 969.

7   Timothy Raylor, *Cavaliers, Clubs, and Literary Culture: Sir John Mennes, James Smith, and the Order of the Fancy* (Newark, NJ, 1994).

8   *Mercurius Britanicus*, 2 September 1644, p. 386.

9   *Ibid.*, 11 November 1643, p. 89; cf. *ibid.*, 11 January 1644, p. 153.

10   [John Hall], *Mercurius Britanicus*, 23 May – 27 June 1648, pp. 16, 30, 37, 54; 1 August 1648, p. 90; Hall, *An Humble Motion to the Parliament concerning the Advancement of Learning* (1649), p. 37.

11   Helen Darbishire (ed.), *Early Lives of Milton* (1932), pp. 44, 74. Hall revered Milton.

'sifted from fables', to present 'the truth naked, though as lean as a plain journal'.[12] That, not poetic conceit, was what historical writing needed if it were to equip Milton and his fellow-countrymen 'to raise a knowledge of ourselves'.[13]

In the late 1640s, when the *History* was written, Milton's poetry had almost dried up. From the years after 1647 and before 1652 there survive only the sonnet to Sir Thomas Fairfax in 1648 and the translations of Psalms from the same year. Milton always knew that if good poetry can inspire virtue, degenerate poetry can inspire vice. Yet in his *Eikonoklastes* in 1649, poetry itself almost seems a suspect medium. Having heard that the king was 'a more diligent reader of poets, than of politicians', and noting the 'poetical ... strains', the 'masking scene', the 'painted feathers', of *Eikon Basilike* and its debt to 'Amadis and Palmerin', 'I began to think that the whole book might be intended for a piece of poetrie.' Milton hit at the 'licentious remissness' of the king's 'Sundays theatre'; 'the old pageantry of some twelf-nights entertainment', 'the polluted orts and refuse' and 'heathen orisons' of that 'vain amatorious poem', Sidney's *Arcadia* – a work whose improving power he had earlier saluted, but which he now deemed contrary to 'religious thoughts'. Shakespeare's 'stuff' is presented in no admiring spirit, for his writings were 'the closet companion' of the king's 'solicitudes'.[14] In the same year John Cook, Solicitor General at Charles I's trial, remarked on the disasters that might have been averted had the king 'studied Scripture half so much as Ben Jonson or Shakespeare'.[15]

Andrew Marvell's poem to the royalist Richard Lovelace, published in 1649 but perhaps written the previous year, makes the connection between royalism and poetry by scorning the writers thrown up by rebellion, 'Of wit corrupted, the unfashioned sons' (line 20).[16] In 1650, in 'Tom May's Death', we learn that the poet and historian May, in deserting the king and writing against him, has demeaned himself much as Nedham was earlier accused of doing: he 'prostituted hast/ Our spotless knowledge and the studies chaste,/ Apostatising from our arts and us' (71–3). Marvell's verse of 1648–50 debates the rival claims of the sword and the pen. In his poem on the death of the young royalist Lord Francis Villiers in battle in 1648, during that brief period when the sword was once more an alternative to literature, 'we hereafter' will 'Not write too

12 Don M. Wolfe et al. (eds.), *Complete Prose Works of John Milton*, 8 vols. (New Haven, CT, 1953–83), vol. V, p. 230.
13 *Ibid.*, vol. V, p. 130.
14 *Ibid.*, vol. III, pp. 342, 358, 361–7, 406.
15 John Cook, *King Charls his Case* (1649), p. 13.
16 I quote Marvell's poetry from Nigel Smith (ed.), *The Poems of Andrew Marvell* (2003).

many' obsequies but 'kill' 'so many' Roundhead soldiers, Cromwell and Fairfax at their head. Villiers himself 'died not ... revengeless', for 'A whole pyramid/ Of vulgar bodies he erected high'. In time the Roundhead army will 'by just vengeance come' to be 'at once' Villiers's 'trophy and his tomb'(14–16, 115–17, 125–8).[17]

By 1650, however, it seems that writing rather than fighting has become the duty of the royalist poet. The frontal contrasts between the two poems that Marvell wrote to mark political occasions of that year reinforce the point. In 'Tom May's Death' the regicide is 'the poet's time'. Since 'justice' has succumbed to the sword, and since 'coward churchmen' – that is, almost all the Anglican divines – are too frightened to write or preach on the murdered king's behalf,[18] the royalist cause is entrusted to the solitary poet, who 'Sings still of ancient rights and better times', and to whose exertions Marvell gives a military metaphor: 'tis then he draws,/ And single fights forsaken virtue's cause' (63–9). Yet when we turn to *An Horatian Ode upon Cromwell's Return from Ireland*, where the royalist cause is – ostensibly anyway – renounced, the 'forward youth' is to 'forsake his muses'. Now the 'time' is not the writer's but the soldier's: 'Tis time to leave the books in dust' and to oil and don armour. Instead of 'singing still' of ancient rights, the forward youth is to 'cease' to 'sing/ His numbers languishing' (1–8). Those opening lines are close in spirit to words written around the time of Cromwell's return by John Hall, whose literary career had its contacts with Marvell's as well as Nedham's. Arguing for submission to the republic, Hall denounces inert royalists who are 'lulled asleep with some small continuance of peace ... as if the body politic could not languish of an internal disease', and associates them with 'speculative men', 'men merely contemplative', who follow 'those notions which they find in books' and 'fight only with pen, ink, and paper'.[19] A month after Cromwell's return, Nedham spoke in a similar spirit in the same cause. In the First Civil War he had identified royalist writing with a weakness for 'ale'[20] and with 'melancholy'.[21] Now he exclaimed:

How sweet the air of a commonwealth is beyond that of a monarchy! Is it not much better then to breathe freely, and be lively, upon a new score of allegiance,

---

[17] I hope it is by now uncontroversial to take the poem to be Marvell's.
[18] For the Anglican reticence see Wilcher, *Writing of Royalism*, p. 272.
[19] John Hall, 'The Grounds and Reasons of Monarchy', in John Toland (ed.), *The Oceana of James Harrington and his Other Works* (1700), pp. 4–5. Cf. *Mercurius Britanicus*, 25 November 1644, p. 72; 10 February 1645, p. 548.
[20] *Mercurius Pragmaticus*, 7 March 1648, pp. 1–2.
[21] See e.g. *Mercurius Britanicus*, 11 January 1644, p. 153; cf. *The Recantation of Mercurius Aulicus* (1644), p. 3; *Mercurius Britanicus*, 28 October 1644, p. 435; 7 July 1645, p. 802.

than pine, and fret, and fume, in behalf of the old non-entity, till wit, soul, and all be drowned in ale and melancholy?[22]

Was the 'wit' of royalist poets being 'drowned' in 1650? Was it a fault of royalist verse to look, not 'forward' with the 'youth' of the *Horatian Ode*, but backward? The second line of Marvell's poem to Lovelace addressed his subject's 'sweet muse', which is the victim of present times. His royalist poem on the death of Lord Hastings in 1649 appears in a volume entitled (conventionally enough) *Lachrymae Musarum* (the tears of the muses). In the second line of the *Horatian Ode*, where the forward youth is to forsake his muses, it seems that Marvell has cleared and dried his eyes.

'Tom May's Death' gives to the shade of Ben Jonson, through whose voice the poem reproaches May, the role that Jonson had awarded to himself and to poetry, as the arbiter and instructor and reformer of the world. No writer had been so widely claimed for Civil War royalism. No writer so fully embodied royalists' perception of the proper relationship of poetry to politics. Not least we find him repeatedly present in the prefatory poems to that ambitious statement of literary royalism, the edition of the works of Beaumont and Fletcher published by Humphrey Moseley in 1647. James Howell's contribution (which, like 'Tom May's Death', introduces Jonson familiarly as 'Ben', without the surname) castigates the present times much as Marvell's poem to Lovelace rebukes 'the times' that are 'much degenerate from' the 'candid age' – Jonson's age – of pre-war literature, and much as Marvell's Jonson castigates May: 'Had now grim Ben been breathing', writes Howell, 'with what rage,/ And high-swolne fury had hee lash'd this age.'[23] Likewise the reminder by Marvell's Jonson that the true poet 'arraigns successful crimes' points back to lines, in the Beaumont and Fletcher volume, of the royalist polemicist Sir John Berkenhead. He, too, invokes Jonson in recalling a pre-war world free from the present literary degeneracy, when, as he recalls, 'high crimes were still arraigned'.[24]

Jonson's role in 'Tom May's Death' recalls, too, the royalist Nedham of the late 1640s. When Jonson is found 'Sounding of ancient heroes, such as were/ The subject's safety, and the rebel's fear' (15–16), Marvell presumably has in mind Jonson's play *Catiline his Conspiracy*, which, despite its failure on the English stage in 1611, had become, in print,

---

[22] *Mercurius Politicus*, 11 July 1650, p. 65. Cf. *ibid.*, 13 June – 18 July 1650, pp. 20, 50, 63, 81.
[23] Arnold Glover and A. R. Waller (eds.), *The Works of Francis Beaumont and John Fletcher*, 10 vols. (Cambridge, 1905–12), vol. I, p. xxvi.
[24] *Ibid.*, vol. I, p. xliii.

a powerful influence on English perceptions of rebellion.[25] The 'ancient heroes' of the play are Cicero and Cato, whom Marvell introduces later in the poem as the kinds of classical figures whose names – as Marvell alleges – May has misused in rebellion's cause (48). Marvell's phrase for the regicide, when 'the world's disjointed axle crack[s]' (68), is taken from Jonson's *Catiline* and from Jonson's own poem on May.[26] Perhaps Jonson is present in the *Horatian Ode* too. In November 1647, and again in a tract of 1648, Nedham had described the leaders of the New Model Army as 'being resolved to follow the example of Catiline in Ben Jonson', and had imagined them saying, as Catiline does at the start of Jonson's play, 'The ills that I have done cannot be safe,/ But by attempting greater.'[27] From a royalist perspective – for in spite of the contrasts with 'Tom May's Death', we shall find, the *Horatian Ode* will sustain a royalist perspective – the lines recall the *Ode*'s concluding couplet: 'The same arts that did gain a power/ Must it maintain.' From the same perspective Marvell's 'restless Cromwell' answers to another soliloquy of Jonson's Catiline, who is addicted to

> That restless ill, that still doth build
> Upon success; and ends not in aspiring;
> But there begins, and ne'er is fill'd,
> While aught remains that seems but worth desiring.[28]

II

In 1648–50 Marvell wrote four poems that declared a royalist allegiance.[29] Two of them, those written on the deaths of Francis Villiers and Tom May, incited or demanded adherence to the Stuart cause. The others appeared in collections of poems, published in the months after the regicide, which proclaimed a collective royalist identity: the

---

25 Its impact is explored in Barbara de Luna, *Jonson's Romish Plot. 'Catiline' and its Historical Context* (Oxford, 1967), ch. X.

26 Jonson, *Catiline his Conspiracy*, Act III, Scene i, lines 175–8; Norbrook, *Writing the English Republic*, p. 279; cf. Nedham, *Honesty's Best Policy* (1678), pp. 7–8.

27 *Mercurius Pragmaticus*, 9 November 1647, p. 63. Nedham made use of the lines again in *A Plea for the King and Kingdom* (1648), p. 10.

28 Act III, Chorus, lines 864–7. Clarendon's famous description of Oliver Cromwell as a 'brave bad man', which from the same perspective sums up the Cromwell of the Ode, has Jonson's *Catiline* behind it: Act IV, Scene ix, 84.

29 Though I hesitate to disagree with James Loxley, who has written with such distinction and insight on royalist poetry, his argument that royalism is peripheral to Marvell's verse of 1648–9 seems to me to rest on too narrow a definition of royalism: ' "Prepar'd at Last to Strike in with the Tyde"? Andrew Marvell and Royalist Verse', *The Seventeenth Century*, 10 (1995), 39–62; 'Marvell, Villiers, and Royalist Verse', *Notes and Queries*, 239 (1994), 170–2.

Lovelace poem, and the poem in memory of the young Lord Hastings. Hastings died, aged nineteen, not, like Villiers, in war, but of smallpox; but the insignia of the volume claim him for his family's royalism. Marvell's royalism, or anyway the record of it, is confined to those years. We do not know what political thoughts he had during the First Civil War, when, in his early-to-mid-twenties, he travelled abroad. From early 1651 he wrote poems for, or favourable to, the new rulers of England. From 1654 (if not earlier) to 1659 he was an open Cromwellian. The two poems that mark occasions of 1650 are the bridge from Marvell's royalist past to his Cromwellian future. It proved hard to cross.

We have seen how 'Tom May's Death' defines the poet's time, whereas the *Ode*, applying the same vocabulary to opposite ends, renounces it (albeit on terms that it takes verse to prescribe). There are further antitheses, on the surface anyway. The 'ancient rights' that, in the May poem, the poet is to 'sing still' are, in the *Ode*, pleaded 'in vain' (38). In the *Ode* the 'successful crimes' that in the other poem are to be 'arraign[ed]' are endorsed, while the 'wretched good' of the May poem (70), which in the *Ode* is Charles I's 'helpless right' (62), is abandoned. In the May poem, Brutus and Cassius are 'the people's cheats' (18): in the *Ode* the death of 'Caesar' (23), Charles I, has history on its side. In the *Ode*'s concluding lines, the symbol of the erect sword unites war with justice: in the May poem the sword, glittering 'o'er the judge's head' (63), is justice's enemy.

If Tom May had died earlier, instead of five months later, than Cromwell's return from Ireland, the contrasts between the two poems might have a straightforward explanation. We could read the *Ode* as the witness to a conversion experience, and think of Marvell directing against the royalist cause the language he had so recently used for it. As it is, May's death came roughly half-way between Cromwell's return and the public occasion which Marvell marked in his next public poem, the decision of the republic, which the poem endorses, to dispatch an embassy to the United Provinces under Cromwell's cousin and intimate friend and ally Oliver St John. It is the poem of a man seeking a patron. The *Horatian Ode* is no such poem. In 1654 Marvell, who had borrowed wording from the *Ode* in the May poem, would take other words from it in his poem on 'The First Anniversary' of Cromwell's assumption of the protectorate.[30] The 'First Anniversary' is a panegyric. The *Ode* is not. There is no reason why Marvell's transition from royalism to Cromwellianism should have taken a linear or uncomplicated path. The *Ode* and the May poem are occasional poems, responses to the separate events

[30] Norbrook, *Writing the English Republic*, pp. 340–1.

that occasioned them. As the events are different, so are the responses. But they are not the straightforward opposites that their antitheses of wording might suggest. The *Ode* is a double-sided poem that itself invites antithetical understandings. The May poem, which is straightforward in its royalism, is opposite only to one of the *Ode*'s two sides.

There is one perception that the *Ode* shares with 'Tom May's Death'. The execution of the king, which in the May poem has cracked the world's disjointed axle, is no less elemental an event in the *Ode*, where 'that memorable hour/ Which first assured the forced power' (65–6) occupies the pivotal lines of the poem. If there are such things as seismic shifts of political consciousness, the regicide brought one. That its impact, to which Marvell's verse is so eloquent a witness, remains elusive is partly due to our divisions of academic labour, which divide poetry from political thought. The one is considered the province of feeling and of literary form, the other of thought and ideas. One, in the wake of the regicide, produced the *Horatian Ode*, the other *Leviathan*. Those works, both written by royalists or ex-royalists, share a political context and a political vision. Both of them vindicate, or half-vindicate, a new order. In 1968 the critic John Wallace persuasively set the Hobbesian – and Machiavellian – logic of the *Ode*, where 'ancient rights' do 'hold or break/ As men are strong or weak' (39–40), beside the arguments from the right of conquest that were deployed in 1649–52 in support of the imposition by the new republic of an engagement of loyalty by its citizens.[31] That initiative, which became acutely controversial in 1650, presented the nation with a stark choice of allegiance: a choice between past and future of a kind that the 'forward youth' of Marvell's poem, wondering how to 'appear', must make. Readers of the arguments from conquest were offered warrants for accommodation to a hostile and illegal political world and a basis for survival within it. The arguments were a huge leap from the constitutionalist thinking, and from the preoccupation with legality and liberty, that had been the normal currency of political debate for long before the Civil Wars, and had remained so during them. The new political language which emerged after the regicide, and which enjoined obedience not to virtue or legality but to might, was a symptom of political deracination – or of the cracking of the axle. So too was the simultaneous outburst of apocalyptic thinking, which extended well beyond the radical sects, and which would come to

---

[31]   John M. Wallace, *Destiny his Choice. The Loyalism of Andrew Marvell* (Cambridge, 1968); and see Quentin Skinner, 'Conquest and Consent. Thomas Hobbes and the Engagement Controversy', in G. E. Aylmer (ed.), *The Interregnum. The Quest for Settlement 1646–1660* (Basingstoke, 1972), pp. 99–120.

the forefront of Marvell's writing in the 'First Anniversary'. The challenge is to recover a mental world where those disruptive ideas could carry such conviction as to subsume the fiercest opposition to them – including Marvell's.

On one side of the *Ode*, the anger and pain that are openly voiced in the May poem have a largely covert but not any less keen presence. We have only to look at the most famous lines of the poem to witness them. Critics debate Marvell's representation of the martyred king, but miss the contrast between Charles's own conduct and that of his killers. In a poem of such metrical perfection, the italicized breach of it – '*He* nothing common did, or mean,/ Upon that memorable scene' (57–8) – speaks loudly. Cromwell is 'The force of angry heaven's flame' (26), and yet his own rise has been won by the sham-providentialism of himself and his fellow-regicides, who in bringing the king to execution 'did call the gods with vulgar spite/ To vindicate' their deed (61–2). Their 'common' behaviour, 'While round the armèd bands/ Did clap their bloody hands' (55–6), is seen through royalist outrage. To illustrate the royalist side of the poem, I shall set Marvell beside two writers to whom he was close, and both of whom, like him, were converts from royalist allegiance or sympathy during the 1650s. They are Marchamont Nedham and the political thinker (and poet) James Harrington.[32]

III

In 1649 Nedham was arrested by the republic and his royalist newsbook closed down. He bought his pardon, and a handsome salary, by turning his pen to the commonwealth's use. If there was an emotional cost to his transition – or to any of his political transitions – he does not reveal it. His writing discloses none of Marvell's depth or anguish of feeling. In May 1650 he produced his first work of propaganda for the republic, *The Case of the Commonwealth*, which enjoins obedience and subjection to any regime which commands the sword, as the republic does. It was at the end of that month that Cromwell returned from Ireland. In mid-June Nedham began to edit his weekly newsbook on the republic's behalf, *Mercurius Politicus*. Normally *Politicus*, like other newsbooks,

---

[32] I have written more fully on Nedham in 'Marchamont Nedham and the Beginnings of English Republicanism', in David Wootton (ed.), *Republicanism, Liberty, and Commercial Society 1649–1776* (Stanford, CA, 1994), pp. 45–81; '"Wit in a Roundhead": The Dilemma of Marchamont Nedham', in Susan Amussen and Mark Kishlansky (eds.), *Political Culture and Cultural Politics in Early Modern England* (Manchester, 1995), pp. 301–37; and 'Milton and Marchamont Nedham', in David Armitage, Armand Himy and Quentin Skinner (eds.), *Milton and Republicanism* (Cambridge, 1995), pp. 156–80; and on Harrington in chs. 2 and 3 of Wootton, *Republicanism*.

was compiled day by day, events being described under the heading of
the day on which news of them came through. Yet its first issue, which
ran from 6 to 13 June, began with an exception to that rule. Since
Cromwell, after his return from Ireland, had entered London on 1 June,
his reception had no proper place in Nedham's opening number. But so
important an event 'cannot here be omitted',[33] and is duly described.
Until now, Cromwell, who had been extravagantly vilified and carica-
tured in royalist publications (not least Nedham's royalist newsbook of
1647–9, *Mercurius Pragmaticus*), had been accorded only limited praise
in pro-government ones. There had, too, been little serious poetry in his
commendation.[34]

Together, Nedham and Marvell transformed his literary standing.
They give him a heroic stature – only to counter it simultaneously with
a villainous one. Nedham cited Cromwell's heroism among the reasons
why his readers should commit themselves to the republic. *The Case of
the Commonwealth* observed that in Ireland

the lord lieutenant hath swept away [his] adversaries with the besom of vengeance and made way by a continued chain of miraculous successes to shackle
that rebellious nation ... every month brings fresh laurels of victory to their
terror and amazement.[35]

The theme is developed in *Politicus*. Its opening issue maintains that if
'reason' and 'interest' are not enough to bring the English to rally round
the regime against the threat from Scotland, 'yet let them stoop with
reverence at the name of that victorious commander, Cromwel', whose
'most famous services in Ireland', 'being added to the garland of his
English victories, have crowned him, in the opinion of all the world,
for one of the wisest and most accomplished leaders, among the present
and past generations'.[36] Even now that he has left Ireland, he con-
quers there by his 'bare reputation', which is 'strong enough against
the stoutest hearts, and most impregnable castles', so that his army
'can not forget to conquer wheresoever it comes'.[37] When, on 11 June,
Cromwell gave parliament an account of the situation in Ireland,
Nedham observed that it is

the wonder of our neighbour nations, that so much should be done in so little
time, notwithstanding so many disadvantages; and for my part, if we take a view

---

[33]   *Mercurius Politicus*, 13 June 1650, p. 3.
[34]   Cf. Norbrook, *Writing the English Republic*, p. 251.
[35]   Marchamont Nedham, *The Case of the Common-Wealth of England, Stated* ([8 May]
       1650).
[36]   *Mercurius Politicus*, 13 June 1650, pp. 3–4.
[37]   *Ibid.*, p. 5.

of his actions from first to last, I may (without flattery) proclaim him to be the only *Novus Princeps* that ever I met with in all the confines of history.[38]

So much is likewise done in so little time in the *Horatian Ode*, where the Irish see themselves 'in one year tamed' and ashamedly acknowledge that 'So much one man can do' (73–5). In October *Politicus* published a letter ostensibly written by an Irishman decrying the failings of his nation's leadership, which, the writer complains, have led a hitherto puissant land to yield all to Cromwell 'in one winter's season; such a winter's successe in war, by so inconsiderable a party, against so considerable a kingdom, was never read, nor heard of: Alexander the Great, or Julius Caesar, or William the Conquerour never had the like successe'.[39] Ruthless as Cromwell's victories were, Marvell's poem has the Irish confessing 'how good he is, how just' (79): Nedham invites his readers to 'take notice of the noble temper of the lord generall, all whose conquests are ever sweetned with acts of mercy'.[40]

Marvell's 'restless Cromwell ... urgèd his active star' (12): Nedham's Cromwell is 'as restless in his own sphere, as the great intelligencers' – the stars – 'are in theirs'.[41] In the last section of the *Ode*, Cromwell will carry his conquests from Scotland to France, to Italy, and to 'all states not free' (102). Nedham, who in *The Case* proclaims 'the excellency of a free state',[42] looks in *Politicus* for Cromwell to lead a European war of liberation:

this brave Scipio, my lord generall Cromwell, after he hath wholly subdued Ireland, and Scotland, to the Common-wealth of England, ought to do the like elsewhere; that so our domineering and insolent neighbours may be brought under.[43]

Politicus expects Cromwell to liberate the Scots, follows the struggles for freedom of the rebels of the Frondes in France, and wishes himself among the monarchy's opponents in Bordeaux 'for one twelvemonth, to teach them to spell the meaning of liberty'.[44] Like Marvell, whose Cromwell will be 'A Caesar...ere long to Gaul,/ To Italy an Hannibal', Nedham looks beyond France to Italy. 'If things thus go on as they

---

[38] *Ibid.*, p. 13.
[39] *Ibid.*, 31 October 1650, p. 346.
[40] *Ibid.*, 12 September 1650, p. 219.
[41] *Ibid.*, 25 July 1650, p. 109.
[42] Nedham, *Case*, pp. 51, 111–28.
[43] *Mercurius Politicus*, 3 October 1650, pp. 281–2 (a letter ostensibly sent from Brussels; but letters published by *Politicus* tended to have, at least by the time they got there, Nedham's literary characteristics); cf. *ibid.*, 27 June 1650, p. 47.
[44] *Ibid.*, 20 June – 15 August 1650, pp. 11, 21–2, 32, 35, 55, 61, 95, 97, 106, 119, 153; 27 May 1652, pp. 1612–14.

begin, in Great Britain, Ireland, and France', foretells the second issue of *Politicus*, 'the pope himself may in a short time be put to live upon shifts, as well as his faction.'[45]

In *The Case of the Commonwealth*, too, Nedham envisaged a European scenario in words that touch Marvell's *Ode*. 'Tis madness to resist or blame', writes Marvell, 'The force of angry heaven's flame' (25–6). 'If it be considered', reflects Nedham,

how the worm works in many parts of Europe to cast off the regal yoke, especially in France, Scotland, Ireland and other places, it must needs be as much madness to strive against the stream for the upholding of a power cast down by the Almighty as it was for the old sons of earth to heap up mountains against heaven.[46]

Nedham, too, represents Cromwell as a divinely appointed instrument: 'it is a privilege of this generall, consigned to him from heaven, to conquer wheresoever he comes; for evidence whereof, collect the many miraculous and signall successes bestowed upon him by God, in England and Ireland'.[47] Marvell, in writing of the anger of heaven, rehearsed the contemporary assumption that the Civil Wars had been the punishment of the nation's sins by a wrathful deity. Even in Marvell's poem on Cromwell's death in 1658, where Oliver, who in the Ode had been a purely or almost purely elemental force, assumes a human face, he remains the force of 'angry heaven' (16).[48] In Nedham's *The Case of the Commonwealth* it is 'the weight of sin' that causes the 'fatal circumvolutions' that overthrow and replace governments.[49] For fate and the divine will are one: 'How fatal it is', reflected *Politicus* after Cromwell's conclusive victory at Worcester the following year, 'for men to fight against [God's] decrees, who hath made so many declarations from heaven of his resolution to support' the new regime.[50]

For fate, to Nedham and Marvell alike, is the motor of history, the irresistible force that, with Cromwell as its medium, has destroyed the monarchy and established the military republic. In the Ode, fate is allied to 'Nature that hateth emptiness' (41). Nedham tells us at the outset of *The Case of the Commonwealth* that political revolutions are wrought by 'a certain destiny or decree of nature'.[51] In the Ode, when 'fate' killed the

45   *Ibid.*, 20 June 1650, p. 26.
46   Nedham, *Case*, p. 13; cf. *Mercurius Politicus*, 22 August 1650, p. 174.
47   *Mercurius Politicus*, 25 July 1650, p. 109.
48   Cf. Andrew Marvell, *The Rehearsal Transpros'd*, ed. D. I. B. Smith (Oxford, 1965), p. 112.
49   Nedham, *Case*, p. 9.
50   *Mercurius Politicus*, 18 September 1651, p. 1063.
51   Nedham, *Case*, p. 7; cf. *ibid.*, p. 34.

king, 'the state' foresaw its 'fate' (37, 72). The argument of the first chapter
of *The Case* is 'that governments have their revolutions and fatal periods'.[52] To help his readers 'understand what fate is', Nedham quotes
Seneca's definition of it as 'that providence which pulls down one kingdom
or government and sets up another', and which 'hurls the powers of the
world'.[53] Those who commit the 'madness' of resisting it merely 'fortif[y]
castles in the air against fatal necessity'.[54] Fate has dissolved the ties of
subjects to their monarch. 'The old allegiance', argues Nedham, 'is extinct
and must give place to a new':[55] in the *Ode*, nature 'must make room' (43)
for the world which 'fate' has decreed. To Marvell and Nedham alike, fate
has laid bare the facts of power. 'The sword', declares *The Case*, 'is, and
ever hath been, the foundation of all titles to government.'[56] In the *Ode*,
the 'justice' that 'complains' against fate has been separated from power
(37), but at the end of the poem justice and power are (it seems) reunited,
in the 'erect' sword that has destroyed the old and will sustain the new
(116). *The Case* rebukes royalists who explain their refusal of allegiance to
the republic on the ground that 'it is by the sword unlawfully erected'. For
as Hobbes, explains Nedham, has shown, 'the sword of war' and 'the
sword of justice', 'are but one' and 'are in the same hands'.[57] In the *Ode*
the 'fate' of the 'free' 'state' will be 'happy' (72, 103). The rhetorically
charged conclusion of *The Case* observes that the English will lay 'the
foundations of future happiness' by securing their 'free state'.[58]

Yet if the Nedham of 1650 is present in the poem, so too is the royalist
Nedham of the late 1640s: the Nedham whose own poem on the death of
Lord Hastings was paired with Marvell's, which it echoes, in *Lachrymae
Musarum*.[59] In the *Ode*, the necessary preliminary to regicide is the
episode of November 1647 when Charles escaped from his imprisonment at Hampton Court, only to be incarcerated at Carisbrooke Castle in
the Isle of Wight. Marvell's inclusion of the episode is by itself enough to
dispose of the notion that the poem is a panegyric. His lines take up the
common royalist accusation that Cromwell, by mixing hints of impending assassination with professions of friendship, had lured the king into

[52] *Ibid.*, pp. 5, 7, 12. 'Fatal periods' were a recurrent theme of Nedham's writing, as were
      'fatal' events, among them the 'fatal stab' of Julius Caesar: *Mercurius Politicus*, 9
      October 1651, p. 1110; 20 May 1652, p. 1594; 15 July 1652, p. 1723; see too his *Plea
      for the King*, p. 22.
[53] Nedham, *Case*, p. 9.
[54] *Ibid.*, pp. 13–14; cf. *ibid.*, p. 8.
[55] Nedham, *Case*, p. 41.
[56] *Ibid.*, p. 5.
[57] *Ibid.*, p. 136.
[58] *Ibid.*, pp. 127–8.
[59] Blair Worden, 'The Politics of Marvell's Horatian Ode', *HJ*, 27 (1984), 533.

fleeing from the captivity of the army's opponents in parliament, so that the army itself could control his fate.[60]

> And Hampton shows what part
> He had of wiser art:
> Where, twining subtle fears with hope,
> He cast a net of such a scope
> That Charles himself might chase
> To Caresbrook's narrow case. (45–52)

Nedham returned repeatedly to that episode. In his first account of it, in *Pragmaticus*, fears and hope are likewise subtly twined: Cromwell and his friends, 'according to Machiavel's gospel', 'went a subtle way' in 'pretending friendship to [the king] by high praises and frighting him with intended attempts upon his person', and thus 'wrought in him a willingness to remove from Hampton'.[61] And it is to Nedham that we owe the report, which casts light on Marvell's lines on the sham-providentialism of the regicides, that in January 1649 Cromwell, in explaining to the Commons the need to bring Charles to trial,

played his cards very cunningly, saying, 'Mr Speaker, if any man whatsoever had carried on this design of deposing the king and disinheriting his posterity, or if any man had such a design, he should be the greatest traitor and robber in the world. But since the providence of God hath cast us upon this, I cannot but submit to providence ...'. By which speech you may see, they entitle God's providence to all their villainies.[62]

Nedham's prose on the republic's behalf points to those 'villainies' too. Why, after all, does he call Cromwell, in June 1650, 'the only *Novus Princeps* that ever I met with'? Machiavelli's *The Prince* – 'that unworthy book' as it is called in *Politicus*, which nonetheless makes maximum polemical use of it[63] – is a handbook for the 'new prince': that is, for the man who acquires control of a state by conquest or usurpation. In his

---

[60] For the place of the episode in royalist verse see James Loxley, *Royalism and Poetry in the English Civil Wars* (Basingstoke, 1997), pp. 147 ss.

[61] *Mercurius Pragmaticus*, 14 December 1647, p. [6]. See too Nedham's newsletter of 28 December 1648, Bodl. Clarendon MS 34, fo. 17v; Nedham, *Digitus Dei* (1649), p. 22; cf. the anonymous work *The Machivilian Cromwellist* (1648), pp. 10–11. We have to guess whether Marvell, in preparing or composing the *Ode*, saw journalism of Nedham from an earlier year, but the notion is not implausible, for Nedham, who longed to transcend the ephemeral nature of journalism, held on to his own writing, which he frequently cited and recycled.

[62] Nedham's newsletter of 11 January 1649, Bodl., Clarendon MS 34, fo. 72.

[63] *Mercurius Politicus*, 6 March 1651, p. 215; 15 September 1651, p. 1077; 3 June 1656, p. 1626; 5 August 1652, p. 1769.

royalist writing Nedham had explicitly compared Cromwell to one of the arch-tyrants in Machiavelli's pages, Dionysius of Syracuse.[64] Under the republic Nedham returned to Dionysius's conduct. This time, naturally, he omitted Cromwell's name, but he allowed it to be visible between the lines.[65] The task given to Nedham's propaganda by the republican government was the discrediting of royalism. But he had another agendum too – perhaps one set by Cromwell's enemies within the regime, or perhaps his own, for Nedham, amidst his superficially craven alterations of side, could sustain, through oblique and indirect writing, a surprising degree of independence of voice. In 1650–2 he portrayed two political struggles. One, the subject on the surface of his prose, is that between Stuart and republic. The other is between the republic and Cromwell. England was ruled by the forcibly purged House of Commons, the remnant of the ancient constitution. The regime had been hastily improvised in 1649 and was rapidly demoralized thereafter. People found its survival less easy to envisage than a return, under Cromwell, to the familiarity of single rule. Nedham warned against that prospect. He urged the Rump to turn itself into a true republic, secured and animated by republican virtue. In his royalist guise he had predicted that Cromwell would seek, like Dionysius, to 'usurp the government to himself'. In his republican guise he shows Cromwell to be what Machiavelli required a 'new prince' to be: a master at once of force and of cunning, at once a 'lion' and a 'fox'.[66]

Alongside Dionysius, Nedham repeatedly hints at parallels to other classical enemies to republican rule, among them Sulla and, above all, Julius Caesar. In alluding to those parallels, Nedham pioneered or helped pioneer a literary practice. Cromwell's eminence was widely attended by interlinear comparisons between his career or intentions and those of Roman and other dictators. Deservedly or not, he inspired almost universal mistrust. It had long been expected that he would try to make himself king. The prospect was enhanced by the final defeat of the royalists in 1651 at the Battle of Worcester, which prompted a debate within the government whether England should remain a republic or return to some form of monarchy.[67] Two characteristics of Cromwell were emphasized by Nedham. There was his secret ambition, on which almost everyone had been long agreed. And there was his readiness,

[64] Nedham, *Plea for the King*, p. 25.
[65] *Mercurius Politicus*, 1 April 1652, pp. 1490–1.
[66] *Ibid.*, 5 August 1652, pp. 1770, 1773.
[67] For the background, see my *The Rump Parliament 1648–1653* (Cambridge, 1974, repr. 2003), esp. ch. 13, and my 'Marchamont Nedham and the Beginnings of English Republicanism'.

which Nedham specially emphasized, to forge and exploit a reputation as the champion of the liberties of the people, which, when the moment of opportunity came, he would sacrifice to his own elevation. Nedham, alert to 'designs laid in the dark for the converting of liberty into tyranny', enjoined the same vigilance on his readers.[68] He stresses the consequences for Roman liberty of Caesar's own moment of opportunity, the crossing of the Rubicon, that 'plain usurpation'.[69] In the month of Cromwell's return from Ireland, Nedham described the 'arts' by which Caesar and other 'tyrants' had 'erected the imperial tyranny at Rome'. He told how that master of 'the sword' had 'insinuated himself into the people's favour' and, with 'ambitious thoughts', had 'turned his arms upon the public liberty'. Caesar, recalls Nedham, had acted in the belief that 'all laws may be violated to make way to a domination'; that 'a man may be wicked to obtain or maintain an absolute sovereignty'; that 'a prince ought to account nothing unjust which is profitable'.[70]

The opening lines of the *Horatian Ode* allude unmistakeably to Lucan's account of Caesar's crossing of the Rubicon,[71] and align that event with the conquering general Cromwell's return from Ireland. The parallel was no remote or merely decorative allusion. At the time of Cromwell's subsequent re-entry into England, in 1651, when he allowed the Scots to invade and followed them with his own army, members of the republic's council of state 'raged and uttered sad discontents against Cromwell, and suspicions of his fidelity'.[72] Because Cromwell would go on to dominate the England of the 1650s, we easily forget how much is stated by Marvell's choice of subject. Cromwell's political eminence had been given no constitutional recognition or standing. He was not yet even Lord General of the army. The authority with the obvious first claim on the gifts of an aspiring poet was the sovereign parliament. Like Nedham, Marvell overtly portrays a conflict between a royalist past and a Cromwellian future, and more subtly portrays one between a Cromwellian future and a republican present. Ostensibly Cromwell is the servant of the republic. He 'can so well obey' it (84). Yet it was widely noticed that he had returned from Ireland only after declining, for many months, to 'obey' parliament's order to do so,[73] an evasion

---

[68] *Mercurius Politicus*, 1 April 1652, pp. 1490–1. I should add that, just as in Marvell's poem there are two Caesars, Cromwell and Charles I, so are there in Nedham's prose for the republic: Cromwell and Charles II (who is more often 'young Tarquin').

[69] *Ibid.*, 27 May 1652, pp. 1611–12; 10 June 1652, p. 1644; cf. 20 May 1652, p. 1596.

[70] Nedham, *Case*, pp. 17, 25, 64, 102.

[71] Worden, *Literature and Politics*, chs. 3, 4.

[72] James Sutherland (ed.), *Memoirs of the Life of Colonel Hutchinson* (Oxford, 1973), p. 202.

[73] Worden, 'Politics of Marvell's Horatian Ode', 529–30.

which the prominent MP Lord Lisle (Algernon Sidney's brother) attributed to the pursuit of 'his interest'.[74]

Besides, the Cromwell who 'can so well obey' seems destined to cease doing so, for by the same token he is – it seems – 'fit ... to sway', 'fit for highest trust' (80–3). In Nedham's writing it is ambition that transformed Caesar, as it threatens to turn Cromwell, from the people's friend into the people's enemy.[75] It is ambition that drives Marvell's Cromwell. To appearances, Cromwell, who before his rise 'lived reservèd and austere' in his 'private gardens', 'As if his highest plot' were to plant a pear-tree (29–32), has had a reluctant rise. He seems to resemble 'the noble Camillus, and Fabius, and Curius' as they are described in *Politicus*, which recalls that they 'were with much ado drawn from the recreation of gardening to the trouble of governing'.[76] Yet Marvell, not for the only time in the poem, contrives by allusion to counter the surface impression of the verse, for the tree, 'the Bergamot', is the tree of kings. Nedham, in the previous issue of *Politicus*, had prominently reprinted, in the translation by Tom May, the description of the virtue of Pompey which Lucan had put into the mouth of Cato. Again, there is a superficial parallel to Marvell's Cromwell: Pompey's 'house' was 'chaste [and] unrioted', and he was

> powerful grown
> Not wronging liberty; the people prone
> To serve, he only privat still remain'd;
> He sway'd the Senate, but the Senate reigned;
> Naught claim'd he by the sword, but wish't what he
> Wish't most, the people's peace and liberty.[77]

But the true Cromwell is not Pompey, whose death, recalled *Politicus*, was a 'catastrophe' of the 'bloody tragedy' that produced 'the domination of Caesar'.[78] He is Caesar himself. To Marvell as to Nedham, Cromwell is a *Novus Princeps* – or one in the making, for to become a prince he must first usurp. Timothy Raylor has shown how Edmund Waller wrote his panegyric to Cromwell of 1655 with Machiavelli's prose at his side.[79] Only an anachronistic distinction between poetry

---

[74] HMC, *Report, De L'Isle and Dudley*, VI (1966), p. 472.

[75] *Mercurius Politicus*, 17 June 1652, p. 1661.

[76] *Ibid.*, 27 November 1651, p. 1222.

[77] It is from *Politicus* that I quote the lines: 20 November 1651, p. 1206.

[78] *Ibid.*, 15 July 1652, p. 1723.

[79] Timothy Raylor, 'Reading Machiavelli; Writing Cromwell: Edmund Waller's Copy of *The Prince* and his Draft Verses towards A Panegyrick on my Lord Protector', *Turnbull Library Review*, 35 (2002), 9–32; Raylor, 'Waller's Machiavellian Cromwell: The Imperial Argument of *A Panegyrick to my Lord Protector*', *Review of English Studies*, 56 (2005), 386–411.

and political thought can inhibit our recognition of Machiavelli's place in Marvell's *Ode*. Cromwell, who rises by combining 'courage high' with the 'wiser art' (17, 48) that lures Charles to Carisbrooke, is at once lion and fox, a master of force and fraud.

We are taken back to Machiavelli, too, by another aspect of Cromwell's ostensible self-effacement: 'Nor yet grown stiffer with command/ But still in the republic's hand' (81–2). Readers of Machiavelli's *Discourses* knew that military rulers on whose commands there are no time limits have a way of rising above their political masters and turning against them (Book 3, Chapter 24).[80] It was a point repeatedly made by Nedham, who cited Machiavelli's chapter.[81] He found support for it too in Lucan's picture of the anti-Cromwell, Pompey: 'The sword/ He took, but knew the time to lay it down'.[82] So if Cromwell has not 'yet' grown stiffer with command, how long will it take? Nedham remembers how Cinna, Marius, Sylla 'and the rest of that successive gang down to Caesar' contrived to 'obtain a continuation of power in their own hands'. Having found means to strip the people, the cultivation of whose favour had won them power, of their liberty, they 'maintained by the same arts' the power they had acquired.[83] Nedham turned against Cromwell the passage of *The Prince* where Machiavelli explains that a new prince is often 'forced, for the maintenance of his state', to break all moral rules. 'Let a prince therefore take the surest courses he can to maintain his life and state, the means shall always be thought honourable.' Nedham then enjoys himself by quoting, 'without adding or diminishing a syllable', Machiavelli's reference to 'a prince ... in our days' who proves the point, and 'whom I shall not do well to name'.[84]

David Norbrook finds 'an activist republicanism' in the *Ode*.[85] The term would aptly apply to the Nedham of 1650, when his argument that the sword is the permanent foundation of government is turned to

---

[80]   I am most grateful to Timothy Raylor for suggesting to me that the couplet alludes to that chapter.

[81]   *Vox Plebis* (1646), p. 66 (which cites the chapter of Machiavelli in a passage that is transparently by Nedham); *Mercurius Pragmaticus*, 18 April 1648, p. 2; *Mercurius Politicus*, 11 December 1651, p. 1256; 25 December 1651, pp. 1288–9; 18 March 1652, p. 1461; 15 April 1652, p. 1522; 6 May 1652, p. 1572; 13 May 1652, p. 1588; 27 May 1652, pp. 1610–12 (where Nedham also dwells on Caesar's crossing of the Rubicon); Nedham, *A Pacquet of Advices* (1676), p. 51, with which compare Nedham, *The Levellers Levell'd* (1647), p. 4.

[82]   *Mercurius Politicus*, 20 November 1651, p. 1206.

[83]   *Ibid.*, 11 March 1652, p. 1461.

[84]   *Ibid.*, 5 August 1652, pp. 1770–2.

[85]   Norbrook, *Writing the English Republic*, p. 264. Though we disagree on that subject, Norbrook's book offers a richly rewarding account of the political and literary contexts of Marvell's verse.

a republican end. The republic, he maintains, can sustain itself against the royalist threat only by the very weapon with which the line of tyrants since William the Conqueror has suppressed the nation's liberty.[86] Yet here we encounter, not Marvell's concurrence with Nedham, but his departure from him. 'Tom May's Death' places Marvell squarely opposite to Nedham, who composed the inscription for the tomb of May in Westminster Abbey, and whose *Politicus* hailed 'the best of poets, Thomas May our English Lucan'.[87] The opposition extends into the *Ode*, which, unless in irony, supplies no counterpart to Nedham's celebrations of republican virtue. The 'emptiness' that is left by the death of the king is filled for Marvell, not by the civilian leaders of the republic, but by the single 'greater spirit' (41–4) who threatens to usurp them. All that we learn in the poem about those leaders is that they were 'fright[ened]' (70), an apt verb for the nervous constitutional improvisation that created the republic in 1649 and also for the mood of alarm and despair which, in Cromwell's absence, settled on the regime in the first half of 1650. Marvell was never drawn to republicanism, or to the idea of sovereign parliaments. In February 1653 his 'The Character of Holland' mocks the kingless polity of the Netherlands, that 'wat'ry Babel' (21). In the 'First Anniversary' the former members of the Rump are 'tedious statesmen' who 'many years did hack/ Framing a liberty that still went back' (69–70). Even after the Restoration, when Marvell would contend to the hilt against the threat of 'arbitrary government', he had little faith in parliaments, where, as he observed on the basis of close acquaintance, the friends of truth and liberty were a minority. Cromwell's Machiavellian character is not, for Marvell, a threat to republican rule or virtue. He is the destroyer of the king who 'nothing common did or mean / Upon that memorable scene'. And he is the future ruler of England, at once its tyrant and – dread thought – perhaps its only salvation. Nedham, though under the commonwealth he recycled material from his royalist period, cast off his royalist allegiance like a suit of clothes. In the *Ode*, Marvell half-clings to his.

IV

Marvell and Nedham, who were born a year apart, were in their late twenties when Charles I was executed. The Civil War was not the responsibility of their generation, only its affliction, to which they must adjust as they could. James Harrington, who is known to posterity as the

---

[86] *Mercurius Politicus*, 12 June 1651, pp. 858–9; 10 July 1651, p. 903.
[87] *Ibid.*, 20 November 1651, p. 1206.

author of *The Commonwealth of Oceana*, was a decade older. Yet John Aubrey, who was himself an 'old friend' of Harrington and who is generally reliable about people he knew, tells us that Marvell, though he 'had not a general acquaintance', was an 'intimate friend' of Harrington.[88] We also learn from Aubrey that on Harrington's death in 1677, the year before his own, Marvell wrote an epitaph for him, which was not used on his tomb as 'it would have given offence' – that is, offence to the government. We cannot tell when the friendship between Marvell and Harrington was formed. What we can say is that if the two men were not friends by the time Marvell wrote the *Ode*, they were missing something.

Like Marvell, Harrington was a traveller and a linguist. Both men, in their youth, journeyed in the Netherlands, France and Italy and learned the languages of those war-torn countries. Like Marvell, Harrington kept out of the First Civil War. In 1647 he was appointed by parliament, with two others, a gentleman of the king's bedchamber. He held the post until Charles's death, when reportedly he was present on the scaffold and was given tokens by the condemned king. Aubrey tells us that Charles, who discussed political ideas with him, 'loved' Harrington's 'company'; that Harrington 'passionately loved his majesty'; and that at the meetings of the Rota Club a decade later – where Harrington's political theory was debated, and where Marvell was among the participants – Aubrey 'often heard' Harrington 'speak of King Charles I with the greatest zeal and passion imaginable, and [say] that his death gave him so great grief that he contracted a disease by it; that never anything did go so near to him'.

Like Nedham, Harrington wanted a true republic. Unlike Nedham, whose writing for the commonwealth is uncompromisingly hostile to royalism, he argued for a republic free from the partisanship of the Civil Wars, one where Cavalier and Roundhead would forget their differences. Though his own logic drove him to reject monarchy, he was temperamentally never a Roundhead. He looked forward to the revival, under a republic free of partisanship, of 'wit and gallantry'.[89] Like his poetry, the fictional dress of *Oceana* is closer to royalist than to parliamentarian literature. So are the literary skits and spoofs of Harrington's intimate friend Henry Neville and Neville's intimate friend Thomas Chaloner. Chaloner was a regicide, and Neville served the Rump alongside him. Yet, like their common friend the MP Henry Marten (whose own verse about Cromwell has the ironic quality we have found in

---

[88]   Aubrey's recollections of Harrington and Marvell are in his *Brief Lives*, ed. Andrew Clark (Oxford, 1898), vol. I, p. 288, vol. II, pp. 54, 185.

[89]   J. G. A. Pocock (ed.), *The Political Works of James Harrington* (Cambridge, 1977), p. 253; cf. *ibid.*, pp. 337–8.

Marvell's *Ode* and Nedham's prose),[90] they were eccentric figures on the puritan side. Chaloner, Neville and Marten, the MPs with whom Nedham as editor of *Politicus* probably worked most closely, were known for their 'wit'.[91] 'Wit in a Roundhead', a royalist critic of Nedham's earlier prose for parliament had maintained, was a contradiction in terms.[92] Yet however sharp and deep the polarization of the Civil Wars, it could not neatly divide humanity into two camps of contrasting outlooks and temperaments and talents.

Harrington despised the partisan rule of the Rump, the 'base itch' of its 'oligarchy', the 'venom' at its 'root'. He compared its Council of State to the thirty tyrants of Athens. He was repelled by its plunder of 'our cathedrals, ornaments in which this nation excels all others'.[93] Yet Harrington, as unsympathetic as Marvell to the Rump, is as troubled as the Marvell of 1650 by the Rump's rival, Cromwell. Like Marvell and Nedham, Harrington uses subtle tactics to portray Cromwell's Machiavellian qualities. Nedham had presented an idealized picture of Pompey to show that Cromwell, who ought to be like him, is the opposite of him. Harrington does the same with his leading character the Lord Archon, the idealized Cromwell whose conduct has been the opposite of the real one's.[94] In passages where the contrast between ideal and reality is underlined, Harrington links Cromwell's aspirations with those of Julius Caesar, a figure 'more execrable than Catiline', whose 'prodigious ambition', Harrington recalls, had reduced Rome to 'havoc'.[95] Other parallels, classical and biblical, assist his characterization of Cromwell. In describing the 'ambition' and 'tyranny' of those who 'usurp the liberty of their native countries', he cites Tacitus's account of the uprising of Piso, who, in urging his soldiers to rise against Nero, observed that 'imperial power gained by wicked means no man has ever used with good arts' ('bonis artibus').[96] In the *Ode*, Cromwell is 'the English hunter' (110). It is a fair guess that Marvell is identifying him, as royalist writing had learned to do, with Nimrod, the biblical 'mighty hunter' and archetypal tyrant. ('Proud Nimrod in Ireland', a royalist writer had recently called Cromwell.)[97] The

[90]   Norbrook, *Writing the English Republic*, pp. 317–9, 496.
[91]   Worden, '"Wit in a Roundhead"', pp. 326–7.
[92]   *Ibid.*, p. 308.
[93]   Pocock, *Political Works*, p. 295.
[94]   Blair Worden, 'Harrington's *Oceana*: Origins and Aftermath, 1651–1660', in Wootton, *Republicanism*, pp. 113–26.
[95]   Pocock, *Political Works*, pp. 338, 345–6.
[96]   Tacitus, *Histories*, I, 30; Pocock, *Political Works*, p. 338.
[97]   *The Man in the Moon*, 2 January 1650, pp. 285–6. Cf. Nedham's use of Nimrod in *Mercurius Britanicus*, 24 June 1644, p. 318; *Mercurius Pragmaticus*, 26 October 1647, pp. 542–3; *Mercurius Politicus*, 5 December 1650, p. 423; *Case*, p. 15.

'English hunter' ostensibly brings the swords of war and justice together in the hands of Cromwell, whom the Irish have called 'how just' (79). But why then has 'justice' complained at his rise (37)? *Oceana* in turn explains that if 'the sword of war' is 'any otherwise used than as the sword of magistracy for the fear and punishment of those that do evil', it 'is as guilty in the sight of God as the sword of a murderer'. On that principle, with Cromwell in his sights, Harrington remarks that the exploits of Alexander the Great, that 'mighty hunter', were 'but a great robbery'.[98]

In *Oceana* Cromwell's 'sword' has conquered the Scots, as, in Marvell's *Ode*, it soon will. It has 'nailed them with his victorious sword unto their native Caucasus'.[99] That is no liberation, for Harrington makes it clear that tyrants can never free foreign lands, which is the prerogative of republics. Here as often he followed his hero Machiavelli (the republican side of Machiavelli), as Nedham had followed him in making the same point. The point is also made, with irony, in the *Horatian Ode*. There Cromwell 'to all states not free/ Shall climacteric be' (102–3). Since 'new princes', or Caesars who have crossed the Rubicon, bring tyranny to the lands they annex, the couplet contradicts the poem's earlier representation of Cromwell. In the previous line, Cromwell will be 'To Italy an Hannibal'. Yet, as Nedham remarked in *The Case of the Commonwealth*, 'the hand of heaven will assuredly be against' princes such as Hannibal, who instigated 'an ambitious war against the Romans' and lost it.[100] In his royalist phase, Nedham had written of 'the arbitrary vassalage of a free state'.[101] To royalists, the conversion of England in 1649 into a 'Commonwealth and Free State' was a symptom of the debasement of language by the Roundheads and of their capacity to make words say the opposite of what they mean. Would Marvell, whose poem to Lovelace had made its own observations on literary degeneracy, have taken up the phrase 'free state' without irony?

Harrington, who calls the rule both of the Rump and of Cromwell a 'tyranny', would never have used that word of the rule of Charles I, which instead he calls 'the most indulgent to, and least invasive of for so many ages upon, the liberty of a people that the world hath known'.[102] There is no more taint of evil in Harrington's Charles I than in Marvell's *Ode*. In both works he is a victim of history. In the *Ode*, ancient rights yield to force and fraud. In *Oceana*, 'a man (you know) though he be

---

[98]   Pocock, *Political Works*, p. 345.
[99]   *Ibid.*
[100] Nedham, *Case*, p. 79; and cf. Marvell's l. 98 with *Mercurius Pragmaticus*, 28 September 1647, p. 13.
[101] *Mercurius Pragmaticus*, 11 January 1648, p. 4.
[102] Pocock, *Political Works*, p. 235.

virtuous, yet, if he do not understand his [political] estate, may run out
or be cheated of it'.[103] The regicide and the end of monarchy are the
fulcrum of Harrington's argument, as they are of the *Ode* and of 'Tom
May's Death'. In the May poem the world's disjointed axle cracks: in
Oceana the regicide was met by 'such horror as hath been a spectacle of
astonishment unto the whole earth'.[104] Like Marvell, Harrington adjusted to it only with pain and difficulty, and only by accepting a logic
that broke with the assumptions of the pre-war world. *Oceana* was published in 1656. But there are indications in its text that it was drafted
earlier, at some point under the Commonwealth of 1649–53, and then
revised under the Protectorate.[105] If so, there is an added interest to some
remarks of John Toland, Harrington's late-seventeenth-century editor,
who had seen papers of the family that have subsequently disappeared,
and who gave an account of the genesis of *Oceana*. Toland was not the
most instinctively truthful of writers, but his detectable inventions have
discernible motives, and none such is visible in his account.

'After the king's death', writes Toland, Harrington 'was observed to
keep very much his library, and more retired than usually, which was by
his friends' – which friends? – 'a long time attributed to melancholy or
discontent'. It was out of that withdrawal, Toland explains, that there
emerged the insights which Harrington would incorporate into
Oceana.[106] Then it was that he concluded that momentous forces of
history were at work, which men were powerless to resist and to which,
if they craved peace and civil life, they must adjust. He traced a process
of economic and social change that removed the feudal base of monarchy
and made inevitable the revolution of 1649 which abolished both kingship and the House of Lords. The fall of kingship had thus derived, in
Toland's fair summary of Harrington's argument, from 'natural causes',
which 'produce their necessary effects' in politics 'as much as in the
earth or air'.[107] In the *Ode*, 'Nature that hateth emptiness' likewise takes
political command.[108] In *Oceana*, Harrington uses the point that the end
of 'the late monarchy' was 'as natural as the death of a man' to explain
that 'the oath of allegiance ... impl[ies] an impossibility, and [is] therefore void'.[109] Marvell's 'nature' renders void allegiances to principles

---

103 *Ibid.*, p. 173.
104 *Ibid.*, p. 312. In Harrington's time, he also observed, 'governments are universally
     broken or swerved from their foundations' (p. 235).
105 Worden, 'Harrington's Oceana', pp. 113–15.
106 *Ibid.*, p. 113.
107 John Toland (ed.), *The 'Oceana' of James Harrington and his Other Works* (1700),
     p. xvii.
108 Cf. Marvell, *Rehearsal Transpros'd*, p. 135, ll. 10–11.
109 Pocock, *Political Works*, p. 203.

that 'hold or break/ As men are strong or weak'. To demonstrate the irreparable destruction of the English Constitution, Harrington draws on the text of which Marvell's poems of 1650 had made so much, the opening of Lucan's *Pharsalia*.

Crassus, remarks Harrington, 'was dead and Isthmus broken'. In Lucan, Crassus is the link that temporarily prevents war between Caesar and Pompey, and is thus likened to the Isthmus of Corinth, 'that small rock of land' which alone prevents the clash of the two great seas, the Ionian and the Aegean.[110]

Between them, the Ode, the poetic masterpiece of the years of the revolution of 1640–60, and *Oceana*, with *Leviathan* one of the two masterpieces of their political thought, convey the scale and profundity of the mental transition wrought by the regicide, and illuminate intense yet vain contentions of royalist sentiment against it.

---

[110]   *Ibid.*, p. 198.

Subject Index

Author Index

Printed in Great Britain
by Amazon.co.uk, Ltd.,
Marston Gate.